BY WATERWAY TO TAUNTON

THE BRIDGWATER AND
TAUNTON CANAL

BY WATERWAY TO TAUNTON

THE BRIDGWATER AND TAUNTON CANAL

TONY HASKELL

TEMPUS

First published 1994, this edition 2007

Tempus Publishing Limited
The Mill, Brimscombe Port,
Stroud, Gloucestershire, GL5 2QG
www.tempus-publishing.com

British Library Cataloguing in Publication Data.
A catalogue record for this book is available from the British Library.

ISBN 978 0 7524 4267 9

Typesetting and origination by Tempus Publishing Limited
Printed in Great Britain

CONTENTS

FOREWORD

For many of us, canals and waterways are a source of endless fascination and interest, the more so since a number are being restored today and offer opportunities for boating and a range of countryside activities. Somerset is scarcely a county whose name springs readily to mind when contemplating our nation's heritage of industrial canals. Yet, whilst the fervour of what we know as the 'canal mania' was sweeping through the industrial centres of England, there were entrepreneurs already thinking of a canal that would enable their waterborne traffic to cross the narrow peninsula between the Bristol and English Channels, thus avoiding the treacherous Cornish coast.

It was a vision that was to exercise the minds of successive generations of engineers and surveyors for more than fifty years, but which, with the coming of the railways, was never to be fully realised.

Only the Bridgwater and Taunton Canal and short lengths of the Grand Western Canal exist today as waterways, reminding us of these once ambitious plans.

This book covers not only the subject of these various inter-channel schemes but also the long-neglected history of River Tone navigation. It was the river which provided the essential lifeline to Taunton along which generations of boatmen laboured with their barges to bring the region all its coal and merchandise for over 200 years, before the canal and later the railways arrived.

However, this book is mainly about the Bridgwater and Taunton Canal; its building, its trade, its demise and subsequent recent restoration to navigation. Its author, Tony Haskell, has been, since 1975, closely involved in planning its restoration whilst he was with the Somerset County Council, and his engrossing and informative account should tempt many to take a fresh look at the canal.

Ralph Clark
Chairman
Somerset County Council
May 1994

PREFACE

Tony Haskell's book carries me back to my youth, for my interest in canal and river navigation history began in the West Country, still 'home' to me in a very special way.

Of points in his book that spoke strongly to me I would first choose the role of the Conservators of the River Tone. Established in 1699, and still actively doing the job for which they were created, they prove the foolishness of those who think that because an institution is old, it must be out of date.

Another is the successful cooperation of the three local authorities that cover the canal's course, with British Waterways its present owners.

These are important both historically and today. Tony Haskell has, however, gone behind them to show the reader that same history being made. Newspaper cuttings, posters, minute book extracts: here is local history as our forefathers made it, or read of it, being made.

This is not so much a book to read through, as one in which to browse, evening after evening, month after month, until you too, dear reader, may decide to go out yourself and contribute something to tomorrow's history.

Charles Hadfield
July, 1993

ACKNOWLEDGEMENTS

As with most books covering historical subjects, and where considerable research is essential, it is inevitable that many people get involved and give freely of their time. For this I am grateful. My thanks also go to many of my colleagues in the various departments of the Somerset County Council, Taunton Deane Borough Council and Sedgemoor District Council who have given me much help, as well as the staff at British Waterways and the National Rivers Authority.

One aspect of the recording of historical research is the frustration of seeking, and indeed finding, suitable illustrations. Few photographs of the barge traffic of the time seem to have survived, but nevertheless I am indebted to a great number of local residents who have allowed me to reproduce pictures from their private collections. Some are so historically interesting that they have been taken into the archive of the Boat Museum at Ellesmere Port, Cheshire. The late Richard Goodland-Hyde gave me valuable information about the coal trade in the area, and, as a Conservator of the River Tone, allowed me access to the many photographs of the Conservators' annual inspections that I reproduce here.

Tony Haskell

ABOUT THE AUTHOR

Tony Haskell trained as an architect and town planner and was involved in many conservation projects before coming to Somerset in 1974.

From 1977 he was deputy County Planning Officer for Somerset County Council, and retired in 1990. During that time he was closely involved in drawing up proposals for the restoration of Bridgwater Docks, and later the Bridgwater and Taunton Canal. In 1989 he was elected a Conservator of the River Tone.

His book aims to acknowledge the work of those who have striven to reopen this canal, and to provide further interest in what has been up to now a somewhat neglected aspect of Somerset's history.

Taunton, Somersetshire. (Courtesy of Somerset Archaeological and Natural History Society)

INTRODUCTION

At a quarter to seven, in the fast fading light of a late April evening in 1989, the canal narrow boat *Croghall-Mor* was carefully eased through the restored Newtown lock. She was passing from the dock into Bridgwater and Taunton Canal to take her place in a commemorative rally to mark the reopening of nearly 6 miles of the canal between Bridgwater and North Newton. Few of the handful of spectators huddled at the lock-side that evening, could have realised the significance of the occasion. It was well over sixty years since a barge had passed through on its way to Taunton and over eighty since the canal was used commercially.

In the mid-nineteenth century while many English canals succumbed to competition from the fast and efficient new railways, the Bridgwater and Taunton survived. How was it, then, that this relatively short, rural and isolated canal, linking no great industrial centres, managed to exist alongside the railway that had acquired it, until the turn of the century? With a nine-year-long programme of restoration now complete, the opportunity arises to investigate not only the story of the Bridgwater and Taunton Canal, but the whole fascinating history of waterway navigation to Taunton and the lives and times of the boatmen who worked long and lonely hours, not only on the canal but the river as well, bringing their cargoes to the town's wharves and to the traders and merchants who depended on them.

It would be misleading to deal with the history of the Bridgwater and Taunton Canal in isolation. Its creation owed much to the business speculators and sponsors and engineers who calculated on handsome profits from the carriage of coal and agricultural produce on a waterway linking the Bristol and English Channels. Looking at the quiet rural charm of the Bridgwater and Taunton Canal, it is hard to appreciate that it once formed part of an ambitious scheme to avoid the treacherous sea journey round Land's End. Nor would the story be complete without mention of the River Tone which served Taunton for over 200 years before the coming of the canal.

For the researcher, the river has a distinct advantage over the canal. It was still operating as a navigation up until the late 1920s and there are still people who can either remember or recall their parents' accounts of the days of the boatmen. I have been fortunate enough to meet some and their comments have been invaluable in gaining an insight into life on the barges.

Few of the original Canal Company records remain. They were destroyed through enemy action during the Second World War, together with the papers of the Bristol & Exeter Railway Co. that bought them out. Most of the story has been pieced together from other sources held principally in the Somerset Record Office. Newspapers of the period, especially the *Taunton Courier*, have been another valuable source. Wherever appropriate, I have reproduced notices from the newspapers of the day so that readers can learn of events in the same way that the townsfolk did at the time, with all the exuberance and expectation that the columnist could conjure up!

A word about the reproduction of canal maps and plans. The original plans deposited by the canal companies are, today, quite fragile and have to be handled carefully. They were often quite sketchy, comprising little more than a single line superimposed upon a survey of the proposed route. The plans were to show proposals stretching over many miles and therefore they tend to be very long and narrow. As neither of these styles is conducive to clear reproduction, I have therefore decided, reluctantly, to redraw some of the plans as faithfully as possible, at the same time taking the opportunity to omit superfluous information while adding helpful facts such as later revisions to the line of the canal. Where this has been done, plans are clearly marked as redrawn. The originals can be seen in the Somerset Record Office.

In 1946, after the canal had been abandoned for more than fifty years, a group of dedicated canal enthusiasts led others to believe that there was a valuable recreational future for these long-forgotten canals. With the encouragement of the newly formed Inland Waterways Association, the long road to restoration of the Bridgwater and Taunton Canal was begun; a task that would have been impossible without the commitment of its owners, British Waterways, working with Somerset County Council, Sedgemoor District Council and Taunton Deane Borough Council. 1994 sees the conclusion of this task that represents countless hours of dedicated work by so many people who have shared their enthusiasm and given their expertise and energy.

In the end, this book is the story of two survivors. Firstly, the Conservators of the River Tone, established in 1699 and still in being, who ensured that the canal remained navigable, even after it had closed commercially. And secondly, of course, the canal itself. While many other canals were abandoned, blocked off or filled in, surviving only as interesting earthworks testifying to ambitious but short-lived dreams, the Bridgwater and Taunton still lives on. We have our canal and our dream!

Tony Haskell
1994

Taunton, 1880. A view across the River Tone – the site of the present cricket ground – showing the churches of St Mary's and St James's from a painting by John William North. (Courtesy of Sotheby's, Belgravia)

And, when the stream
which overflowed the soul was passed away,
A consciousness remained that it had left,
Deposited upon the silent shore
Of memory, images and precious thoughts
That shall not die, and cannot be destroyed.

Wordsworth

THE RIVER TONE

Early Trading

During the seventeenth century, as sources of iron and coal were located and exploited in many parts of the country, Britain's economy slowly changed from its reliance upon agricultural production to one based upon industry and the growing manufacturing capabilities of a number of major town and cities. Central to this change were the rivers, upon which the fuel, raw materials and manufactured products would be transported. The tidal reaches of many of the country's main rivers were already being used, but it would now be necessary to improve and control the upper reaches, beyond the tidal limits and make them navigable to carry this new trade.

Most of the employment in Somerset at this time was still based upon the needs of agriculture and the woollen industry, but its main rivers, particularly the River Parrett and its tributary, the River Tone, were to become increasingly important in bringing supplies of coal from South Wales to towns such as Langport and Taunton.

Much of the land through which these rivers flowed, the moors and meadows, the rich agricultural pastures and indeed the watercourse itself had for years been under the control of ecclesiastical foundations. These included Wells Cathedral and the abbeys of Muchelney, Glastonbury and Athelney. They had once derived a large income not only from the produce of their land, but also from the rivers which provided both food from the fisheries, and revenue from the supply of water power for the mills, important buildings in any settlement at that time.

One of the earliest references to work on the Tone appears in a manuscript from the Dean and Chapter of Wells Cathedral, dated 1325, where it is proposed to make a new water course 24ft wide from the River Tone below 'Hamme' to a new mill to be built at 'Cnapp'.[1]

The Dean and Chapter owned Stathmoor and the Tone down to the 'weir at Athelneye' and with it the rights to the fishery in the river. Fish was an important source of food for both rich and poor in these times and catches from the river were assisted by the construction of 'fish weirs'. This, no doubt, accounts for the mention of the weir at Athelney. In 1379, the Bishop of Bath and Wells needed to remind his clergy that 'persons would be punished who have fished and taken fish in the rivers and waters of the Tone'.[2]

In 1494 there is mention of a proposal to build a watermill in the manor of North Curry on the Tone, and, from references in 1504, the mill was clearly in operation. Penning back the waters up-river would have been necessary so as to provide a sufficient head of water to power the waterwheel. A year later, the Bishop of Winchester is relaying a complaint to the Dean and Chapter that before the mill was built, 'the poore tenauntes within the tythying of Ruyssheton (who) were never troubled in theire copyholdes by grete floodes of water of the ryver that commeth from Taunton towardes Brigwater until now, by reason of beldyng a myll called Hammyll',[3] pointing out that, after heavy rains and with the stopping of the flood gates, the water could not pass.

The earliest mention of the use of the Tone for navigation is made at this time. The Dean is informed that the inhabitants and merchants of Taunton:

> … have had course, recourse and free passage upon the water of the Toon, Bathpolemyll and Brigewater for all manner of marchaundyses, corne, cole and stones … bought and sold until the tyme a mylle, called Hammyll, which was newe made … by reason wherof your said petioners bee stopped'.[4]

THE DEVELOPMENT OF THE NAVIGATION

Even by the end of the sixteenth century cargoes were regularly hauled up the tidal waters of the Parrett from Bridgwater to Langport, and the 7 miles of the Tone from Burrowbridge to Ham Mills. Whilst Langport and Ham Mills were at the limits of the high spring tides, the slacker tides would not allow barges to reach these towns without the help of horses and cargoes could still be taken the further 4 miles up-river to Taunton. This last stretch was considerably more difficult to navigate for it was winding and narrow and the mills needed to be bypassed, often occasioning long delays for the boatmen while they waited for the waters to be released.

The upper reaches of the Tone were in a poor state for anything but the smallest tubs. In the winter months the journey would have been arduous and prone to delays, due most often to ice and flood, while in summer the water would be shallow, exposing shoals and mudbanks. The result was that the cost of goods, principally coal, became well beyond the means of many inhabitants of the town.

In one of those interesting displays of seventeenth-century public concern for the well-being of the poorer residents of Taunton, John Malet, MP for Bath and Sheriff of Somerset, sought, in 1638, to provide an improved means of conveying coals to Taunton. He was a wealthy man who had estates at Enmore in the west of Somerset and was therefore in a privileged position to take the necessary action. He obtained a commission under the Great Seal from Charles I, which enabled him to improve the River Tone navigation at his own expense as far as Ham Mills, and thereby was granted sole navigation rights over the river between Bridgwater and Taunton and authorised to levy tolls on the cargoes carried:

> This waterway, one of the earliest built in England, carried much general merchandise but was most important in assuaging the fuel famine as woodlands became exhausted, for it supplied to a very large area, even to south coast towns, coal carried across the Severn from Wales. He [John Malet] carried out the works, not to make money, but to help the poor by reducing the price of coal, and to aid the local economy by improved transport.[5]

During the time of John Malet's involvement in the navigation project, a family named Bobbett were carrying coals to Ham Mills. During the sixteenth century it is recorded that the Bobbetts had leased a piece of moorland from the Dean and Chapter of Wells at Ham Mills, in the Parish of Creech St Michael where they had set up premises as 'dealers in Sea coles'. Richard and his brother, Robert, were apparently complete masters of their trade, for they owned trows for bringing the coals from Wales, lighters (small barges) to take it up the river and packhorses to carry it to Taunton, North Curry, Langport and Wellington. In 1672, the Corporation of Bridgwater had become a little uneasy and brought an action against the brothers alleging 'conbynacon' (a monopoly) but it was proved 'that no abuse of power had occurred'.[6] Another coal haulier at the time was John Culverwell (1645–1716), who is noted as living in Ham Mills and his family based in North Curry and Creech St Michael. Also involved in this trade were his sons Anthony (1674–1716), John (1684–1741) and Edward (1688–1735). John's son Edward, who died in 1752, and later a cousin, Robert (1716–1810), was based in Taunton with his son William. Inevitably disputes arose between traders and it is not surprising that, in 1739, it is recorded that there was a dispute that went to law concerning the Culverwells and the Bobbett brothers. In later years, around 1778, William Culverwell was to become clerk to the Conservators of the River Tone.[7]

The improvement works to the river 'had been a great charge to the said John Malet'[8] but, by his death, they were not completed and the duties of maintaining and improving the river passed to his son, another John. Upon the son's death in 1656, the responsibility then passed to his daughter and, later still, the responsibility passed to her children, but it is likely, and perhaps understandable, that their commitment to maintaining the Tone was not great, and the condition of the river for navigation slowly declined once more. Maintenance was neglected and there was growing anxiety, particularly with the merchants in Taunton, that this would ultimately affect their trade in the town.

THE CONSERVATORS OF THE RIVER TONE ARE ESTABLISHED

In 1697 'thirty-four gentlemen' representing traders and merchants living in or around Taunton were persuaded that if matters did not improve, they would need to consider purchasing the navigation rights from the Malet family, and take over the responsibilities for maintaining and improving the condition of the river themselves. To do this they would first need to petition Parliament for the necessary powers. A year later, as there was no sign of improvement, they formally established themselves as a body and drew up 'General Proposals', which included not only the purchase of navigational rights from Bridgwater to Ham but the additional length of river to Taunton. Amongst their number they included a gentleman, various merchants, a doctor of physick, an apothecary, a tallow chandler, a goldsmith, a woolstapler and a grocer.

Their submission to Parliament stated that:

'Tis proposed that the River Tone, washing the Town of Taunton and emptying itself into Bridgwater, may be made navigable home to the Town of Taunton. That it hath been for many years last past the general opinion of the inhabitants of Taunton and the country around about that the bringing up Coal-Trows and Boats will be incouragement to trade, and an exceeding benefit to the Poor, and great good to the country round.

'Tis agreed that when the Moneys Subscribed shall be paid and the work wholly finished; that every Subscriber shall be reimburst, both the Principal Money and Profits, at the Rate of Seven Pounds per cent, with all Costs and Charges they shall be at for the carrying on and effecting the said work ...[9]

They appreciated that the necessary works would still need a considerable sum of money, but in a short time nearly £4,000 was subscribed. Immediately negotiations were opened to purchase the necessary land, together with the rights of navigation on the river. A figure of £330 was agreed with the vendors, and in 1699 the Tone Navigation Act was passed,[10] which authorised the setting up of the Conservators of the River Tone, as they were to be called, and set out the works still to be done, the method of financing them, how the profits were to be disbursed and the level of tolls to be levied.

There were to be thirty Conservators, elected from time to time by themselves, who would be, 'enabled to cleanse and keep the said River Tone navigable from Bridgwater to Ham Mills, and thence to the town of Taunton.'[11]

The Conservators were given powers to dig banks and to carry out works to remove impediments to the passage of craft upon the river, to cut new channels, after making due recompense, and to build bridges, wharves, locks, weirs, and turnpikes to improve the navigation. They were also permitted to make a path along the riverside for watermen, boat or bargemen, or others.

The mention of the word 'turnpike' is interesting, if not somewhat confusing. This fifteenth-century word means a 'barrier' preventing passage until a toll has been paid. In the early years of river navigations it referred to a lock weir, where a toll would be levied before a boatman could pass. In later years the word would be more commonly linked to highways, where, again, a toll would be exacted before a traveller could pass.

These extensive powers suggest that the river at this time was in a rather poor condition for navigation, despite the attempts of John Malet fifty years earlier. The responsibilities the Conservators were taking on were heavy, added to which they were now empowered to keep the navigation open through to Taunton, a 4-mile stretch that for many years had been notoriously difficult to navigate and would need considerable sums of money spent on it.

The 1699 Act included provisions to allow these costs to be defrayed, together with the initial capital investment 'that for reimbursing the Conservators the principal money of the said purchase, and what they shall lay out in making and keeping the said river navigable, etc, with interest at six per cent per annum, till they shall be repaid.'

The Conservators were also authorised to levy tolls, the level of which was strictly laid down in the Act:

... every boat, barge or vessel, that shall pass up the said river, from Bridgwater, or other part thereof, towards Ham Mills, shall pay, to the use of the said Conservators, a toll of not above

4*d* for every weigh [3 tons] of coals so carried, … and 2*d* for every ton of other goods, as often as they shall pass … to be paid and received at Knapbridge.

For barges passing Ham Mills through to Taunton there were additional charges that reflected the great cost of the works the Conservators would need to put in hand. Shrewdly, these were to be collected before the barges reached the lock at Ham Mills:

> … every boat, barge or vessel passing from the said Ham Mills, or any part of the said river, towards Taunton, shall pay at the first or lowermost lock on the said river at Coal Harbour, a further toll not exceeding 4/- for every weigh of coals so carried, and 2/- for every ton of other goods.[12]

The place called Coal Harbour, which most probably contained the wharves of the Bobbett family, was situated on the north side of the river, just below Ham Mills itself.

The majority of the cargoes carried up-river by barge would be destined either for Ham Mills, where they would be taken by waggon and distributed locally, or for Taunton. There was also a smaller but equally important trade carried down-river consisting mainly of agricultural produce, grain, flour, apples and cider and manufactured items including cloths and basket work, the former woven in towns such as Chard and Taunton, and the latter made locally from the abundant willow which grew alongside the river. These would have to pay tolls to the Conservators as well, not exceeding 1s between Taunton and Bridgwater.

Once the Conservators had both 'perfected the navigableness' of the river between Bridgwater and Taunton, and had been reimbursed for the costs of both the initial purchase and the subsequent improvement works, they were authorised to reduce the tolls by 75 per cent.

THE CONSERVATORS OF THE RIVER TONE TAKE CONTROL

This was the time when rivers in many parts of the country were being improved and extended for commercial navigation beyond their tidal limits. The building of locks and bypass channels around mills, together with the dredging of shoals and shallows, was costly and demanded continual maintenance. The River Thames, for example, was capable of being used by small boats for well over 100 miles beyond the limit of its tide at Teddington, although its upper reaches were increasingly difficult to pass due to the usual obstructions of weirs and shallows. As early as 1605, nearly 100 years before the setting up of the Conservators of the River Tone, James I had authorised an Act appointing eighteen commissioners to have powers to 'cleanse' the Thames for navigation. After successfully purchasing the navigation rights from the descendants of the Malet family, the Conservators of the River Tone, by all accounts, lost no time in getting some works underway to improve the navigation on the river.

That tireless traveller, Celia Fiennes, who visited the county at the end of the seventeenth century, recorded her impressions of the Tone and the activity at Ham Mills. She said:

… this river comes from Bridgewater, the tyde comes up beyond Bridgewater even within three miles of Taunton, its flowed by tyde which brings up the barges with coale to this place, after having pass'd a large common which on either hand leads a great waye good rich land with ditches and willow trees all for feeding cattle, and here at this little place where the boates unlade the coale, the packhorses comes, and takes it in sacks and so carryes it to the place all about; this is the Sea Coale brought from Bristole, the horses carrying 2 bushell at a tyme which at the place cost 18*d* and when it is brought to Taunton cost 2 shillings; the roads were full of these carryers going and returning.[13]

The 'little place' referred to is undoubtedly Coal Harbour.

It is more than likely that as the river between Ham Mills and Taunton was still a difficult navigation at the time and the tolls levied to use it so expensive, many traders chose to unload their cargoes at either Ham Mills or Coal Harbour and use horse-drawn waggons to take them into Taunton and further afield. In order to achieve an early return on their investment, the Conservators chose, understandably, to concentrate their efforts in those first years on improving the 7 miles between 'Borough Bridge,' where the Tone joins the Parrett, and Ham Mills. This was, after all, the most heavily used length and the receipts from tolls would be a good income to help fund the more costly works nearer Taunton. Indeed, in October 1699, the year of their inauguration, the Conservators engaged a Joseph Powell to bring gates for Obridge lock from Tewkesbury, by water, at a cost of £3 15s 0d. Repairing 'Barpool' lock cost £30 0s 0d. Within the first year of their control of the river, the Tone was carrying cargoes of timber, lime, stone and bricks in addition to the main cargo of coal. In June 1700, a boatman was paid £2 16s 0d 'for expenses and allowances and time for bringing up the first boat to try all the locks.'[14]

Joshua Toulmin, in his *History of Taunton*, states that over £3,000 had been spent within the first ten years of the Conservators taking over responsibility for the river and still it was not completely navigable: 'It was not navigable in the winter, much less in summer, for want of a lock, or half-lock, at a place called Round Island, and removing the shoal called Broad Shoal.' Both these obstructions were near what is now known as New Bridge.

The Conservators petitioned Parliament for powers, not only to carry out this work, but to levy additional tolls to recoup the extra expense they would be put to in attending to these obstructions. This action had the support of the inhabitants of Taunton and other surrounding towns who would clearly benefit from barges getting through to Taunton. The petition stated that 'unless some further Considerable sume be expended in Building or Erecting an half-lock or turnpike below a place called Knapp bridge … and cleansing a great shoal called Broad shoal … the river will never be completely navigable from Bridgwater to Taunton'.[15]

In presenting the petition to the House of Lords, it was requested that the Conservators be able to 'finish the Navigation of the said river from Bridgwater to Ham Mills'. In an interesting commentary on the conditions of the time, the petition continues:

… it would be much to the Advantage of this Part of the Country by keeping down the Price of Coals and Culme, preventing the Monopolies of these goods as formerly, Promotion of Trade by Carriage of all sorts of Tunnage goods by water for less than half the price of land carriage, the Preservation of the Highways, Increase of duty on water-borne Coals to

the Government by the Greater Consumption of them, and the preservation of estates of
neighbouring Gentlemen from the spoils and damages of the Poor … do in Winter season by
Topping and shrouding their trees, cutting and breaking their hedges with other disorders.

This last comment refers to the habit of the 'poor' who could not afford to buy coal and
would cut down trees and hedgerows for their fuel instead!

The petition was acceded to and in 1708 another Act[16] was passed enabling the works
to be undertaken and the tolls raised.

In order to remedy certain disagreements that had arisen over the use of the river banks
as towpaths, the 1708 Act amended earlier provisions in the 1699 Act, which had stated
that 'watermen, boatmen, bargemen and others may use winches, ropes, etc to draw up
vessels through the said river, with men and horses going on the banks thereof.' Unlike a
canal, which from the outset would be cut with a towpath, a river navigation would not
necessarily have such a path, particularly if private land extended to the river frontage.
What paths existed were probably used only for the occasional bank maintenance and
would not provide a continuous route along the entire length of the river. There were
instances where the boatmen were accused of trespassing upon private land with their
horses whilst towing the barges. The new Act placed a duty upon the Conservators to set
out a towpath and suitably compensate the owners of the land involved.

Work Begins

The Conservators quickly dealt with the sand shoal in the river and erected a half-lock at
Round Island, as authorised by the Act. It was to be known as the Curry Moor half-lock and
was situated some 300 yards down-river of the present-day New Bridge. The original Articles,
drawn up between the Conservators and William Roe (a stone mason of Bridgwater) and
dated 1708, still exist. He was paid £150 for his work and, 'he and his executors, administrators
and assignes shall from the completion of the half-lock meet out of their own costs and
charges any repairs for twenty years and to suffer, uphold and maintain the lock.'[17]

This lock must have helped considerably, for it was now possible to 'pen back' behind
the lock gates between three and four feet of water thereby giving a sufficient depth in
the river between here and Ham Mills. By 1724 it was recorded that it had been possible
to complete a towpath through to Taunton. By September 1728 it was obviously felt
that some further lock was required before Ham Mills, for an agreement was drawn up
between the Conservators and Robert Bennet of 'Michael Creech', a stone mason, to
build a new half-lock in the Tone at the 'hopyard' below Ham Mills for a sum of £50,
and maintain it for ten years.

However successful the Conservators were in keeping the river open for navigation,
the presence of mills along the river would always be an obstacle. It can be assumed that
they were kept continually aware of the conflict that would arise if the free flow of water
that millers had enjoyed for centuries was to be interfered with in any way. Each mill
would have a weir behind which the water up-river would be penned until it was released
through sluices to power the mill wheel. In summertime, when the millers' work was at

its busiest, the water in the river would be at its lowest. It is not surprising, therefore, that the miller guarded the amount of water in his millpond jealously and was not prepared to lose all or part of it in letting barges through. The millers could almost hold barge traffic to ransom and charged exorbitantly for the right to pass. It is no wonder that delays were caused and tempers flared.

> When a miller opened the weir (for barges to pass through) the amount of water available to turn his wheel was substantially reduced. So millers were unwilling to let barges 'flash' through, except at times, and prices, that suited them. Consequently tolls at weirs became heavy, and there were frequent disputes between millers and bargemen.[18]

In an interesting comment from a boatman that has survived down the years, William Kitch, who was born in 1822, recalled that:

> … when I was a boy I used to go with barges up the River Tone from Bridgwater to Taunton. At this time there were locks and half-locks on the river to enable it to be navigated. There was a half-lock just below Bathpool Mill. If there was no water running over the weir at Bathpool Mill, the millers did not allow us to take water to fill the lock, and we had to keep our boats until the water rose. I have known boats stop there for six or seven hours in a day until the water came. Sometimes the men would try to take the water, but the millers came and stopped them.[19]

There were no mills below Ham Mills, largely because the river up to Ham was tidal, but above Ham there were two, at Creech St Michael and Bathpool, both being flour and grist mills.

In the Conservators' Minute Book, for December 1763, it was resolved 'to purchase Firepool Mill, to pull it down for the benefit of the navigation at a sum not exceeding £45.' It was in fact purchased for £32, although the cost of demolishing the building is not given. Four years later, further expenditure of £39 was incurred in repairing a breach at Firepool, near where the mill had stood, and again that year they resolved to purchase Obridge Mill, possibly for the same reasons as at Firepool.

As well as building half-locks, and undertaking the cutting of passing channels at the mills to circumvent the mill ponds, the Conservators were required to repair, and more often rebuild, the old timber bridges that they had 'inherited'. These were generally of low headroom and with narrow openings, causing considerable difficulties and obstruction to the boatmen. In February 1766, the Conservators contracted John Robins of Langport:

> … within four months to take down the old Knapp Bridge, build over … the River Tone and erect a good and substantial new Bridge across the same river in the place and Head of the said old bridge now to be taken down. The new bridge to consist of one arch of one and twenty foot clear to be built entirely of good Pibsbury stone, except only the ringing which is to be of Hamhill stone. Parapet walls 2½ft high and 16ins thick … for his natural life and at his own proper charges provide and keep the piers and bridge from sinking.[20]

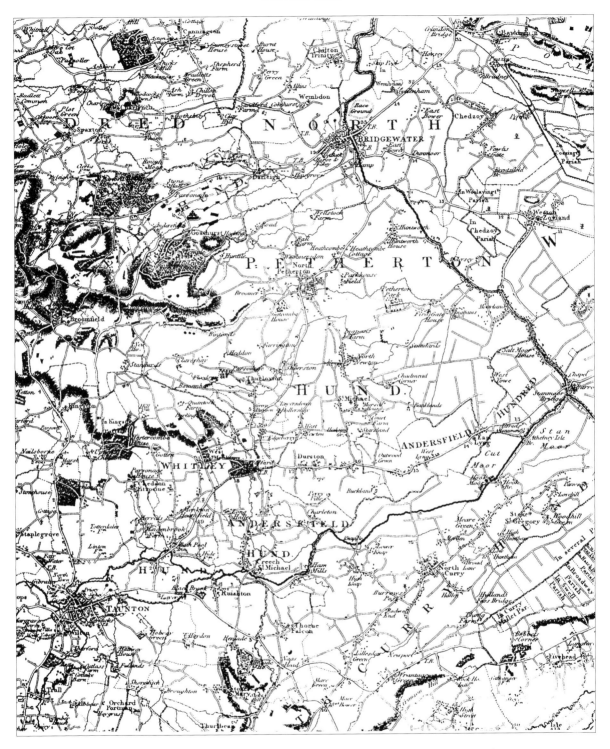

An extract from Greenwood's map of Somerset, 1822 – published before the line of the Bridgwater and Taunton Canal was known.

He was to be paid £45 for the entire work, £15 when the old bridge was taken down and the balance when the new bridge was complete. It is likely that poor Mr Robins underestimated the cost for the work, for, on 11 July, William Spiller 'charged £45 for the supply of the stone, the lime and for labour for Knapp Bridge.'[21]

This mention of Knapp Bridge is interesting, for there is little doubt that it refers to the bridge that preceded the present one at the point now called New Bridge near North Curry and was probably the reason for the name 'new bridge'. Pibsbury stone was specified by the Conservators as the main stone to be used; the quarries were situated between Langport and Long Sutton and, being close to the River Yeo, the stone could easily be brought to the site by barge using the River Parrett.

The Conservators were soon to realise the difficulties they would be continually facing to keep the River Tone navigable. The river below Ham Mills was largely tidal and while barges could expect to reach Coal Harbour without the need of horses on the few high tides, most of the time they would be needed from Burrowbridge. Beyond Ham Mills there was no question; horses were needed all the way to Taunton.

The Conservators' problems seemed to have fluctuated between those brought about either by insufficient water, or too much of it! In 1768, the season's heavy rains and floods had caused damage to many weirs and locks on the river and their minute books contain frequent references to the need to carry out essential repair work. One of the two half-locks at Bathpool was converted into the more conventional pound lock, up-river of the Mill, whilst, at about the same time, a similar lock was installed at Ham.

Spencer, in his 1769 *History of Somerset*, gives an interesting insight into the cargoes that were carried on the river at that time, and makes some prophetic comments about the use of canals, which were then very much in their infancy! He writes that:

> … coals are extremely reasonable, being brought to Bridgwater by ships from Swanzey and Neath, in Wales, and from Bridgwater to Taunton in barges. By the same conveyance, all sorts of heavy goods are brought thither from Bristol, such as iron, lead, oil, wine, flax, pitch, tar, grocery, dying drugs, and the like. This navigation is supported by means of a toll paid by the barges at each lock entered on the river. There is no doubt that this navigation might be considerably improved, by connecting some parts of the river, where the stream is rapid, and, in consequence of that rapidity, the course is very crooked, by canals cut from one part to the other; perhaps when the modern improvements in inland navigation are better known, this may be attempted.

In 1777, another well-known Taunton author, Joshua Toulmin, whose book the *History of Taunton* gives considerable information on the river navigation, was elected a Conservator, a position he held until 1804.

A somewhat unusual situation occurred in the mid-1770s when the country as a whole was being affected by an influx of counterfeit coins, usually halfpennies and pennies. These coins were obviously showing up in the tolls taken, particularly at Ham Mills, and, in 1778, the Conservators resolved, on finding a 'quantity of bad half pence tendered for the payment of tolls', that; 'the Clerk to the Conservators do not take or receive of any person or persons for Tolls at the lock any greater sum in half pence at any one payment, than one shilling, and that he be careful to take good half-pence'.[22]

It was at the same meeting, held at the George Inn at Taunton, that the Conservators decided, in order to avoid too much water running to waste during the dry summer months, because boatmen were not closing the half-locks properly, that instructions be given 'to all boatmen to let down the lashes and strut the gates, after they have passed the locks, up or down.'[23]

In November 1794 it is recorded that floods caused damage to the new lock at Ham which not only stopped barges from passing through, but affected the working of the Mill as well. 'The struts and the stonework under the struts at Ham Mill was driven away by a flood, which struts was kept in repair by the occupier and proprietor of Ham Mill.'[24]

Three years later, the Conservators put in hand repairs to the half-locks at Ham, just below the mill there, as well as repairs to the half-locks at Bathpool and Curry Moor, the lock at Creech beside the mill, and stone repairs to the arch of Knapp Bridge. They must have felt that there was no end to the constant repairs, and that maintaining a clear navigation to Taunton was fraught with continual and costly problems.

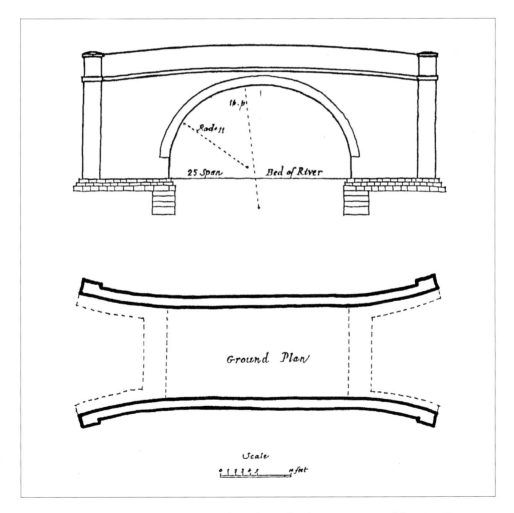

Knapp Bridge, redrawn from John Easton's plans of 1817, for the Conservators of the River Tone.

By 1796 the Conservators had become increasingly concerned at the condition of the 'old timber bridge' that carried a well used trackway over the Tone from Knapp across the moor to Creech St Michael. Apparently the boatmen experienced difficulties in passing through the narrow openings between the piers. And they were, indeed, narrow. There still survives the survey measurements taken that year by two stone masons, John Fry and William Drewe, noting that:

> No 1 opening was 10ft 3ins clear, not arched.
> No 2 opening was 11ft 11ins clear.
> No 3 opening was 10ft 7ins clear.

They also noted that the boats used the centre opening as the others were 'stopped up by the Parishoners of North Curry'.[25]

Their annual inspection the following year, 1797, revealed a host of other improvements that would need to be done, such as removing shallows and sand-shoals, repairing lock walls and gates and attending to the half-locks and bridges, including the bridge at Knapp. It would all take a lot of money and could not be done at once. For example, it was to be a further two years before the lock at Ham received its 'four new sashes', and twenty before the bridge at Knapp was attended to.

For this bridge they engaged the services of John Easton, a surveyor from Bradford on Tone, and son of the well known surveyor Josiah Easton. He was to work with his brother, William, from Hillfarrance, on erecting a new, single-span, stone bridge, very

Knapp Bridge in 2006.

similar in design to the one built sixty years earlier at 'New Bridge'. Pibsbury stone was again specified, but with two rings 'in the arch in Hamden Hill stone'. For this work they were paid £380. Today, this elegant bridge still stands in splendid isolation on the moors, for the trackway is not used to the extent it once was. It is in surprisingly good condition, considering the minimal maintenance it would have received over the intervening years, testimony to the high quality of craftsmanship that the Conservators brought to bear upon the work they undertook.

As the eighteenth century drew to a close, and almost 100 years had passed since those 'thirty-four gentlemen' agreed to form themselves into a body of Conservators of the River Tone, their successors had every reason to feel a degree of contentment with the success of their venture, and the amount of trade that was carried on the river. However, this would have been tinged with some concern over the growing popularity of canals. The period known as 'canal mania' had set in motion an ambitious, if largely unrealistic, euphoria so that virtually every town in the country wanted a canal. Certainly, these purpose-built waterways could offer a more convenient means of water transport; they were free of obstructions such as weirs and mills, the boatman could depend on a consistent depth of water and they were largely unaffected by problems of flooding although could suffer from lack of water in long dry summers.

The Conservators had always been aware that their river navigation would need to be every bit as efficient as a canal in order to be competitive. Their tolls would need to reflect this and as these tolls were the only income the Conservators had, this in turn would dictate the amount of maintenance and repair they could carry out.

The country was now involved in the Napoleonic Wars which had broken out in 1793, at the time when canal building was getting into its stride. The protracted campaigns, which did not end until 1815, were to have the effect of bringing considerable financial austerity to the country. Money was scarce, and many would-be canal promoters and subscribers were simply not prepared to finance further expansionist canal schemes, at least for a time. For a while the Conservators could enjoy a short respite from the attentions of the canal builders.

REVENUE FROM TOLLS

The tolls that the Conservators were able to levy were strictly laid down in their authorising Act of 1698, but they were also able to pay themselves a 'dividend' of 6 per cent per year on their outlay, which they termed their 'debt', and which was made up of the initial purchase, together with the costs of subsequent improvements. After that, any monies remaining would be given 'in Trust for the use of the poor of Taunton and Taunton St James'.[26]

Charles Hadfield states that the debt, as recorded by Joshua Toulmin in his *History of Taunton*, had amounted to nearly £5,700 by 1717, the first year that the undertaking had paid its way, and 'dividends were subsequently paid on that sum … it was considered that the Conservators were entitled to 6% upon this … and, because earnings did not then allow it to be paid, 6%, less the years profit, was added each year to the total of the debt. The nominal debt, therefore, ceased to have any relation to the actual sum spent on the navigation.'[27]

As the Conservators carried out further works to the river over the years, the 'nominal debt' increased to such an extent that it became clear that there would be no monies left over after all disbursements, for the Conservators to assist the charities in Taunton as their Act required.

It is not surprising, therefore, that some found the method the Conservators used in keeping their books rather disturbing and considered that they were, themselves, benefiting financially from the navigation, leaving no surplus for the town charities. In 1734 a local resident petitioned the Commissioners for Charities in Somerset, accusing them of '… having illegally entered and charged … several exorbitant, unnecessary and unwarrantable charges, by means whereof the charity for the benefit of the poor of Taunton, was, and had been long protracted and delayed'[28] The effect of this was that, for four years, the accounts of the Conservators were suspended whilst matters were investigated. By 1737, however, they had successfully appealed against a decree of the Charity Commissioners, when they stated that they had only paid themselves the principal money and interest disbursed for making the river navigable. The decree was reversed, 'affording an honorable testimony to the truth and integrity of their accounts.'[29]

By 1760, after the Conservators had been involved in considerable expense in maintaining the river, this 'dividend' that they paid themselves (or as it would be more properly termed today, the debt), amounted to nearly £14,500, whilst the toll receipts for the same period were just £464. Thirty years later the toll receipts amounted to £734, whilst by the beginning of the nineteenth century, it had risen to £1,100, when over 11,000 tons of coal alone had been hauled through to Taunton. But the notional dividend had also risen to an astronomical £85,000. At this point, the Justices to the Quarter Sessions who examined the annual accounts of the Conservators, refused to pass them on the basis that they had been improperly kept and, despite many commercially successful years of trading by the Conservators, the poor of Taunton had yet to receive any benefit! After some initial resistance from the Conservators, they agreed to recalculate their debt, and by 1803, it was agreed at £13,000.

The next two decades were to be their most successful trading years, despite the continual problems the Conservators experienced over the state of the river. Their Treasurer was able to report, in 1823, that over 28,000 tons of coal had been brought to Taunton from Bridgwater, together with a further 2,000 tons of general goods, and over 700 tons brought in from Langport. In the reverse direction, over 800 tons had been taken to Bridgwater, mainly serge, woollen goods and agricultural produce. All this represented nearly £2,500 in receipts to the Conservators, a figure which was to be repeated the next year and very nearly equalled in 1825.

The tonnage brought to Taunton represents almost 100 tons each working day throughout the year and probably indicates the maximum that could be handled on the river, bearing in mind the obstructions and difficulties with which the boatmen had to contend. With each barge carrying, on average, around twenty tons apiece fully laden,[30] a conservative estimate would show that around seven to ten barges would be unloading at Taunton wharves each day.[31]

It is easy to picture the scene of activity on the riverside as dozens of labourers and coal-porters busied themselves in unloading the barges with barrows and baskets and loading the waiting wagons for the carters and merchants to distribute further afield. For the boatmen, bringing up the barges, it was heavy work; in summer, they would need to steer clear of shallows and sand shoals in the river and interminable delays at the mills, while in winter, ice and floods must have made hauling a heavily laden barge up-river against the current far from easy. At the end of the journey, they would also be expected to assist in unloading the cargoes, while others would lead the horses away to stables.

There were a number of traders who owned their barges and who traded on the Tone up to Ham Mills, and on to Taunton. The receipt books of the toll collector at Ham Mills for 1822 state that there were fifteen separate traders in business. They included John Culverwell, Joseph Davey, Charles and John Goodland, Benjamin Hammett, Richard Sharman, Joseph Potter, Joseph Kingsbury (senior), James Locke, James Gridley and Joseph and Thomas Smith. Stuckey and Bagehot, from Langport, also operated barges to Taunton.[32]

The number of barges coming to Ham Mills was nearly two dozen a day, but not all of these would have continued through to Taunton. In June that year, for example, Joseph Kingsbury (senior), who largely carried coal, made over forty trips to Ham Mills from Bridgwater, as did his colleague, William Grainger. At the time, the toll charged was 4s a weigh of coal. For other goods it was 2s 2d a ton. During the month of July that year, a staggering 990 weighs were recorded as being received at Ham Mills, nearly 3,000 tons, earning the Conservators over £224 for the month. Other cargoes upon which tolls were levied that month were 11 tons of bricks and tiles, 7 tons of sand and 29 tons of stone. Lime, timber and salt would have made up much of the remaining cargoes.

THE CONSERVATORS' RIVER INSPECTIONS

The Tone Conservators met once a year, apart from the river inspections and any special meeting that may be called, and held their meeting usually in a hotel or inn in Taunton. Their Minute Books record that, in 1763, for instance, they met at the George Inn, whilst, in 1798, the Old Angel was the venue, and in 1826, the Bell Inn.

Their membership was drawn from the gentlemen, professional men and traders in and around the town, and never exceeded thirty. In 1830, for instance, a meeting was called to elect new members:

> Notice is hereby given that the surviving Conservators of the River Tone in the County of Somerset do intend to assemble at the Bell Inn, in Taunton, to choose some other persons to be joined to them to be Conservators of the said river, in the room of such Conservators as are dead or have been removed since the last election, so as to make up the number of

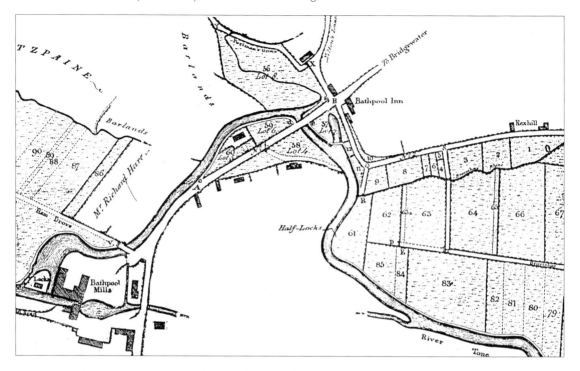

An inclosure plan, around 1830, showing the original course of the River Tone at Bathpool before the new cut was made.

the said Conservators to thirty, conformably to an Act of Parliament made and passed in the tenth and eleventh years of the reign of King William the Third, entitled an Act for making and keeping the River Tone Navigable from Bridgwater to Taunton.

Their duties and responsibilities in keeping the River Tone navigable were well known and appreciated by the many townsfolk and merchants who benefited from the trade that was able to reach the town. Anyone unjustly criticising their work was immediately taken to task, for the Conservators were held in high esteem, and their efforts respected.

Such was the situation, when in October 1824, a traveller to Taunton saw the town submerged by floods. He wrote that from his observations, this had been caused by a great amount of timber from an adjacent timber yard being washed into the river and blocking up the narrow archways of the old bridge. He stated that he was informed that the river was under 'the special care of twelve Conservators, who met regularly once a month, took a speculating walk round the environs of the town, and then adjourned to a sociable dinner.' To this, the editor of the *Taunton Courier* replied that 'our Correspondent is quite wrong respecting the Conservators, who are very respectable gentlemen and highly useful Functionaries and whose services being entirely gratuitous, entitle them to public respect. Whatever is expended in their personal indulgence, is entirely at their individual expense. The mischief complained of is neither within their province or power to obviate'.

They would be well aware of the condition of their navigation, both from comments made to them by traders and from their own Inspector. The course of the river between

Ruishton and Taunton must have caused them many problems with a series of locks and weirs and troublesome shallows on the numerous bends of the river, particularly in the vicinity of Bathpool and Obridge. The original course of the Tone, in the early 1800s, took it past the present day Bathpool Inn, on the Bridgwater Road and then in a wide arc to Bathpool Mill. Today, this line is still visible, with its group of waterside cottages tucked back from the main road, where it is said many boatmen lived. On Christmas Eve, 1821, 'the local blacksmith, of the name Southwood, on coming out of the Bathpool Inn, near this town, in an intoxicated state, is supposed to have mistaken the path and fallen into the river, which was very high at the time, as nothing has since been heard of him.'[33] A week later his body was found in the river at Creech.

A survey of the old bridge at Burrowbridge, May 1824. (Courtesy of the Somerset Record Office)

The Conservators' annual inspection of the river commenced at Taunton and they would be able to see at first hand the condition of the navigation throughout these difficult lengths, although, apart from constructing locks, such as those at Obridge and Bathpool, and reducing the mud-banks, there was only a limited amount of improvement they could carry out. There were some sceptics in the town, however, who misconstrued these annual inspections as a pleasant day out affording an opportunity to eat and drink well.

Few descriptions survive of these inspections, apart from brief records in the Conservators' minute books, but a Conservator did describe, in a letter to the *Taunton Courier*, the details of such a day in 1811 when the Conservators went as far as the half-lock at Curry Moor:

A boat, with an elegant awning was provided, and a plentiful store of the luxuries and delicacies of the season, were laid in to satisfy the cravings of those on board, when we arrived at the half-lock. I never went down in the boat, but took care to be at the place of destination when the viands were produced and did my share in the destruction of the eatables and drinkables.

After this, began the amusements, such as cards, backgammon, smoking, bowls and skittles, pitch and toss, etc. These continued till the time arrived for returning as far as Ham Mills, to the house of the person who collected the Tolls, and did most of the business as to the management of the river for the Conservators. Here again, was an ample supply of cream, cakes, toast, and everything requisite for a sumptuous tea, the amusements were revived till the voice of the bargeman signified it would be dark before the boat would be back to Taunton; they then embarked, and tales, songs and witticisms filled up the time till the boat was safely moored near one of the arches of the Tone Bridge; here the evening was ended in a jovial and convivial way, the party being joined by a number of their friends (male, and I have known females also) who had been anxiously awaiting the return of those bold navigators from so perilous a voyage![34]

Whether the journey was perilous or not, talk of canals was again rife in the region and the Conservators could not afford to let the condition of the river deteriorate. As a body, they would not be qualified to comment on any engineering works necessary to improve their navigation and they would need to call in experts. They appointed William Armstrong, a surveyor from Bristol, with a remit to inspect and survey the river to ascertain its state for navigation, and to point out any improvements that might appear necessary and practicable. He was also asked to show that 'the river was capable of supplying a trade on a very extensive scale'.[35] The survey was to be made in two sections: between North Town Bridge, in Taunton, and Burrowbridge, and between Burrowbridge and Bridgwater.

William Armstrong's Report, 1824

This report,[36] when submitted, must have caused some anxiety, for William Armstrong found many obstructions and difficulties that would need attention if the river was to become an efficient navigation. There were sand-shoals, low-lying and waterlogged towpaths (particularly impassable in times of wet weather), lengths of river too narrow for barges to pass and obstructions caused by the narrowness of many bridge openings. Two comments he makes are interesting: 'at a place called Swans Neck, between Obridge and Bathpool, it was difficult to navigate a barge in blowing weather, and, with a head wind and strong current, it is difficult to pass'. In another, he was concerned at the state of the towpath alongside the River Parrett below Burrowbridge, observing that, 'It is obstructed by the proper gates having been replaced by stiles, which the horses are obliged to jump over'. How this was managed whilst towing a barge needs some imagination! Interestingly, his view was that the number of sand-shoals present in the river was a direct result of the 'decrease in current' caused by obstructions, such as dams and weirs, penning back the water.

However, it was the old, three-arched bridge at Burrowbridge that caused him most concern. He commented not only on the number of barges waiting at the junction of the Tone and Parrett which 'formed a barrier to the tidal influx, with water becoming stagnant and alluvium deposited', but also upon the need for the removal of the bridge itself, '…which now constitutes a dam … this would afford a greater influx of tide which would flow with a greater rapidity for boats coming up-river, and greater velocity of the ebbing tide, an increase which will help scouring'. Referring to the need to carry out some additional dredging of the river, he added, perhaps hopefully, 'I propose generally to employ a horse and a couple of men with an iron drag line for the purpose'.

Whilst William Armstrong recommended the removal of the bridge at Burrowbridge, it was not within the powers of the Conservators to do anything about it. However, they were no doubt instrumental in assisting the Turnpike Commissioners in immediately promoting a Bill to Parliament and an Act was passed for its rebuilding that same year.[37]

All this must have been a body blow to the Conservators, for how could they ever hope to argue that their navigation was in every way as efficient as any possible canal that might be built? By the end of the second decade of the century, however, the Conservators' attention was being directed, somewhat reluctantly, to the increasing threat posed by the very real possibility of a canal to Taunton. There had been proposals for various canals in the county put forward over the years, many involving the county town, but as yet nothing had materialised. The day was not far off when they would have to take the threat of a canal to Taunton very seriously indeed.

CANAL SCHEMES IN SOMERSET
1768–1828

When the industrial and manufacturing areas of the Midlands and North East England were developing during the mid-1700s it was the need to transport fuel and raw materials over areas of the country not immediately served by rivers, that brought about the demand for canal building. When, subsequently, these canals were linked to the navigable rivers they formed vital inland trade routes across the country providing a communication network that was used, in many instances, for well over 100 years.

The main thrust for canal building in the south-west, however, developed from a desire, long cherished in the hearts of many surveyors and entrepreneurs of the time, to construct a waterway across the peninsula, linking the Bristol Channel with the English Channel. At its narrowest point these two channels are only 33 miles apart, and although connecting them would be a formidable undertaking, it was a challenge that was to fascinate a succession of leading engineers in the eighteenth and nineteenth centuries as more and more ambitious barge and ship canals were considered.

Not only would such a link save many days sailing on a journey round the south-west peninsula (some reports of the time mention a saving of as much as four weeks), but it would avoid the treacherous Cornish coast and Land's End, where the small vessels were vulnerable to the powerful south-westerlies.

In a vivid description of these dangers, *The Sun*, as late as 1824, was to say of the seas around the Cornish peninsula and the lower stretches of the Bristol Channel that they were:

> … particularly dangerous … the velocity of the tide, which frequently comes up with a head of five or six feet when added to the prevalent winds from the south-west, makes it, under such circumstances, next to impossible to beat down, even in the chops of the Channel, whilst in a gale of wind, the iron-bound coast of the North of Devon and Cornwall threatens certain destruction; there is no friendly port for which a distressed vessel can bear, except the distant ones of Padstow and Milford. Those who have witnessed, during the fair moments of summer, the perilous situation of a ship embayed below Hartland Point, with the usual wind blowing inshore, can only form an adequate idea of the wintry terrors of that long barrier of cliffs opposed to the fury of the Atlantic.[1]

As early as 1768, James Brindley was commissioned by a group of Taunton businessmen to survey a line for a canal linking the Bristol Channel with Exeter, using part of the navigable River Tone between Burrowbridge and Taunton. Despite the enthusiasm of the sponsors the scheme did not proceed further than a survey and it is unlikely whether, in those early days of canal building, the engineering knowledge would have been available to take a waterway over the 300ft contour of the hills between Taunton and Tiverton. A year later, Robert Whitworth, James Brindley's assistant, was commissioned to investigate a more direct route across the Blackdowns from Bridgwater Bay to Seaton, using the River Parrett and the River Axe, but like Brindley's scheme this proposal got no further than the drawing board.

Variations on these two approaches, an east–west line between Bristol and Exeter and a north–south route between Bridgwater and Seaton, occupied the minds of canal promoters and engineers again towards the end of the century, as 'canal mania' gripped the country. Each had its own supporters and advocates, and whilst some never got further than surveys, others progressed with varying degrees of success towards the necessary Parliamentary measures.

By the 1790s engineering and surveying skills had improved, the economies of moving goods about the country by water were appreciated and the working requirements of the canal users themselves better understood. Robert Whitworth was commissioned to review his original proposal and confirmed that his line over the Blackdowns was still feasible. Again, no action was taken. The Napoleonic Wars now occupied the concerns of many and sponsors found it difficult to raise the money to embark upon such schemes. There was also the lingering thought that, if a canal were to be built at all across the peninsula, it would probably be better to think in terms of a ship, rather than a barge canal.

Many a fine vessel came to grief on the rocks of the Cornish and Devon coasts.

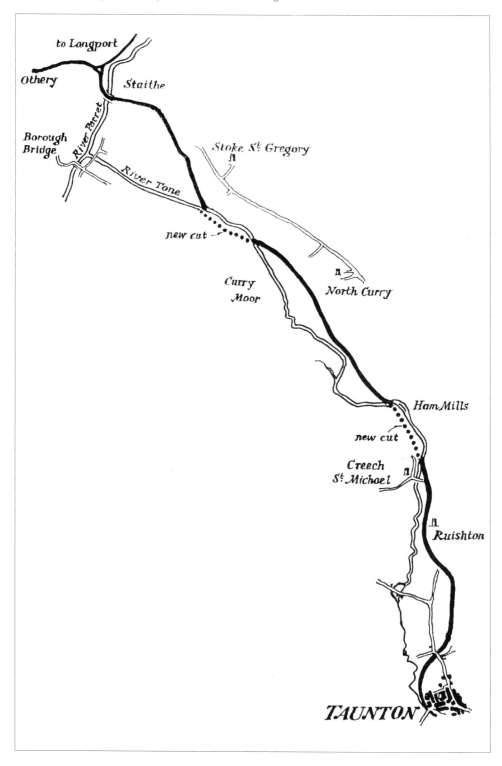

A redrawn plan showing the Bristol and Western Canal Co.'s proposals of 1796. From Othery, the canal crossed the River Parrett and used sections of the River Tone on its route to Taunton. The river was, in these places, accommodated in a new cut.

It was the proposal to link London to Bristol by means of the Kennet and Avon Canal which provided the impetus for a renewed approach to promoting canals in the West Country. Not only would a route between Bristol and Exeter provide the sought after inter-channel link, but, by joining with the River Avon, a connection could be made with the Kennet and Avon, opening up opportunities to bring the great wealth of agricultural produce from the West Country into the capital.

At the beginning of the 1800s, sea trade in the Bristol Channel and River Avon was growing considerably, and the Port of Bristol itself was, at the time, a major port for the region. A large proportion of its trade was manufactured goods, brought down the River Severn from the Midlands, and coal from South Wales, although overseas trade was also using the port.

The River Avon was navigable as far as Bristol for moderately sized vessels, but the wharves and warehouses in the centre of the city were some 8 miles from the sea, up a winding and heavily tidal river, such that, 'It was becoming increasingly unsuitable for large ships, at a time when rival ports such as Liverpool were expanding rapidly and overtaking Bristol in commercial prosperity.'[2]

In April, 1792, the Kennet & Avon Canal Co. received its authorising Act, and, as work got underway two further West Country Canals were put forward. The first proposal envisaged a canal between Taunton and Exeter, to be known as the Grand Western Canal. Although Brindley's scheme for such a route had not been taken further than initial surveys, there were many in the West Country who felt that a renewed effort should be made to get a canal underway. William Jessop, already working on the Kennet and Avon at the time, was commissioned to survey a route in greater detail, and in 1794, assisted by that well-known Taunton surveyor, Josiah Easton, he suggested a line between Exeter and Taunton, together with an additional canal extension beyond Taunton to Uphill, so that the Canal Company would have its own outlet to the Bristol Channel, and thereby, directly attract the coal traffic from South Wales.[3]

The other canal scheme was to link Bristol to Taunton. A group of promoters commissioned William White to outline a possible canal that would link Bristol to the newly opened collieries at Nailsea and continue to Bridgwater and Taunton, taking coal to these towns and returning with agricultural produce for the London market, via the Kennet and Avon Canal. Promoted as a 'Proposal for a Navigational Canal from the River Avon, (near Bristol) to Bridgwater and Taunton…whereby an inland communication will be formed between BRISTOL, BATH and LONDON and the Northern and Western Counties', it was to be known as the Bristol and Western Canal. The line chosen took the waterway from Morgan's Pill on the Avon, via Nailsea, through a tunnel to Banwell and thence to the east side of Bridgwater where a small basin alongside the Parrett was to be formed.

Strangely, instead of taking a line directly to Taunton from Bridgwater, the canal turned eastwards and connected with Westonzoyland, Middlezoy and Othery, before turning westwards, crossing the Parrett at Staithe and running alongside the River Tone as far as Athelney. Here the canal used a short length of the course of the River Tone, whilst the river itself was accommodated in a 'new cut'. The proposed waterway then continued to Ham Mills taking a new course through Creech St Michael and Ruishton to avoid the

inadequate river navigation that existed beyond Ham. The entry into Taunton was along
the line of the Black Brook, through the fields between Lambrook and Holway, rejoining
the River Tone at Priory Fields and terminating at the wharves at Coal Orchard.[4]

Why such a circuitous route was felt necessary between Bridgwater and Taunton is
not clear; the length of the proposed waterway was over 20 miles compared with a direct
distance of a little under 11 miles. It is possible that, by suggesting use of short lengths of
the River Tone, the Bristol & Western Canal Co. had hoped to build upon the existing
barge traffic of the Conservators and so win them over, when a Bill was eventually laid
before Parliament. However, from an engineering point of view, it was easier to cross the
River Parrett at Staithe, where it was narrower than at Bridgwater and close to its tidal
limit, and thus avoid the construction of an expensive aqueduct. At any rate the resultant
line would have been a considerably costly affair for any group of promoters.

With three separate canal schemes now before the Somerset landowners, it is not
surprising that there was considerable confusion as to just what was being seriously
proposed and concern as to whether there was sufficient trade to meet the expectations
of each. To add to this confusion, Josiah Easton, that year (1794), also drew up proposals
for an inter-channel scheme to link Uphill, on the Bristol Channel, with Seaton, on the
south coast. This may have been more of a political than a practical move, for it spurred
both the Grand Western Canal promoters and those supporting the Bristol and Western
Canal to seek the necessary Parliamentary powers for their respective canals, both being
submitted in 1796.[5]

The locks at Keynsham near Bristol on the short length of the River Avon navigation that linked
Bristol to the Kennet and Avon Canal at Bath. From a painting by A. Wilde Parsons. (Courtesy of
Taunton Deane Borough Council)

Although Easton's Uphill to Seaton proposal was never submitted to Parliament, either the Bristol and Western or the Taunton to Exeter would have provided that elusive inter-channel canal. Mainly due to objections from local landowners, of which there were a considerable number, the Bristol and Western Canal Bill was defeated, although the Grand Western Canal Co. was more successful, obtaining its Act that same year, 1796.

With the country still at war with France, economic prospects for trade were uncertain and sponsors and speculators held back from any long-term investments. This was certainly no time to undertake grandiose canal schemes and accordingly, the Bristol and Western Canal promoters abandoned their attempt to link Bristol with Taunton. As for the Grand Western Canal Co., this was no time to construct a canal in isolation. The glorious expectations of only four years before had come to nothing. Thus it remained until 1810, when the Kennet and Avon Canal was opened, providing yet again the incentive for a fresh look at the possibilities for further canals in the south-west.

A REVIVAL OF INTEREST

Many of the share-holders of the Kennet & Avon Canal Co. harboured ambitions to extend their interests further than Bristol, and foresaw great potential for a canal linking that city with the south coast. Who better to ask than John Rennie? – particularly now that he was free of his duties at the Kennet & Avon. Early in 1810, he was instructed to consider a line for such a canal, but, this time, 'it was to be capable of navigating vessels of all descriptions of not less than 120 tons register measurement, and also to report generally on the subjects of a canal on any other scale.'[6]

A ship canal had many advantages, for it could avoid the costly and time consuming operation of transhipment from vessel to barge. Any observer at the port of Bridgwater in those days would have witnessed the extraordinary labour and delay that was involved in double handling the cargoes into the barges. There were, however, disadvantages. No longer could river navigations be considered, as had been the case with the earlier inter-channel canals, for they could not provide the depth of water the ships would need. Furthermore, the canal would need to be cut from coast to coast, and would have to be constructed to larger dimensions than a barge canal. Its larger locks would require considerable quantities of water.

John Rennie chose for his proposed English and Bristol Channels Ship Canal a route from Bridgwater Bay, taking advantage of 'the open and capacious mouth of the Parrett, at its entrance to the Bristol Channel [which would] render it an easy matter for vessels to pass into any canal.'[7]

From Combwich, where there would be a tidal basin and lock, the proposed Ship Canal would run alongside the River Parrett, crossing the River Tone at Burrowbridge by means of an aqueduct to Langport, Ilton and Donyatt, reaching a summit near Chard before descending beside the River Axe to Seaton, where another tidal basin and lock would gain access to the English Channel. The summit would be at nearly 300ft above sea level and two reservoirs were incorporated in the proposals to provide sufficient replenishment water for the top locks. The canal was to be a massive 92ft wide and 13ft deep, far larger than anything that had been proposed previously.[8]

Rennie incorporated in his tidal basin at Combwich a 'wet dock' or floating harbour, which, when closed off from the river, allowed the sailing vessels to load and unload irrespective of the tides, thus predating the floating harbour that was eventually built at Bridgwater by over a quarter of a century. He estimated the costs, exclusive of the harbour works on the south coast, at just over one million pounds, but added that the expected income from tolls could include over £12,500 per year 'in carrying coals, for over 200,000 tons of coal, culm and stone coal (anthricite) are consumed annually in the region through which the canal passes.' There was also over £2,500 per year to be earned, he said, from carrying 'over 1,000 tons of merchandise from Bristol, Bridgwater, Wolverhampton, Sheffield, Manchester, and the Bar Iron works of Wales.'[9]

Despite receiving considerable support from many quarters, Rennie's scheme did not progress further 'on account of the then scarcity of money, and the general pressure of the times, [it was] agreed to postpone all further proceedings in the matter until a more favourable period should arrive.'[10]

A Canal Between Bristol and Taunton

With the abandonment of the ship canal proposal, attention returned to the concept of a direct waterway for barges between Bristol and Taunton, particularly if interest could be rekindled in undertaking the Grand Western link to Exeter. Some shareholders in the Kennet & Avon Canal Co. were predisposed to invest financially in such a proposal, particularly as the Grand Western Canal already had Parliamentary authorisation.

In 1810, John Rennie was commissioned to review the earlier proposals of the Bristol & Western Canal Co., whose scheme had been shelved some fourteen years earlier. He was assisted by John Easton, who would survey the Taunton to Bridgwater length while William White would concentrate on the route from Bridgwater to the River Avon. At the same time, the Grand Western Canal Co. decided to make a start on its canal, and appointed John Rennie to oversee the work on a length between Tiverton and Holcombe Rogus. Unfortunately, the missing link in this strategy, a canal between Holcombe Rogus and Taunton, was still many years away!

John Rennie's line indicated a route for a canal that would leave the River Tone at Firepool and cross the River Parrett by an aqueduct at a height of nearly 30ft east of the village of Huntworth. So that Bridgwater could receive direct benefit from this canal, John Easton surveyed a proposed short linking canal, from the aqueduct, that would take it, via two 15ft-deep locks, through Hamp to the south-western outskirts of the town, with a further lock and tidal basin to the river-side quays and wharves there.[11] Such was the foresight of John Easton that it would be more than a quarter of a century before a somewhat similar connection would ultimately be built between Huntworth and Bridgwater!

The Conservators of the River Tone would have watched this latest proposal with considerable concern for they must have felt that, despite many false starts, the time would surely come when a canal would be constructed between Bridgwater and Taunton and their monopoly of water-based trade to Taunton lost. When the Bill was presented to Parliament the Conservators, predictably, objected along with many others, but to no avail, and in 1811

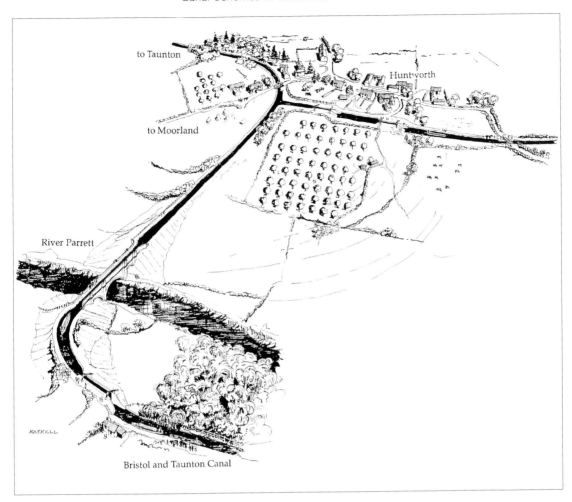

to Taunton

Huntworth

to Moorland

River Parrett

HASKELL

Bristol and Taunton Canal

This conjectural view shows how Rennie's projected plans for his Bristol to Taunton Canal of 1811 might have looked at Huntworth, Somerset, had it been built.

Here he proposed taking the canal over the River Parrett by means of an aqueduct. The sketch indicates a design similar to his structure of Avoncliff, on the Kennet and Avon Canal, which was built some four years earlier.

To avoid expensive embankment works, Rennie chose a location close to the village of Huntworth for his river crossing, where the ground rose to a height convenient for his canal. This sketch also shows a suggestion put forward by Rennie's assistant, John Easton, for a linking canal from the Bristol and Taunton, to the town of Bridgwater and the Parrett quaysides, which involved the construction of two sets of locks at Huntworth.

the Canal Company, who had dropped the title 'Bristol & Western' and adopted the more accurate one of 'The Bristol & Taunton', was granted its authorising Act.[12]

Priestley, in 1831, wrote, 'The object of this canal was to facilitate the communication between the Ports of London, Bristol, Bridgwater and Exeter, and to afford a better mode of conveyance for the produce of the agricultural and mineral districts through which it passes, the utility whereof can only be appreciated by that portion of the public which partakes of such important benefits.'[13]

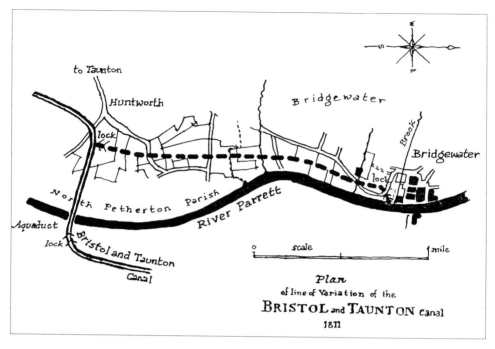

A redrawn plan showing John Easton's suggested link between the proposed Bristol and Taunton Canal and the town centre of Bridgwater.

The Bristol & Taunton Canal Co., however, shelved plans to undertake the necessary work, for, although 'a sum of £571,800 was actually subscribed before the application went to Parliament',[14] it would appear that there was still some concern that the economic climate in the country had not sufficiently recovered and would affect the projected level of trade upon which their scheme depended. As Rennie had estimated the costs of the 42-mile canal to be a little under £430,000, it would have been a heavy financial commitment in the circumstances. They could afford to wait a while.

The Grand Western Canal Co. completed the short length of canal between Tiverton and Holcombe Rogus, thus providing a source of income, mainly from agricultural produce and the carrying of lime from kilns at Whipcott, near Holcombe Rogus. However, the expectations of earlier years began to evaporate when, with the heavy costs the company had already incurred, there was still the link to Taunton to provide before it could attract any income from the lucrative coal traffic from Bridgwater. For the shareholders of the Bristol & Taunton Canal, this was disheartening. Although they themselves had not yet started their own canal, but were keen to see the Grand Western achieve the hoped-for connection to Taunton, they purchased in 1818, further shares in the Grand Western Canal Co., as well as some Tone shares held by the Conservators.

By 1822, the Bristol & Taunton Canal Co.'s authorising Act had been in existence for eleven years, and although its powers to build the length between Bristol and Bridgwater had lapsed by 1815, confidence to undertake the remaining section of the canal between Bridgwater and Taunton was beginning to return, a change that reflected a national mood of expansion.

THE BRIDGWATER AND TAUNTON CANAL

The port of Bridgwater in the early 1820s was emerging as an important harbour, not only for overseas shipping, but also for a growing number of colliers and coasters that were now regularly using the River Severn and the Bristol Channel. Like Bristol, coal was the main cargo, shipped across from the coalfields of South Wales, although there were sizeable quantities of timber and slates brought into the port, whilst bricks, tiles and agricultural produce were exported. In 1822, the port is recorded as receiving over 75,000 tons,[15] which probably represents well over a thousand berthings a year or between three and four vessels a day.

There is little doubt that the Bristol and Taunton Canal promoters felt that the port of Bridgwater was every bit as satisfactory for their business as Bristol would have been, and with the increase in coal traffic to the port in recent years, it could well be a more attractive financial undertaking if they limited their ambitions to a canal between Bridgwater and Taunton. As their 1811 Act had been for a canal that by-passed Bridgwater and crossed the River Parrett by aqueduct, the Canal Company was reminded that it would require an amended Act, if it wished to make a connection directly to the River Parrett and cut the canal on a different alignment to that authorised. Indeed, as shown in the next chapter, the company actually made a start on cutting the canal at Taunton in 1822 before it was halted by the serving of an injunction to this effect.

The necessary plans for a basin at Huntworth to link the canal to the River Parrett, and the revised alignment of the canal were drawn up, almost certainly by John Easton, although the deposited plans are not signed. A revised Bill was submitted to Parliament in September 1823.[16]

The Canal Company would certainly have realised that the submission of a new Bill would give the Conservators of the River Tone further opportunities to oppose its plans, and in this it was not to be disappointed! In a statement issued by the Conservators in March 1824, in which they also graciously included the 'inhabitants of Taunton', they stated that the annual income from the river was now about £2,300, and 'debt on the river is now in a rapid course of liquidation … and it has to be fairly deduced that in about six years time it will be entirely discharged.' The mention of six years is probably deliberate, for they would guess that would be the time taken for the Canal Company not only to secure any Act but to build the canal. The Conservators even added that:

> … if business on the river does not increase, it will be more than sufficient for keeping the same in good repair, because by the time the debt is fully paid off, the necessary locks and other buildings for rendering the navigation complete will be erected and all the works on the river will be in a perfect state.

It would appear that there was considerable public disquiet that the Canal Company had not undertaken the canal sooner, particularly as a decade earlier it had been supported with so much enthusiasm. At a public meeting the opportunity presented itself to find out why! In a report in the *Taunton Courier* for 17 March 1824, it is recorded that a meeting was held, at the Guildhall, Taunton:

... of the inhabitants of this town; to consider the propriety of opposing in Parliament, the progress of the Bristol and Taunton Canal Bill. At which meeting, Mr James Bunter, Treasurer to the Tone Conservators, and a leading Taunton banker, read from a paper printed and circulated by the Canal Company, in which they 'assigned other reasons for not having commenced their undertaking. First, the prevailing commercial distress in 1811, and secondly, what do you think, Sir? All sorts of crimes have been imputed to Bonaparte, but I have never heard before – and who would have thought that he had anything to do with the Bristol and Taunton Canal! (laughter). Yes, Gentlemen, said Mr Bunter, this paper informs us that the company were prevented commencing their work by the return of Bonaparte from Elba!' (laughter).

One of the main concerns of the Conservators at the time, apart from the competition for trade, was the inadequacy of the water supply. There had never been enough to satisfy all the needs of those who worked on the river, including the millers, and now it would be required to supply a canal as well. This particular point was emphasised by the Conservators when a Committee of the House of Lords considered the amended Canal Bill in 1824, postponing their deliberations so that 'an engineer of the Canal Company could meet the Conservators to explain to them the method by which the company was to be supplied with water from the Tone, and also how the company proposed to secure the Navigation of the Tone from Injury.'[17]

The Bristol & Taunton Canal Co., as it was still called at the time, proposed to construct for the Conservators a 'complete lock' (i.e. a pound lock) between their half-locks at Curry Moor and Ham. By doing so they could raise the level of the water in the river for the benefit of both the Conservators and the Canal Company. The reasoning behind their suggestion was simple: all the water flowing down the Tone from Taunton was required to feed the mills at Taunton, Bathpool, Creech and Ham. Below Ham, however, the course of the river ran close to the line of the intended canal. The Canal Bill contained powers allowing the company to abstract water from any river, stream or brook within 400 yards of the canal.

It was perfectly feasible, the engineer explained, and within their proposed rights, to pump water from the river at this point; water which had been ponded behind the suggested pound lock on the river. A pound lock would most certainly have assisted the boatmen on the river, but surprisingly, the Conservators found 'this proposition altogether inadmissible', and this was conveyed to their Lordships. Despite these objections, The Bristol & Taunton Canal Co. obtained its Act in 1824,[18] after the Conservators had agreed to withdraw their opposition on the understanding that they would be compensated for their loss of trade.

The Bridgwater & Taunton Canal Co., as it was now to be called, more accurately reflecting its new responsibilities, then re-invited subscribers to support the shortened line from Huntworth to Taunton, insisting that it was still its wish to link up with the Grand Western Canal. By joining its canal to the River Parrett at Huntworth, a mile or so up-river from Bridgwater, the company felt possibly they could attract the existing barge traffic from the River Parrett to their canal, and not proceed up-river and on to the River Tone to Taunton.

Before a start would be made to cut this canal, however, there were to be two more attempts to provide a canal across the peninsula to link up the Bristol and English Channels.

A Tub-Boat Canal Linking Taunton with the South Coast

With the abandonment of Rennie's 1810 proposal for an English and Bristol Channels Ship Canal, interest now turned to an altogether less costly, but hopefully, equally effective solution. The West Country was already witnessing the construction of what some felt was a daring scheme at Bude in Cornwall, where a tub-boat canal was being cut, relying upon water-driven inclines to haul each craft over the steep hills of the area.

Could this be the solution for an inter-channel canal? The engineer to the Bude Canal Co., James Green, was approached and asked to survey an appropriate line between Taunton and the English Channel. Just before Christmas 1822, he outlined his proposals for a similar type of canal to his Bude Canal, which would connect 'either the River Tone, or the canal now cutting from Bridgwater to Taunton', with Beer, near Seaton on the south coast, 'by which a communication will be effected between the English and Bristol Channels'[19].

Notice in the *Taunton Courier*, September 1822, announcing James Green's proposal for a tub boat canal between Taunton and Beer.

NOTICE IS HEREBY GIVEN, to all persons whom it may concern, that Application is intended to be made to Parliament, in the enfuing Session, for leave to bring in a Bill for forming, making, and maintaining a NAVIGABLE CUT or CANAL, with communicating rail roads, inclined planes, tunnells and other works, at certain parts in the line thereof, for boats and barges, with proper and neceffary carriage roads, ways, tunnells, archways, approaches, drains, and water courfes, to communicate therewith, and fupply the fame from Beer Cove or Harbour, in the county of Devon, unto the River Tone at the parifhes of Creech Saint Michael, Weft Monckton, and Ruifhton, or fome or one of them, in the county of Somerfet, and unto a canal which is intended to be cut or made in the faid parifh of Creech Saint Michael; which faid canal, rail roads, inclined planes, tunnells, drains, water courfes, and other works, are intended to pafs through, along, by, and into the feveral parifhes, chapelries, townfhips, or places of Beer. Seaton, Beer and Seaton, otherwife Seaton and Beer, Colyton, Kilmington, Shute, Widworthy, Axminfter, and Membury, in the county of Devon, the parifh of Chardftock, in the county of Dorfet, and the feveral parifhes, chapelries, townfhips, or places of Chard Borough, Chard, Chaffcombe, Knowle Saint Giles, Combe Saint Nicholas, Ilminfter, Donyatt, Broadway, Whitelackington, Buckland Saint Mary, Ilton, Whiteftaunton, Afhill, Beercrocombe, Staplefitz paine, Bickenhall, Barrington, Curland, Hatch Beauchamp, Weft Hatch, Thurlbeer, Thornfalcon, Stoke Saint Mary, Ruifhton, Weft Monckton, Creech Saint Michael, Taunton Saint James and Taunton Saint Mary Magdalen, in the county of Somerfet.
Dated 5th September, 1822.

He estimated that his canal, to be called the English and Bristol Channels' Junction Canal, would cost around £120,000 including the building of a pier at Beer. Compared with the million pounds that Rennie had estimated for his ship canal, this announcement must have been sweet music to the ears of his sponsors and was, no doubt, influential in their ready acceptance of his plans. The draw-back, of course, was that although Rennie's canal could have accommodated sea-going vessels, and thus avoid trans-shipment into barges, this would be a narrow canal, with tub-boats in sets of six, each carrying around five tons apiece, hauled by one horse.

There was hardly any comparison. One supporter remarked that 'half a loaf was better than no bread', and stated 'that even on the diminutive scale now proposed it would be advantageous to the Country at large and beneficial to the subscribers'. [20]

James Green's canal was to be 31 miles in length, and would join the Bridgwater and Taunton Canal at Hyde Farm, near Bathpool. There would be four inclines, taking the canal to over 260ft above sea-level; the longest incline being at Stoke St Mary, where, after crossing the River Tone on an aqueduct at Black Brook, the canal would rise 190ft to take it through Stoke Woods and past the Henlade Quarries. After this, a further incline of 50ft just south of Bickenhall would bring the canal to the summit level. With much ingenuity, James Green was able to provide at the summit a pound of level water of over 13 miles in length, 'being three times the length ever before contemplated', [21] before descending to Titherleigh with an incline of 129ft. At Yarty Bridge there was to be another incline of 61ft which would bring the canal to Colyton and Seaton, although there would still have to be a quarter-mile tunnel to reach the wharves at Beer where the terminus was some 70ft above sea-level. [22]

Compared to the customary design of canals, where pound locks were used to raise or lower the water levels over any gradients, these long inclines were audacious proposals, derived from the principles of the pit inclines but where horse power was replaced by water. James Green argued that with his inclines great heights could be reached in a relatively short length and although the Stoke St Mary incline was not the highest he had designed (Hobbacut Down, on the Bude Canal, was 225ft), it would be testing enough for the unsophisticated winding machinery of the time. 'The inclined planes would be so constructed as to be worked by water instead of steam engines and would be capable of passing 60 tons per hour.' [23] On the Bude Canal the boats were chain-hauled up the inclines one by one, using a drum turned by heavy water-filled caissons which acted as counterbalances.

There was much enthusiasm for the proposal, and early the following year a Bill was presented to Parliament. Despite its attractions to the local economy there were other businessmen and sponsors waiting in the wings with their own ideas for a further ship canal scheme. In the light of this James Green's proposals were withdrawn in favour of this far more ambitious ship canal proposal, which again was to involve the Bridgwater and Taunton Canal for part of its length.

ENTER THOMAS TELFORD

In 1822, Thomas Telford had achieved national acclaim when the long and arduous work of cutting the Caledonian Canal in Scotland was at last completed and opened to traffic. On this he worked with William Jessop, and, at the time when James Green was proposing his tub-boat solution, was working on plans to construct the deep-water Gloucester and Sharpness Ship Canal, linking the Severn Estuary and the Severn Navigation. Who better to ask for suggestions for a ship canal across the south-west peninsula than Thomas Telford?

In 1824 he commenced his survey, working with his surveyor, Captain Nicholls, and shrewdly engaging the assistance of James Green, for his obvious knowledge of the area. Between them they selected a line to link Bridgwater Bay with Seaton, where a small harbour would be built, tucked under the cliffs near Beer, away from the prevailing south-westerlies. Although the southern part of his proposed canal, south of Chard, would take a route alongside the River Axe rather similar to that suggested by John Rennie some twenty years earlier, it was the northern part where James Green's involvement was particularly noticeable.

North of Chard there would be a new line where:

> … the canal would descend via Donyatt and Broadway, through Ashill Forest and West Hatch, … crossing the River Tone about half-a-mile below Ham Mills, and then on to the Bridgwater and Taunton Canal on the western side of Buckland Farm.

Here Telford envisaged that much of the route of the Bridgwater and Taunton Canal would be widened and deepened to allow the passage of sea-going vessels along it, whilst, beyond Huntworth it would pass 'on the western side of Bridgwater, to Combwich'.[24] A report in a local newspaper at the time added, 'that if it is found to be difficult to route the Ship Canal around Bridgwater to Combwich Reach, then the Port of Watchet is found to be the most advantageous entrance into the Bristol Channel, crossing the River Tone between Taunton and Wellington.'[25] With the spate of canal schemes that had come before the people of Somerset during those few years, it is little wonder that there were some who were tempted to join in and draw routes for canals all over Somerset!

At the time of this proposal, work on cutting the Bridgwater and Taunton Canal had already started, so in March 1825, the Company of Proprietors of the Bridgwater and Taunton Canal were approached by certain of their own shareholders to ascertain whether the company should sell their interest in the land of their canal to the ship canal promoters. When the Bill was presented to Parliament later that month, it contained a provision for the:

> … Company of Proprietors of the said proposed Ship Canal, to purchase, and the Bridgwater & Taunton Canal Company to sell … the whole of the bed of the said Bridgwater and Taunton Canal so far as the same has been cut, and all the land … of the Company between Bridgwater and Taunton, together with all works and property.[26]

A figure of £90,000 had been agreed by the Bridgwater & Taunton Canal Co. as the price the Ship Canal Co. would have to pay to buy them out.[27]

In contrast to James Green's modest tub-boat canal, this ship canal was going to be a large and expensive undertaking to cut and equip. Telford estimated the cost of the 44-mile canal to be around £1¾ million. It would be designed to accommodate vessels of up to 200 tons, and throughout its length there would be sixty locks. The volume of water that would be needed to replenish these very large ship-locks every time a vessel passed through would have been considerable but Telford was confident that sufficient water could be supplied from the River Axe by the use of reservoirs and feeder canals, 'which themselves are to be navigable for small craft, thereby supplying Crewkerne and the intermediate country with coals and other merchandise.'[28] Commenting upon the preliminary report then before Parliament, *The Sun*, on December 1824, remarked that the proposal for the Ship Canal 'met well-founded expectations'.

As if to give added purpose to Telford's ship canal, the winter of 1824 witnessed storms of unprecedented ferocity along the Cornwall, Devon and Somerset coasts:

> … the disastrous consequences of the late gales which occasioned such dreadful and melancholy loss of lives and property on the South Coast, affords proof sufficient, if indeed, proof were wanting, of the vast importance and utility of the measure. The dangerous, as well as circuitous navigation round the Land's End has already been admitted and dreaded by our sailors.[29]

Enthusiasm for the canal was high and there was little opposition. Towards the end of 1824, the editor of the *Taunton Courier* observed, somewhat poetically, that 'the loss of land to be destroyed by the line is no more to be regretted, compared with the anticipated resulting benefit, than the spot of ground occupied by the acorn, when it has grown into the magnificence of a wide spreading oak.'

In 1825, the promoters of the ship canal received their authorising Act, but time was running out once again for such grand and costly engineering schemes, and like so many before, this ambitious proposal was not pursued. Later that year, mainly because the Bridgwater & Taunton Canal Co. required the Ship Canal Co. to purchase not just part, but the whole length of its own canal bed, Telford was forced to rethink his construction costs. In the following session of Parliament, the Ship Canal Co., in reducing their costs, sought leave to bring a Bill to amend the earlier Act. This time the idea was to bring the ship canal into Taunton itself, where there would be trans-shipment wharves to transfer goods to and from canal barges using the Bridgwater and Taunton. However, to any onlooker, it was all getting too complicated and expensive, and eventually the whole concept was shelved.[30]

By this time the canal age was slowly coming to an end and even in 1824 it was unrealistic to think of a ship canal climbing over the hills of Somerset and Devon. Although other ship canals were still to be built (the Gota Canal in Sweden was

Opposite: Thomas Telford's proposed ship canal between the Bristol and English Channels, 1824.

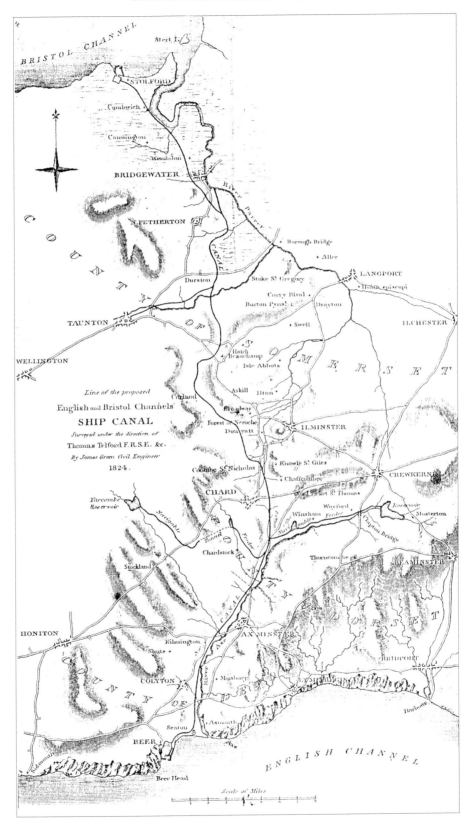

completed by Telford some ten years later) the new iron-hulled steamships that were appearing on the scene in the 1820s were ushering in a safer form of sea travel which would render the need for small ship canals largely unnecessary. Such boats would find the journey round the Cornish peninsula less hazardous than in the days of wood and sail. Certainly, by 1820, steam ships of over 240 tons were being built,[31] larger than could have been accommodated upon Telford's ship canal, had it been built. By the time Telford was submitting his plans for this canal, steam packets were already operating across the English Channel. An iron steamship, the *Aaron Manby*, made the journey between London and Rouen with a cargo destined for Paris, being 'the first attempt to traverse the ocean in a vessel composed of any material but wood'.[32]

There was to be yet another, half-hearted attempt to cut a barge canal between Beer and Bridgwater in 1828, estimated to cost only £600,000, and, although the *Taunton Courier* said at the time that 'it is confidently expected that the measure, so long talked of and so much desired, will at last be carried into execution',[33] there was no longer any great enthusiasm to invest in such canals, and the expectations were not fulfilled.

SURVEYING AND CUTTING THE BRIDGWATER AND TAUNTON CANAL

During the second half of the eighteenth century, when the country witnessed much canal-building activity, the maps available to those early canal surveyors were very elementary, whilst their understanding of the geology was limited. They would traverse the route on foot or horseback, assessing the most suitable line, and making their own surveys. The canal engineers would need to be ingenious in their designs to find a level course through the contours of the hills and valleys, whilst the contractor would have to face the practical problems of building the works, of hiring and accommodating armies of labourers and craftsmen, often in remote and inaccessible regions of the country, and transporting the materials to site. For the canal promoters there was the need to raise the necessary capital, almost exclusively from private sources, with loans and subscriptions through share issues. Needless to say, their worries were rarely over until the canal opened, for the original estimates seldom bore any similarity to the final costs.

By the time the Bridgwater and Taunton Canal was cut there had been nearly seventy years of development in canal building and its promoters could take advantage of the improvements made during that time. Firstly, calculations over the most suitable width and cross-section of the canal could be determined with greater accuracy, once the range of cargoes likely to be carried was known, together with the most suitable and economical size of barge to be used. The surveyors' assessment of the route would determine the number of locks to be provided and this information would be crucial to the engineer so that he could satisfy himself that there would be sufficient sources of water available on the route he was proposing; bitter experience had shown that some canals were notoriously short of replenishment water at one time or another during the year, thereby affecting their efficient functioning and consequently their overall profitability.

As works on canal construction continued over the country, there developed a better understanding of geological matters and soil conditions that would remove much of the uncertainty that attended the cutting of the earlier canals, particularly where such knowledge could reduce the ever-present risks in digging deep cuttings and tunnels. Furthermore, the preparation and issue of maps prepared by the Ordnance Survey gave the surveyors mapping out their routes for canals and roads and later the railways an accurate basis for their work. By the 1820s there were Ordnance Survey maps available for most parts of southern England, printed to a scale of 1 inch to the mile. The map that covered the area of the Bridgwater and Taunton Canal was surveyed in 1808 and first published in October 1809. It showed the location of rivers, streams, roads, trackways and areas of woodland. Hills were shown, together with the extent of the built-up areas of towns and villages. These maps, prepared by the military surveyors, used a method of triangulation based upon prominent landmarks.

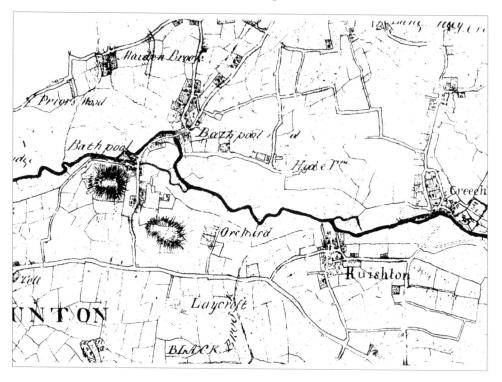

An Ordnance Surveyor's draft map of Bathpool to Ruishton, 1808. (Courtesy of Local History Library, Taunton)

During 'canal mania' in the early 1790s, when so many canal Bills were being presented to Parliament, accurate information on the exact nature of the propoals, and more importantly, the ownership of the land affected by the route, was often either not forthcoming or of insufficient detail. When work started on the ground this could, and often did, lead to costly delays when unsuspecting landowners were likely to be obstructive or hold the Canal Company to a virtual ransom over permission to cross their land. After 1793 Parliament[1] required all information on estate and land boundaries, together with the names of all landowners and occupiers affected by a proposal, to be recorded and to accompany the Bill, with a second copy placed on public deposit. This not only related to canals but other public works such as railways and roads. By 1837, an Act was passed[2] requiring the deposit of such plans with the Clerks of the Peace of the districts within which the works were proposed, although in some instances this practice had taken place many years earlier – some in Somerset as early as 1791.

Apart from the work of assessing estate boundaries, the surveyor would engage assistants to help him check out the levels of the surrounding land relative to the canal, noting the positions of streams and other watercourses. Generally, they would aim to leave such streams untouched and culvert them, for fear of affecting the natural drainage of the adjacent land. Over the 14 miles of the Bridgwater and Taunton Canal, where the route passes through the low-lying land of two river valleys, over fifty culverts were constructed to carry the canal over stream and drainage ditches.

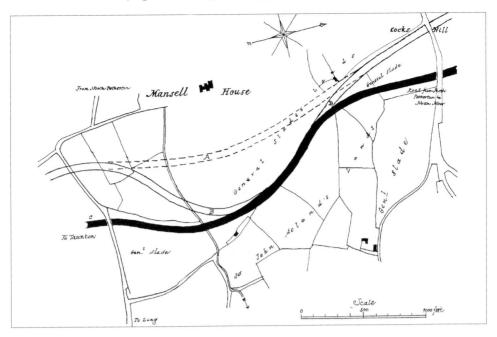

A plan based on John Easton's 1822 proposals for the route of the canal across the grounds of Mansell (Maunsel) House. Route A shows the conjectional 1811 alignment, whilst B indicates a revised route acceptable to General Slade, 1822, taking it further away from the house. The 1824 Act further revised the route, which is shown in black, although when built a lock was added, C, where it passes under the lane to Lyng.

The surveyors travelled on foot or, where possible, on horseback, recording in their notebooks the relevant levels and dimensions of the ground, and taking overnight lodgings in nearby inns and farmhouses. They were keen to keep the costs of construction to a minimum and, adopting methods that would be familiar to later generations of railway and road engineers, they needed to balance 'cut' with 'fill' to avoid the unnecessary labour of removing surplus spoil. They also aimed to retain as many existing field boundaries and hedgerows as possible, thereby appeasing local landowners and avoiding the severance of farm holdings, for, where a farm unit was split by the line of the canal, the Canal Company would be required to construct 'accommodation' bridges.

Although John Easton, had, over the years, surveyed the various routes for a canal between Taunton and Bridgwater, the Canal Company chose a little known engineer, James Hollinsworth, to oversee its design and construction with John Easton acting under his direction as his senior surveyor. Not much is known of the early career of James Hollinsworth but it is likely that he was an assistant engineer with John Rennie, when he was working on the earlier Bristol and Taunton proposals in 1810. John Easton would have been entrusted with much of the detailed surveying work, including negotiations with landowners, matters of compensation, and agreeing any necessary accommodation works for the neighbouring farms.

In 1822 Easton drew up plans for a slight alteration to the original 1811 line of the canal at Maunsel House (then called Mansell House), following a request from its owner, General Slade, to 'carry the line of the canal out of sight of, and further from Mansell House'. He would also have been involved in the resulting land negotiations; a record survives which gives an interesting glimpse of the land values at the time. A Mr Thomas, one of the Committee of the Bristol & Taunton Canal Co. (as it was still called at the time) offered to purchase from the adjoining owner, Sir John Acland, the necessary land '… at a price of £95 per acre, for two acres and one rood, together with timber from the hedges, for a price of £223.15.0d'.[3] In another transaction Richard King, of Sellicks Farm, 'part and parcel of Newton Place', was paid £174 for the purchase of 'three roods and ten perches of land at Slow Meadow, taken for the purposes of the said canal, together with the land tax and also the tithes of corn, grain and hay'.[4]

With much of the line of the Bridgwater and Taunton Canal already surveyed on previous occasions, and some land already purchased, James Hollinsworth would now need a few months to consider the designs of the canal structures before work started on site. He engaged a Mr Hodgkinson as his principal engineer, who with a few assistants would handle the engineering work and the letting of contracts. Unfortunately Mr Hodgkinson died in September 1826, four months before the completion of the canal. Whether he was related to the Mr Hodgkinson who after 1836 was the resident engineer to the Parrett Navigation Co. is not known, although the coincidence in name and profession suggests a family connection.

The proposed route of the canal which the engineers and surveyors submitted was no more than a single line superimposed upon a base of the surrounding countryside together with a long section drawing of the canal, showing the relative levels of the adjacent land and the water level proposed. This section would also have shown the location of locks, bridges and any culverts if necessary.

The authorising Act would contain provisions allowing the company to vary the line of the canal within certain limits either side of the centre line shown on the deposited plan, in order to allow the contractor to avoid local obstacles and ground conditions not appreciated during the original survey and to meet landowners' wishes. The company '… shall not deviate more than twenty Yards from the Lines or Courses there of described on the said Map and Plan.'[5]

The main difference between the 1811 and the 1824 proposals between Bridgwater and Taunton concerned the connection with the River Parrett. Instead of the original aqueduct which carried the canal over the river and which would have required the canal approach to be set on higher ground from North Newton eastwards, the canal would now link directly into the river by means of a tidal basin at Huntworth. This would mean that the canal could now be rerouted along 'lower' ground, closer to both Standards and Fordgate Farms and the river itself.

The plans deposited with the Canal Bill[6] in 1823, show the suggested position of locks below Maunsel. There was to be one near Standards Farm, in much the same position as it is today, but two others were proposed, very close together, just on the Taunton side of North Newton. These were never built; one at Kings and two at Maunsel replaced them. The lock at Higher Maunsel was located on a country lane which had to be rerouted around the chamber itself.

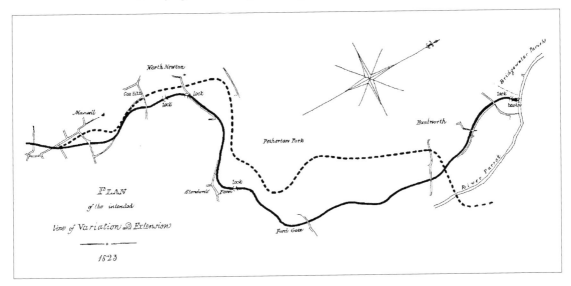

The plan (redrawn), produced by John Easton, showing the revised line of the canal between the River Parrett and Maunsel which accompanied the 1823 Bill. The earlier route is shown by a broken line.

Just below Lower Maunsel lock, a realignment shows that Easton removed the line of the canal further from the grounds around Maunsel House than he had agreed a year earlier. His line for the canal was now superimposed upon a trackway from the estate, for which, in compensation, the owners of Maunsel House were allowed to ride their own horses along the towpath.

However carefully the canal was plotted it was inevitable that there would be certain odd corners of land or thin strips remaining from fields that the Canal Company would be required to purchase, but these could be of value to them as space to provide 'winding holes', a widened point along the canal where maintenance barges could turn, or for stacking and drying canal dredgings.

Land taken for the canal was approximately twelve acres per mile. The line of country through which the canal was to be cut presented few difficulties. The change in levels between the River Parrett, at Huntworth and Firepool Weir at Taunton was no more than 35ft, and this could easily be accommodated by the provision of five locks, together with the locks at the tidal basin at Huntworth. Furthermore, the company would be fortunate in that they would not have to provide a summit reservoir, as this canal would be fed naturally from the River Tone at its upper end. In the later years of the canal's history, this source of water was not always entirely satisfactory and would cause many problems.

James Hollinsworth was fortunate in that the line mapped by John Easton took the canal, for most of its length, through thick grey clay which proved to be an ideal impervious lining. However, this stratum of clay becomes overlaid with a layer of gravelly shale from Durston to Taunton and along this length it was necessary to line the canal bed and sides with clay brought from other parts of the digging. This would be puddled to form a watertight seal, a method used by James Brindley since the earliest days of canal building and still very effective. Puddling the new clay lining could be carried out in a variety of ways. Usually teams of workmen would be assembled after the clay had been laid to a depth of between 12 and 30in when it would be hammered down with timber pummels, although in some cases 'the puddling was achieved by driving a herd of cows along its bed'.[7]

The clay was also of a quality that made it ideal for brick-making; indeed Bridgwater, at the time of the construction of the canal, was developing brick- and tile-making at a number of sites along the sides of the Parrett, and this was to become a major industry in the town throughout the nineteenth century. The Canal Company took advantage of the bonus of the extracted clay to make bricks for their own structures. It is possible that the Reverend Robert Gray of Buckland Farm, in consenting to the purchase of his land for the canal, permitted the company to extract clay from some of his fields adjacent to the canal at Durston when they needed bricks to construct bridges and culverts nearby, particularly the road bridge carrying the Turnpike Road to East Lyng,[8] the present A361.

Surveying equipment of the day was remarkably sophisticated, and could easily be recognised and used by a surveyor today. The principles of land surveying were well known and formed the basis of land surveying well into the twentieth century until the recent advent of computerised and laser technology. Angles were measured and distances taken using a theodolite, fitted with a sighting telescope and cross hairs to assist in tacheometric surveying. A spirit level attached to the theodolite would be used for levelling with staff and ranging rods. Distances would be measured with a Gunter chain, which, whilst only 22 yards long, was conveniently divided up into 100 links.[9]

Plotting the contours of the ground and the levels of the proposed canal was particularly important, for there would be little room for error. The Canal Company would wish to reduce the amount of both heavy earth moving, and the numbers of bridges, locks and cuttings, which could be both expensive and time-consuming to build. Any work on building the bridges and lock chambers would be undertaken as soon as the contractors started on site and it was therefore essential that the levels were accurately plotted and double checked. This would be the prime responsibility of the engineers and surveyors in charge.

The line of the canal would be marked out on the ground by a series of pegs at between two and three chain intervals (approximately 50 yards). Where the canal was in a cutting or on an embankment, it would be necessary to mark the outermost extent of the earth works as well as the line of the canal itself. It would be at this stage that the landowner could see for himself for the first time the effect the canal would have on his land and no doubt discussions often took place to make minor revisions.

James Hollinsworth estimated the cost of the canal to be £34,145, comprising £15,291 for the section between Firepool and Maunsel, and £18,854 for the remainder to Huntworth. The canal was to be 12 miles long and would take a course roughly parallel with the River Tone for its last few miles to Taunton. One major earthwork was unavoidable: at Lyng an embankment would need to be built over 700 yards long, and 40ft high. There were also two short cuttings, one at Maunsel and the other at Durston. Both the Huntworth and Firepool locks were to be provided with reverse-facing flood gates; those at Huntworth would allow both the basin and the canal to be dewatered for maintenance purposes behind the tidal River Parrett, whilst the flood gates at Firepool could allow the canal to retain its water if, for any reason, the level in the River Tone was lowered.

THE CONTRACTORS START WORK

An advertisement by the Bristol & Taunton Canal Co. in early August 1822 sought the interest of contractors to cut the canal, and raised the hopes and expectations of many townsfolk in Taunton that, after so many years of waiting, at last a start was in sight. It announced:

> ## TO CANAL CONTRACTORS.
> ### *Bristol and Taunton Canal.*
> ANY Persons disposed to contract for Making and Executing that Part of this Canal which lies between the town of TAUNTON, in the county of Somerset, and a certain place called MANSELL, in the parish of North Petherton, in the same county, in six distinct lots of about one mile each, may see the plans, sections, and specifications, at the BATHPOOL INN, in the parish of West Monckton, near Taunton, from Monday the 26th, till Saturday the 31ft of August next; during which time the Engineer will attend to shew the Line.
>
> Sealed tenders to be delivered at our office in Shannon Court, Corn Street, Bristol, on the Monday following the 2d of September, at Ten o'clock in the forenoon, when the Committee will attend to Let the Work.
>
> By order of the Committee of Management,
>   COOKE and BENGOUGH, Principal Clerks.
> Bristol, July 23d, 1822.

The Canal Company must have made speedy decisions for within six weeks not only was a contractor, Wawman & Haughton, appointed, but a workforce had been assembled.

Upon the commencement of the work, the engineer would be keen to get bricklayers started on the bridges and work to Firepool lock. From a letter sent to the editor of the *Taunton Courier*[10] we find the contractors calculated that ten men could complete digging a mile of canal in twelve months and that their wages were 20s per week.

> ## *TAUNTON.*
> ——
> Within the last three days, upwards of 200 labourers, called Navigators, lately employed on the Bude Canal, have arrived in this town for the purpose of commencing their operations on the projected Taunton and Bristol Canal. They are immediately to open the ground at Fire Pool Weir, near this town. A party of the workmen are also to commence their labours at Creech, and a bridge, near the present one at Bathpool, is to be erected. The line will terminate in the Parrat, about a mile from Bridgwater.

James Brindley *c.*1770, indicating the surveying equipment that was in use at the time. (Courtesy of British Waterways Archive, Gloucester)

Within a few weeks of starting, however, the Canal Company had an injunction served upon them by the Reverend Robert Gray, of Buckland Farm, Durston, to stop work. Although he owned land required for the canal, the grounds for his action were that works were to be undertaken that were not correctly authorised.[11] As has already been mentioned, the Bristol & Taunton Canal Co. were proceeding under the authorisation given to them in 1811 but matters were now quite changed, and the route of the shortened canal to Bridgwater would not follow the authorised line. The company were advised to seek fresh powers, which resulted in the 1824 Act, under the auspices of the renamed Bridgwater & Taunton Canal Co.

During this period of enforced delay, James Hollinsworth was able to revise his costings as more details were drawn up, and in January 1823 he raised his estimate for the canal from £34,145 to £60,000,[12] which could scarcely have pleased the new company. It is possible that the labourers remained on the site, certainly until the beginning of 1823, as contracts had already been made to cut the canal at Firepool and Creech and to build a swingbridge at Bathpool. These details at the Taunton end of the canal were not likely to

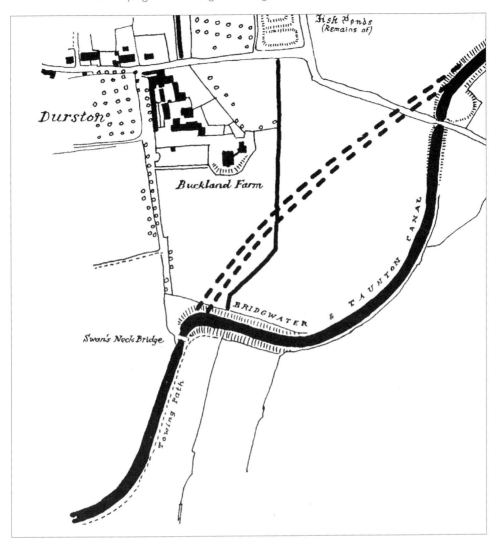

Buckland Farm, Durston, showing, in solid line, the canal as constructed and, in broken line, the original route lying closer to the farm.

be changed in the revisions John Easton and James Hollinsworth were drawing up, which concentrated upon the phase of work from Maunsel to Huntworth.

A critical editorial, which appeared in the *Taunton Courier* of 11 December 1822, gives a rare insight into the way in which the workforce were expected to purchase food and other provisions from the contractor whilst on site:

A practice prevails in discharging the wages of the labourers employed in making the Canal lately commenced near this town, which loudly calls for exposure and reprehension. The poor, industrious workmen, instead of receiving in money the amount of their hard earned wages, are compelled to obtain them in supplies of provisions and other articles, for which they are charged, as might be expected, from such a mode of paying them, an advanced and unfair price. A truckster, or keeper of what is termed a TOMMY SHOP is appointed by the contractors for the line of the work, and to this shop the poor men are compelled to apply for their various supplies, under pain of expulsion from the course of their honest labours. To such a shameful excess has the practice … been carried, that instances have frequently occurred wherein the men after receiving part of their wages in meat, have actually brought them into this town, and sold it, at a loss of 30% to furnish themselves with articles of which they stood in need.

Whether this practice was discontinued after this broadside is not recorded; maybe the injunction on the Canal Company came just in time!

By September 1823, the Canal Company had submitted their revised proposals with their Bill to Parliament. During the passage of the Bill the Reverend Robert Gray, who had earlier served the injunction, took the opportunity to request the company that the earlier line which passed to within sixty yards of his house, be realigned. The Canal Company, possibly in an effort to appease the gentleman, did not oppose the suggestion, with the result that the Act contained provision for the realignment of the canal at this point. Today this amended line can clearly be seen as an abrupt change of direction just south of Buckland Farm at a spot appropriately known as 'swan's neck'.

The 1824 Act further stipulated that three years were to be allowed for '… the execution of these works, if not then done, the powers to cease, excepting as to such parts as may have been completed'.[13] Within two months of the Act being passed, the contractor, Wawman & Haughton, was again advertising:

BRIDGWATER AND TAUNTON CANAL,
SOMERSETSHIRE.

——

WANTED IMMEDIATELY, One Hundred CANAL DIGGERS on this Navigation. Apply to Messrs. WAWMAN and HAUGHTON, the Contractors, at Bathpool, near Taunton.   August 19th, 1824.

It is likely that the Canal Company appointed another contractor to conclude the works from Maunsel to Huntworth, in order to speed up work on the ground and take advantage of the additional labour force from the area around Bridgwater. The contractors would be keen to cut as much of the straightforward canal work as soon as possible, and the long pounds, the lengths of canal between locks, such as the lengths between Firepool and Maunsel, and Standards Farm to Huntworth, would have been a priority. It was not until the last months of the canal work, in September 1826, that work appears to have started on perhaps the hardest part of the job; the building of the tidal basin at Huntworth. This involved the construction of two lock chambers as well as the basin itself. Interesting archaeological discoveries were made:

In cutting out the intended basin for the Bridgwater and Taunton Canal, there have been found two strata of horns, bones and shells, one at a distance of sixteen, and the other thirty feet below the surface of the earth … the bones were of four or five wild deer, which are now found on Exmoor Forest.[14]

This item also gives an indication of the great depth needed to excavate for the basin. The digging of the lock adjacent to the River Parrett would have been carried out behind stout timber baulks in order to ensure the river did not flood into the works. It is fair to assume that shortly after the basin works were completed the company would have constructed the cottages alongside for company employees, as well as a house for the basin inspector (see chapter seven).

There were to be eleven brick-built road bridges spanning the canal and the towpath and, as the line of the canal would sever a number of farm holdings, over a dozen timber accommodation bridges would need to be provided. These were at towpath level and were designed to be swung sideways to allow a barge to pass. They were to be of similar design to those already used by John Rennie on the Kennet and Avon Canal and relied upon an early form of ball bearing and counterweights to make them capable of being opened by one person.

A heavy boat horse, similar to those that would have been used on the river navigations, where their strength was needed to move the heavily loaded barges through the flash-locks, or half-locks, and up the shallow waters of the Tone to Taunton.

On the canal it is likely that smaller horses were used, as well as mules and donkeys, working in tandem. (Courtesy of British Waterways Archive, Gloucester)

THE LOCKS

It was the lock chambers that took most time to build and all four of the central locks were probably started at much the same time, with one contractor handling the two at Maunsel whilst the other built Kings and Standards. In this way the company could take full advantage of the transport and storage of bricks, lime, sand and timber, as well as the presence of the craftsmen needed for the brickwork and the assembling of the timber gates.

From the records of other canals it is known that baulks and planks of timber, usually oak and elm, that were needed in both shoring up the deep excavations of the chambers and the construction of the lock gates would have been brought to the site by waggon and horses from the river wharves and been fashioned on site. A blacksmith would have set up his hearth and anvil close to the carpenter's compound, to forge the iron straps, braces and brackets that each gate required, as well as the mechanisms for the ground paddles and sluices.

The chambers to all the locks on the canal were built to the same dimensions, i.e. 13ft wide by 54ft long. Over the years, due to the effects of lateral ground pressure on the chamber walls, these dimensions have altered very slightly at several locks. Built in local brick with lime mortar, the locks were brick-lined across the bottom, to a thickness of over 2ft, except for the area where the gates swung, called the bay, where a firm framework of heavy timbers was required against which the elm-wood threshold for the gates themselves was attached. The chamber walls were over 4ft thick at the base, diminishing in thickness towards ground level, for experience had taught the canal engineers that the horizontal force exerted by wet ground against the walls of an empty chamber could be considerable, and many locks had failed because the chamber walls had not been strong enough.

An estimate of the number of bricks needed in building a lock chamber on this canal is in excess of 250,000. At Maunsel, approximately halfway along the canal, two locks, Higher and Lower Maunsel, are situated within 100 yards of each other. Each has a brick-built canal bridge alongside, which would have required around 50,000 bricks. With a further canal bridge at Cox Hill, a swing bridge at Maunsel, and a lock-keeper's house at Lower Maunsel, it is likely that the Canal Company had to find space for nearly a million bricks in the confined space of their ownership.

With many demands upon the narrow strips of land purchased by the Canal Company, on which they would have to accommodate the contractors' workforce, the horses, waggons and the spoil taken from the cut, it was necessary for the company to resort to short-term leasing of other land that was near to hand and on which they could store the more bulky building materials. It has been suggested that the present-day Brickyard Farm, at Maunsel, possibly got its name because part of its land was leased to the Canal Company for the storage of bricks, for there is no evidence that brick-making was ever carried out there.

Pound locks operate on the principle that whilst the top gates are closed and the bottom gates have been shut behind the entering craft, water can fill the chamber by means of ground paddles operated by sluices and windlasses, allowing a controlled amount of water to slowly lift a craft to the upper canal level. For the reverse direction, sluices, often called paddles, and again worked by a windlass or key, are positioned in the bottom gates to let out the water from the chamber. When the lower levels have equalised, the

The heavy baulks of timber used at the locks, both for shoring up the deep excavation before the brick lining was built and for the lock gates themselves, had to be delivered by wide-wheeled waggons with a team of horses, for the trackways they needed to use were frequently barely passable and often deep in mud.

Delivery of the bricks and stone used at the lock chambers was also by waggon and horses.

bottom gates can be opened to allow the craft to leave. On the Bridgwater and Taunton Canal the counterbalance weights to the ground paddles are of a cast-iron 'ball and chain' design, considered unique to a canal in this country.

Working on the Canal

The men employed on the laborious task of digging the canals were termed navvies, a word derived from navigators, which itself related to the navigations, as the canals and waterways were frequently termed. They were well accustomed to the work, usually travelling from one canal contract to another. Their skills continued to be sought long after the demise of the canal work, for they were engaged on the equally arduous task of constructing the railways a decade or two later. The canal would be cut, the embankments formed, and the cuttings achieved entirely by hand, using picks, shovels and barrows. Horses would be employed to assist the hauling of spoil away to embankments and bringing of materials to site. The 1824 Act permitted the use of steam engines so long 'as they consumed their own smoke'. The degree to which steam engines were used is not known, although it is more than likely that some were employed as pumps to keep down water where springs were encountered.

Loading up and carting away surplus soil was a laborious task, which often had to be carried out within the narrow confines of the 'pegged-out' area of land purchased by the Canal Company. This work in itself was not necessarily dangerous on the relatively flat terrain of the Bridgwater and Taunton Canal, and no records have come to light relating to any serious injuries or fatalities. However, in 1837, when the Chard Canal was being cut, a fatality was recorded at Ashill Wood. 'A labourer, George Bear, aged forty-eight, whilst employed with others filling waggons to remove the cutting, was buried under a quantity of earth which suddenly and unexpectantly gave way'. The reporter at the time was keen to emphasise that 'it appeared that all the men were perfectly sober and attentive to their work and no blame was imputable to any one.'[15]

In cutting the canal the navvies worked in groups, using picks and shovels and barrows.

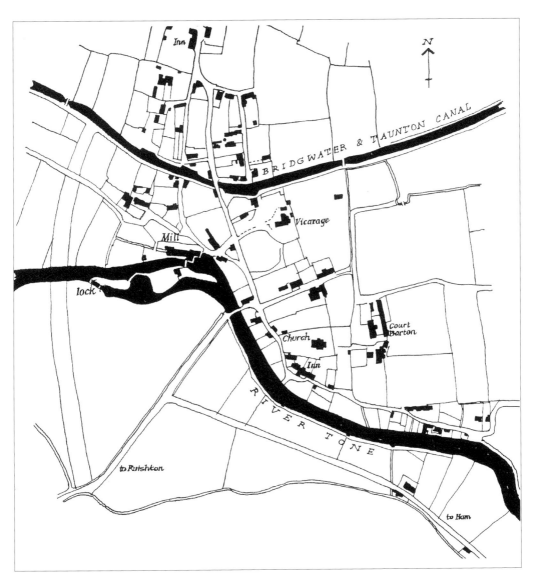

A redrawn map of Creech St Michael, from the tithe map prepared by the parish, 1839. Whilst the intended line of the Chard Canal is already indicated, the route of the railway is still not shown.

Working in such constricted areas, with the land quickly becoming muddy underfoot and the constant movement of horses and waggons, timber duckboards and catwalks for the wheelbarrows would be needed, usually not more than a single plank wide, which would be placed along the side of the working and down into the canal bed to assist in the hauling out of the spoil. Bearing in mind that most of the canal was cut through thick clay, it needs little imagination to appreciate the enormity of the task confronting the navvies.

The largest settlement along the route of the canal was at Creech St Michael, some 3 miles from Taunton. Here the canal passed through the centre of the village and ran close to the River Tone. The old road to Creech flour mill had to be diverted onto a new alignment a little to the east and today this diversion can clearly be seen. However, in 1824, when work was soon to get underway, the records of the vestry meeting record that 'they wrote to the canal authorities that they must not take away any material belonging to the old road, or cut through or stop the same until such time that they have consulted the wishes of the Parish and gained consent of the Vestry.'[16]

Throughout the length of the Bridgwater and Taunton Canal, between Huntworth and Firepool, over 600,000 cubic yards of soil were excavated! Some of this would have been used to form a level towpath, as required by the Act, whilst much would have been used in building up the necessary embankments and bridge approaches. The Act also provided that any surplus spoil could be spread over adjacent areas of farmland, with the owner's permission, in order to fill up unwanted hollows brought about by the building of the canal.

After two years work was progressing well on the canal, but construction costs were higher than those originally estimated, despite the fact that much of the work was through relatively easy terrain. It is possible that these were due to unforeseen works connected with the installation of side drains, the re-routing and joining of various streams and the construction of more culverts under the canal than had been envisaged. The Canal Company was running out of available funds from its own shareholders and other avenues needed to be explored to raise sufficient finance to finish the work.

In July 1826, a special meeting was called by the Canal Company 'for the purpose of executing a Mortgage of the said Navigation, and Undertaking, and of all Tolls and Receipts arising … from all other Property, Chattels and Effects belonging to the said Company of Proprietors for the purpose of securing the repayment of £7,500, being the first Moiety of a loan of £15,000, granted by the Commissioners for the issue of Exchequer Bills.'[17]

Fortunately for the contractors, the summer of 1826 was very hot and dry. 'The extreme heat and long prevailing drought is affecting stock – waste water from the Mills is watched for by owners of cattle. Feed of all sorts is all quite scorched up, and the fields are everywhere looking lamentably arid and brown'.[18] No rain fell between 3 May and 19 July and, as the *Sherborne Mercury* reported at the time, it was the worst drought since 1762. With a fortnight to go before the scheduled completion of the works, the *Taunton Courier* for 20 December 1826, drew attention to the animosity that existed between the Canal Company and the Conservators of the River Tone concerning the use of the river by the Company to reach the town wharves. In an editorial it was pointed out:

… that the Proprietors of the Canal affirm that they have the authority of their Act of Parliament for effecting, and made no secret of their intentions to avail themselves of such of their alleged power, in case no amicable adjustment of their interests, with those of the Conservators can be accomplished.

The article continued:

The proceedings of the Canal Company, it is well known, have been contemplated with jealousy, and opposed with firmness by the Conservators of the River Tone, from their imputed tendency to injure the vested interests dependent on the navigation of the River; and have also been viewed with hostile feelings by some of the inhabitants of the town.

Indeed, in May that year, a correspondent had expressed grave concern that with the Canal Company owning land at Firepool:

… on which to form wharves, with a road-way from the turnpike road, (they could) sell their coals lower than the merchants here now can, that the trade will be transferred to their wharves, and a very considerable injury accrue to the town, and particularly to the wharf property on the river.[19]

This view was reinforced when it was learnt that the Bridgwater & Taunton Canal Co. were involved at the time in initial discussions with the Grand Western Canal Co. to cut a link between their two canals at Firepool, which would avoid the use of the River Tone and the approved line for the Grand Western through French Weir. It was all seen at the time as a sinister plot by the Bridgwater & Taunton Canal Co. to set up wharves at Firepool and thus deny the town wharves the benefits of the lucrative canal trade. This was certainly an option for the company if negotiations with the Conservators over their joint use of the river broke down.

As 1826 drew to a close, the Canal Company had more immediate interests to attend to. The canal was due to be completed and ready for opening on New Year's Day, 1827, but 'on account of insufficient forwardness of the works' the opening was delayed until 3 January, 'the junction with the Tone having been effected at Firepool Weir yesterday afternoon'.[20]

Bearing in mind the long, dry summer the preceding year, it was perhaps fortunate for the Canal Company that the connection to the River Tone was made during the winter months when water levels would have been higher and sufficient to fill the canal. 1827 began with snow and hard frosts, and we can picture the onlookers, well wrapped up against the cold, as:

… several boats laden with coal and merchandize brought up to the established wharves on the river; an event which was hailed with satisfaction by a great concourse of people, as a fore runner of increasing prosperity to the ancient town of Taunton.[21]

One onlooker recorded later that the event had not been quite the occasion the newspaper had suggested:

> It was a day of snow, sleet and rain. I went to see it with one of my big brothers, and was obliged to put my hands alternately into the pockets of his trousers to keep them from freezing. It was intended to be a gay day, but there was not a bit of gaiety or cheerfulness about the whole affair. The first boat that came up this canal was called the *Mary Ann Joyce*.[22]

THE BRIDGWATER & TAUNTON CANAL CO.

THE COMPANY AND THE CONSERVATORS OF THE RIVER TONE –
A PERIOD OF DISTRUST

By 1827 Taunton had two separate waterways to Bridgwater. The Conservators must have realised that, compared with their River Tone which was both longer and more arduous for the boatmen, the canal was an attractive alternative and that they would be bound to suffer in any competition. The only trade they could safely count upon was the reduced traffic from Bridgwater to Ham Mills and back, with a little from Langport. Anything destined for Bridgwater would now use the canal. Competition was to become bitter and relationships between the Canal Company and the Conservators grew increasingly less trusting and, at times, openly hostile. As both were operating within their own legal powers, there seemed little room for compromise.

There were two factors in the Conservators' favour. First, the enabling Act of 1699 allowed them the use of the River Tone up to and including the town wharves whilst the Canal Company, whose Act enabled them to cut a canal to Firepool Weir, would need the Conservators' consent to gain access to these wharves. Secondly, the Conservators, by having control of the water, were able to control the flow going into the canal at Firepool.

The canal 'was cut into the River Tone and navigated upon' on 3 January 1827, and for the next seven months or so, it seems that they eyed each other distrustfully. However, at the end of August that year, the Canal Company served notice upon the Conservators that, under the powers that they considered they possessed in their 1824 Act, they were going to take over the Tone and with it access to the town's wharves. In November, 'the Canal Company, relying on their original Act of Parliament, took possession of the river and forcibly ejected a William Goodland, Inspector and Servant of the said River from his house at Bathpool'.[1]

The Conservators immediately brought a successful action of trespass against the Canal Company, with the Court of King's Bench ruling that 'the Conservators were a Corporate Body, created by Act of Parliament, with all the powers and privileges of Corporations, and that the provisions of the second Canal Act (5th Geo IV) related only to the canal and had no sort of application to the River Tone'.[2] The Canal Company were required to return the river to the Conservators and reinstate William Goodland. Whilst they acted promptly in the case of William Goodland, who resumed his duties, they refused to give up their possession of the river, claiming that their authorising Act of 1811, as amended in 1824, allowed them to keep it.

Litigation followed in the High Court and judgement was found in favour of the Conservators on the basis that neither the 1699 Act establishing the Conservators nor the 1824 Act of the Canal Company contained powers that would allow the Conservators to be compelled to give up their rights of possession of the river. It was not until February 1830 that the river was returned to the Conservators, with much ill-will, and to make sure the Canal Company understood the position, the Conservators, perhaps unwisely, proceeded to construct a dam across the mouth of the canal at Firepool that would not only prevent barges from entering Taunton but deny the canal replenishment water from the river.

Such action was bound to be provocative, and this time it was the Canal Company which instigated litigation. This resulted in an Order of the Chancery Court that the dam be removed. On 14 August 1830, the Conservators removed the dam, although they reserved the right to take action in future against persons 'entering with boats or other vessels, the River Tone from the Bridgwater and Taunton Canal.'[3] In fairness, the Conservators had some justification in their concern over the ability of the river to supply the canal with water. During the summer months, particularly, the River Tone was perpetually short of water. How could any be spared to feed the canal, when the millers at the Taunton Town Mills and at Bathpool, Creech and Ham had an equal right to the water alongside the Conservators?

The powers the Canal Company enjoyed to abstract from any convenient watercourse within 400 yards of the line of the canal allowed them to construct a pumping station alongside their canal at Charlton, near Creech St Michael, as a means of supplying their canal with water from the Tone. The steam-powered pumps drew water from the river below Ham where the two waterways were only 300 yards apart.

Relations between the Canal Company and the Conservators remained strained and the continued ill-will began to undermine the high hopes and aspirations of those who had witnessed the opening of the canal less than three years earlier. The Canal Company, in an effort to break deadlock, offered to buy outright the interests of the Conservators but the latter declined on the basis that they had no powers themselves to relinquish their rights and duties as a trust. Quite clearly matters could not continue in this manner, with recourse to expensive litigation every time there seemed to be a transgression.

The treasurer to the Conservators reported, in 1831, that:

> … the tolls up to the time the Canal Company cut into the river (3 January 1827) had been for many years at 4/– per weigh of 2 chaldron, or 3 tons. They were lowered to 8d per ton, or half, on 14 March 1827. Almost as soon as the Canal Company had taken possession of the river, they raised the rate of tonnage to the highest sum allowed by the Tone Acts, that is, from 8d to 16d per ton in coals. They also raised the tolls on the canal from 1s to 2/– per ton, this being the highest rate allowed by the Canal Act, and while the river was in 'their possession' they suffered some of the works to get so much out of repair as to render it impassable and no boat could, by any possibility, navigate upon it up to Taunton.

He explained that, before the Canal Company 'took possession of the River', and denied the Conservators its use, they had had an income from tolls of over £538. During the two years, 1828 and 1829, there had been no income, but by 1830 when they were once again able to use the river and, in their turn, deny the Canal Company its use during the summer months, their income had risen to over £630. The Conservators claimed compensation from the Canal Company for their losses during the years 1828 and 1829, although, not surprisingly, the company refused to consider it. This led the Conservators' treasurer to state in 1830 that:

> It is quite clear that the business done by the River must, in quantity, be as great, or nearly so as before the Canal was cut, and as the Canal certainly did considerable business at this time, it shows that we may fairly conclude that the River would have been increasingly productive and consequently the income much larger than we have taken it at £2400 per annum.

The constant confrontation between the parties was not only becoming expensive in legal costs, but hindering the prospects of increased trade to Taunton. Possibly with a sense of exasperation, linked with a realisation that the canal would ultimately carry the major coal traffic to the town, William Goodland, the Conservators' inspector and toll collector, sought to change his employment and set up on his own as a coal merchant. It is likely that his eye caught the advertisement that appeared in the *Taunton Courier* on 6 August 1828, offering an existing coal-yard to let in St James's, Taunton (see below).

WHARF AND COAL YARD TO LET, TAUNTON

TO BE LET,

For a Term of Twenty-one Years, determinable at Seven or Fourteen

A MOST convenient WHARF, near the BRIDGE, in TAUNTON ST. JAMES'S, with a COAL YARD adjoining to which there is an Entrance from St. James's Street, with TWO TENEMENTS, now in the occupation of Mr Trood, as Tenant to the Feoffees of Taunton Town Charities, whose Term therein expires at Christmas next.

Also, TWO TENEMENTS adjoining, one in the occupation of John Clarke, Stonemason, or his Undertenant, the other of Thos. Richards, Smith. These Houses are most eligibly situate for Trade, being at the bottom of North Street and St. James's Street, in a very populous part of the Town, and will be Let on Building Leases, or for such Term as may be determined on at the time of letting.

☞ A SURVEY will be held at the Castle Inn, Taunton, for letting the above Premises, on Tuesday, the Twenty Sixth Day of August next, at One o'Clock in the Afternoon.

J. and W. P. PINCHARD,
Stewards to the Feoffees.

Taunton, 29th July, 1828.

CAUTION.

THE Public are cautioned against believing certain statements which are abroad respecting the effects of the CANAL BILL now before Parliament, whereby the Public are told that they will be at the mercy of the Canal Company, to charge them whatever price they please for Coals. THIS IS UTTERLY FALSE, as the *Canal Company's Powers are limited*, and the very utmost Toll they can levy under their Act, is 2 shillings per Ton. Their present Toll is 1 shilling; so that if they were to do the utmost they are empowered to do by Law, it would only be an increase in price of 1 Shilling per Ton, or not quite *three farthings per hundred* above the present price.

TROOD, Printer, Bookbinder, and Auctioneer, TAUNTON.

TENDER MERCIES,

INTENDED BY THE

Canal Company.

IN answer to a Handbill I have just seen, headed "CAUTION," evidently emanating from the Friends of the Canal, and consequently, the enemies of the People of Taunton, I do assert, that before the Canal Company seized on the Old River, I used to pay *Five Shillings* for every Boat Load of Timber sent from my Wharf at Bathpool; but immediately the River was seized on by the Canal Company, they gradually increased their demands, and ultimately extorted *Ten Shillings* per Boat. God only knows what they would now charge had they not been dispossessed of the River! So much for the Tender Mercies to be expected from the Canal Speculators, who intend to engross to themselves all the Trade of Taunton, and all the benefits to be derived from the River Tone.---Fie on them!!

WM. YATES,

Timber Merchant,

BATHPOOL,

W. TOMS, PRINTER, TAUNTON.

Above and *left:* Caution and Tender Mercies: There was much indignation to the coming of the canal to Taunton and these two handbills show the depth of feeling! *Taunton Courier,* 6 August 1828.

The Old Mill and Penstocks at Creech St Michael, River Tone, 1897. Taken from a painting by H. Frier, 1889. (Courtesy of Somerset County Council)

He was thirty-one at the time, and that year set up his own business in St James's Street, close to the river and Coal Orchard. A short while afterwards, his brother, Charles, also established a coal merchants' business close by in North Town, again with riverside wharves. Whilst it would be a few years before the two separate firms in Taunton merged, the two brothers did set up together as coal merchants in Tiverton, relying on the Grand Western Canal to supply that branch. Soon after William Goodland had opened his business, a tragic family bereavement must have cast a dark cloud over his success, for his son, Walter, only two and a half years old at the time, was drowned in the River Tone adjoining his father's yard, being found later at the 'mill tail'.[4]

Although the Conservators probably felt confident that their river was in a sufficiently good state to sustain a reasonable degree of trade despite competition from the canal, there was one area in Taunton where, due to circumstances beyond their control, both the merchants and boatmen experienced great problems. This was at the North Town Bridge. The main coal wharves were down-river of this bridge on both banks, but chiefly because of the narrowness of the arches, barges found it increasingly difficult to navigate through them to the upper reaches of the river. This four-arched medieval bridge had, for years, caused considerable navigational difficulties, not only for the Conservators but also for the merchants and wharfingers who had premises close by. Apart from its narrow openings, there was also a mud bank, Sealey's Island, in the middle of the river adjoining the bridge on the north side, which also considerably impeded the turning of the barges at the coal wharves. In wintertime, when the river was full, the dam-like mass of the old bridge severely constricted the flow of the river; debris blocked the arches, causing flooding in the North Town area.

Proposals to replace this bridge two decades earlier had come to nothing, but in 1826 a new single span bridge at Burrowbridge replaced the old multi-arched medieval bridge. The flow that had caused the boatmen trouble on the River Parrett was no longer constricted. Was this not the time to consider a new bridge at Taunton? In 1828, therefore:

> The project for throwing a cast iron bridge over the River Tone, at the end of North Street, in this town, has lately engaged the consideration of the (Turnpike) Commissioners, and is now resolved to be immediately carried into execution. The floods at North Town, [they had been very extensive during the preceding month, and had caused much inconvenience and damage] so injuriously felt in wet weather, will be one of the evils obviated by this measure. The 'island' near the site of the present bridge, will be removed, in the arrangements for this one to be constructed. [5]

Unfortunately, the enthusiasm shown by this report was not sustained and for reasons that were no doubt financial, the project proceeded no further. It would be another decade before it received the attentions of the Bridgwater & Taunton Canal Co.

CREECH MILL

Whilst the Conservators were still at loggerheads with the Canal Company, and before any reconciliation could take place, another incident occurred in October 1830 which was to cause them further anguish and even more litigation. This time the Canal Company were not involved. It centred around the renewal of a millwheel at the mill at Creech St Michael, a water grist and flour mill jointly owned by Thomas and Samuel Dyer and John Fry. In the action heard at the King's Bench at Westminster the following year it was alleged that in the course of carrying out repairs to their mill, work that involved the fitting of a new millwheel, the owners of Creech Mill had drawn up the flood gates (also known as sluices) for a period of sixteen days when, in fact, they had had permission for only three days. They had also constructed a dam across the river with the result that the boats 'were entirely prevented from going up the river to the great loss of the Conservators'. In a rather enlightening submission the Conservators stated that the millers 'have always been on bad terms with the boatmen and have continual bickerings with them'. The Conservators contended that 'the millers felt they had a primary right to the water and may use it for the purpose of a mill, and draw it off at the flood gates at their pleasure, and that the rights of the Conservators are entirely dependent on them'.

This was going to be an important point to establish. With the increased bitterness and mistrust between the Conservators and the Canal Company, any loss of river trade to the Conservators as a result of action taken by others would ultimately be to the benefit of the Canal Company who, it was strongly suspected, were behind the 'trespass'. By such action, it was alleged by the Conservators that 'the Canal Company would have no difficulty in putting an end to the Tone Navigation by purchasing the Mill and keeping the flood gates raised'. The judgement was that each party had a right to use the water for both navigation and the mill, and that each had to exercise that right in a manner that did not injure the other. [6]

RECONCILIATION – THE CONSERVATORS OF THE RIVER TONE AND THE BRIDGWATER & TAUNTON CANAL CO. AGREE TO WORK TOGETHER

Towards the end of 1831, and within weeks of the Creech Mill judgement, the acrimony between the Conservators and the Canal Company appears to have subsided to the extent that the company resolved to meet the Conservators before promoting a new Bill in Parliament aimed at clarifying the differences between them. On 17 October 1831, the secretary to the Canal Company, Isaac Cooke, a name well known in Somerset as one who had supported many canal schemes in the region, wrote to the chairman of the Conservators:

> Sir,
> I am authorised by the Committee of the Canal Company to propose that a meeting should take place between a deputation from their Body and a deputation from the Conservators with a view, if possible, to effect an amicable arrangement of the differences between the respective parties, or, if it would be more agreeable to the Conservators, the Canal Company are willing to refer the circumstances to three Gentlemen to be chosen in the usual manner, investing them with powers to direct what shall be done by the respective parties.

The Conservators agreed immediately to a meeting and within four days Mr Cooke had responded:

> Sir,
> The Canal Company … have directed me to name the following basis for the proposed conference, viz:
> ★ That the Canal Company shall pay the debt due from the River Tone.
> ★ Also the sums assessed for the Parishes of Taunton. [This refers to the charitable aid to the poor.]
> ★ And a further sum for improving the River Tone from Firepool to the wharves in Taunton and towards erecting an iron bridge instead of the present North Town Bridge.
> ★ That the River Tone be then vested in the Canal Company.

Thus, the 'agenda' had been set which subsequently formed the basis of the provisions within the new Bill the Canal Company presented to Parliament. It is interesting to note that the proposal to erect a new bridge at North Town and to remove the 'island' was now included as one of the responsibilities of the Canal Company.

In November 1831, the Conservators re-commissioned William Armstrong who had previously prepared a report on the Tone in 1824, to survey the river once again, and also the canal, and to 'go to London and present the case for the Conservators at the enquiry into the Bill'.[7]

The Bill was subsequently presented to Parliament and approved. It was to be known as the Bridgwater and Taunton Canal Navigation Act and received Royal Assent in July 1832. It provided for the Conservators to sell all their rights and interests in the River Tone Navigation to the Canal Company but the Company also had to comply with strict and costly provisions to satisfy the Conservators in giving up their ancient rights, including strict limitations on the levy of tolls. They also had to reimburse all the money the Conservators had subscribed (although the remaining Tone debt had already been paid by the company) together with a sum of £2,000, which was an amount assessed for the discharge of the Charitable Trust for the Poor of Taunton, as set out in the original Act of 1699. The Conservators were entitled to retain a small strip of land on the north-east side of North Town Bridge in Taunton so that they could have access to the river and to a landing stage.

In line with the earlier discussions with the Conservators, the company was required to carry out some major works to the river and to keep the river navigable, as it was considered that this would have been work the Conservators would have carried out anyway, had they had retained control of the river. These works included the removal of Sealey's Island and the refashioning of the old bridge itself in order to widen the span and thus allow barges through to the mills and wharves upriver of the bridge. As the Canal Company would have no jurisdiction over any works to the bridge itself, it would be left to the town's surveyor and the trustees of the Turnpike Trust who would organise and supervise the work at the expense of the company.

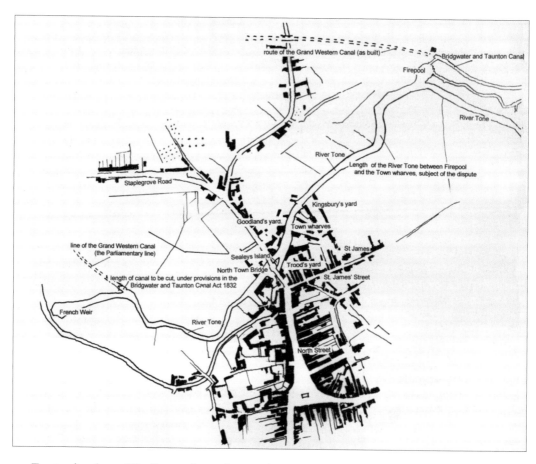

Taunton, based upon Wood's map of 1840, showing the disputed area of the River Tone between Firepool, where the Bridgwater and Taunton Canal joined the River Tone, and the town wharves. The authorised line of the Grand Western Canal (the Parliamentary line) and the route as built is also shown.

Furthermore, as the river through Taunton would be used by barges negotiating the Grand Western Canal (the parliamentary line showed this canal entering Taunton at French Weir), the 1832 Act also required the Bridgwater & Taunton Canal Co. to cut a short length of the canal at French Weir with a lock as a means of completing all works associated with the Tone once and for all.

However, the Act also contained a clause that must have given the Canal Company considerable misgivings. They were to submit their canal to a regular inspection by the Conservators, at least once a year, '… in order that the inhabitants of Taunton would not be denied a communication by water between Bridgwater and Taunton', and to make sure it was 'kept open for the passage of boats and other vessels laden with goods and merchandise'. Any complaints about the condition of the canal that were not dealt with in a reasonable time could be brought by the Conservators to Quarter Sessions, with the Justices having powers to ensure any necessary works were carried out. In default, the Conservators had powers to resume their possession of the river.

The Canal Company could well have asked themselves whether the idea of seeking a new Act had been such a good idea after all, although it had at least succeeded in bringing to an end the perpetual and damaging battles between the parties. With goodwill on both sides it was now possible for the company to settle down and establish a regular and profitable trade between Bridgwater and Taunton. By the beginning of the 1830s, James Bunter, a Conservator of the River Tone, was able to write in a letter to the *Taunton Courier*:

> Sir,
>
> I once heard a medical practitioner expatiate with great earnestness on the wonderful cures that had been effected by some nostrum with which he had just fallen in love, and I was amused when a by-stander, who seemed to be astounded by the wonders he had heard, asked, 'how the medicine operated'. He replied, 'Why, Sir, like a charm'… such seems to be the working of the Bridgwater and Taunton Canal; it is a good – a superbly good – thing, it saves thousands of our money at Taunton, and causes a reduction in the price of coals.[8]

In 1838, the Conservators decided to seek the permission of the charity commissioners to lay out £1,000 'in building a wing to the Taunton and Somerset Hospital and maintain the same', and the balance of £1,000 to be invested in bonds of the Taunton Market Trust; the bonds to be kept in the custody of the Treasurer of the Conservators. The Chancery Order was granted in 1843 and the construction of the hospital wing was commenced shortly afterwards. It was to be known as the Conservators Ward, a name that fortunately has been retained today in the new hospital at Musgrove Park.

1838 was also the year that another coal merchant, John Kingsbury, who for many years had operated coal barges on the River Tone and now used the canal, opened up a wharf at the bottom of North Street, announcing at the beginning of that year, that he would be selling 'the very best Welsh coal at 1/1d per cwt, and Forest of Dean coals at 1/1½d per cwt; coals delivered to Town and Country'. This was a time when Taunton boasted no fewer than twenty-six different firms of carriers providing regular contact with, not only the areas around Taunton, but much further afield, such as Minehead, Dulverton and Wellington.[9]

BRIDGWATER GETS A HARBOUR

The tidal River Parrett, at the time so important an artery to the sea-borne trade of Bridgwater, was not an easy river to navigate for the mariners and ship-owners who brought their small sailing ships up to the riverside wharves in the town. Due to the tides, the strong currents and the long periods of slack water, it required fine judgement to manoeuvre a vessel up the twisting course of the river and arrive on the right state of the tide. The town bridge was always a barrier preventing larger-masted craft from gaining access further up-river and therefore, during the eighteenth century, the schooners, brigs, ketches, colliers and coasters moored alongside the east and west quays, in increasingly constricted conditions.

It must have been a magnificent sight in those days; vessels of all shapes and sizes from many parts of the United Kingdom, Europe and North America, slowly making their way up the Parrett, and, with furled sails, negotiating the last few yards of their journey to their moorings in the town. Yet, because of the growing number of vessels wishing to berth at the quays, handling their cargoes became increasingly difficult. It could only safely be carried out during the short periods of high tide; during slack water the boats settled on to the mud, on occasions some even slumping over slightly, causing cargoes to shift and possible damage to the timber hulls. Facilities had to be improved.

Bristol was a port that, whilst larger than Bridgwater, encountered similar problems during the 1790s in that its quays and warehouses in the town were at the end of a long, winding tidal river, with dangerous mud banks and long periods of slack water. The reputation of Bristol had been going down since the early eighteenth century at which time it had been second only to London amongst seaports and cities in the realm.[1]

Like Bridgwater by the beginning of the 1800s, its ability to handle shipping was becoming inadequate. As early as 1802, William White, who was later to work with both William and Henry Jessop, was engaged to survey the port, and put forward proposals for 'Improving the Harbour of Bristol'[2] by damming the river and building a new floating, or wet, harbour capable of taking the larger vessels. It would be a simple and effective way to achieve safe harbourage alongside a tidal river, whilst still keeping and using the wharves and warehouses in the town. An almost identical scheme, by William Jessop, was later undertaken, being completed in 1809, during the height of the Napoleonic Wars, but in time to meet the scheduled opening of the Kennet and Avon Canal the following year.

The Corporation of Bridgwater was quick to see the advantages that Bristol had achieved and were keen to do the same. John Easton, in 1811, the same year that the Bristol & Taunton Canal Co. gained their Act, put forward a somewhat similar proposal for the town, undoubtably to enhance the canal's prospects. He suggested a new 'cut', 16ft deep and just 2½ miles long between Combwich and Bridgwater, thus avoiding the long,

Bridgwater's medieval town bridge, drawn in the late eighteenth century by John Chubb. (Courtesy of Sedgemoor District Council)

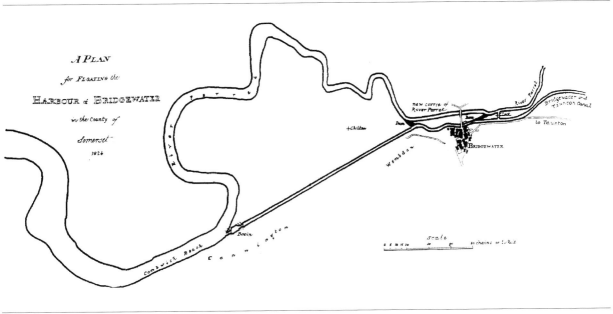

John Easton had prepared many proposals since the early 1800s for a ship canal linking Combwich to Bridgwater. Most utilised the River Parrett through Bridgwater as part of the canal, with the tidal river being taken along a new 'cut', through Eastover. This 1824 proposal was drawn up to link in with the Bristol & Taunton Canal Co. proposals. (Redrawn)

5½-mile course of the Parrett, damming the river at Saltlands and using the old river through Bridgwater as a long floating harbour.[3]

With the ending of the Napoleonic Wars in 1815, trade began to grow again, particularly with the ports of France and northern Europe. The need to transport larger quantities of freight led to an increase in the size of sailing craft. Not only was there a growth in the demand for coal to all parts of the kingdom, but coastal and deep-sea fishing also flourished, bringing an increased urgency for better harbours and more efficient handling facilities at the wharves themselves.

When, in 1824, the Bristol and Taunton Canal Co. obtained their Act for a canal to link Bridgwater with Taunton, John Easton, never one to let an opportunity pass, resubmitted his proposal for a floating harbour for Bridgwater to provide a link between the town's quayside and the proposed canal.

It had been nearly fifteen years since the Corporation of Bridgwater had first entertained the idea of improving their port. Being so conveniently close to the coalfields of South Wales it was essential that something was done before further delay affected the trade to the town, especially at a time when other ports were fast becoming more attractive to use.[4] In January 1825 the *Taunton Courier* stated that, 'Trade in the Port of Bridgwater has been entirely suspended, in consequence of the immense masses of ice which have congealed together and prevented the vessels from coming in or going out'. The town could no longer afford such loss of trade and better facilities were long overdue, although it would be a few years yet before anything was done.[5]

Further Schemes – Will Anything Ever Be Done?

In 1828, a year after the opening of the Bridgwater and Taunton Canal, the Corporation of Bridgwater resolved, at long last, to seek the advice of Henry Jessop, one of William Jessop's many sons, to see if he could propose a solution. That Easton had worked closely with Jessop, and indeed Rennie, was an advantage but Henry Jessop was an engineer and probably the Corporation felt the enormity of the harbour undertaking required the attentions of an engineer rather than a surveyor.

The views expressed to Jessop by the merchants and ship owners could not have been a more damaging assessment of the situation:

> The Port and the accommodation it affords are altogether inadequate to the existing state of the trade, and that great delay, and loss of time and danger often arise to the vessels frequenting the same for want of sufficient 'quay-room', from their being left dry during the reflux of the tides and the circuitous course of the River, and from water during neap tides not being deep enough to float vessels up to the quay. Three or four days are lost during neap tides, and the foreign trade of the Port is stopped at Combwich on account of the dangers to the navigation.

He accepted the commission, submitting his report and plans the following year. They were identical to Easton's earlier proposals in every way, such that there can be no doubt that Easton drew them up! Local opinion was enthusiastic:

To overcome the problems of vessels leaning over whilst moored at the wharves when the waters in the River Parrett ebbed, a grillage of stout timbers was provided below water level upon which a boat could be positioned. The top-sail schooner *Ideal* of Stavanger is stationed upon the grillage for a survey after a collision with SS *Devon*, with a cargo of timber from Sweden, in August 1903. (Courtesy of the National Rivers Authority)

> … the projected improvement of the Port of Bridgwater is one of most desirable importance that ever occurred to that town and will transmit no inconsiderable benefit to the trading and manufacturing interest throughout a great part of the West of England.[6]

Henry Jessop, in presenting his proposal, observed that 'trade on this river has long been increasing at a rate of about 5,000 tons a year'. In 1822, the tonnage was somewhat more than 75,000 tons; whilst in 1829, 113,000 tons had already been registered. He reported to the Corporation of Bridgwater that:

> … these inconveniencies may be effectively removed by making a canal from Combwich Reach to Bridgwater for vessels of 500 tons burthen if not drawing more than 16ft of water, by converting part of the present river into a floating harbour, connected with the Taunton Canal and providing a new course for the River Parrett through the town.

He estimated the cost of his proposals to be £97,371, with a further £3,809 to provide an extension to the Bridgwater and Taunton Canal, from its then terminus at Huntworth, and to reroute it to link into his proposed floating harbour. At a public meeting held in the Town Hall at Bridgwater on 11 December 1829, the plan was again enthusiastically endorsed and subscriptions opened, £10,000 being raised quite quickly towards the total cost of £101,180. Bridgwater Corporation must have been delighted that at long last progress was being made towards improving their inadequate port facilities, although the details of the project should have come as no surprise as they were identical to those put forward on their behalf nearly eighteen years earlier.

Some sixty years before this photograph was taken in 1906, mariners would have experienced the same cramped accommodation for their vessels at both East and West Quays, as shown here. (Courtesy of The Colin Wilkins Collection)

Whether the price quoted by Henry Jessop was considered to be more than could be confidently expected to be raised by public subscription or whether there were doubts as to the financial viability of the undertaking or the amount of trade the scheme could attract is not recorded, but no further action was taken and the scheme, like so many before it, was shelved.[7]

The inadequacies of the existing moorings at the wharves, however, were becoming pressing. By 1835, tonnage of over 130,000 was being recorded, although it is likely that this figure also included a small number of moorings at Combwich. Not only were spaces at the wharves severely restricted, but vessels often experienced difficulties in tacking upon the tidal river, both coming up to Bridgwater, and returning to sea. The *Taunton Courier* reported in that year that 'The *Carleon*, from Bridgwater to Ireland, ran aground in working out of the river, about a quarter of a mile from the Bridge, and fell over when the tide receded. The cargo consisted of flax and cloverseed, which was entirely spoilt.'[8]

This was the year that another engineer, Henry Habberley Price, submitted yet another report to the Corporation of Bridgwater for improving the Port and providing a ship canal. Henry Price was an engineer, with considerable experience of river navigations. He had been retained as Engineer to the River Tees and he was also engaged on improving the River Lea at Cork, the Suire at Waterford and the River Towy at Swansea.[9]

Whilst he proposed two alternative ship canals, to link Bridgwater with the Parrett near Combwich, one on each side of the river, he clearly preferred and recommended to the Corporation a proposal on the west side. Again, this was a variant of the schemes that had already been produced by John Easton and Henry Jessop for a line between Combwich and the north side of Bridgwater, although in his scheme Henry Price did not seek to utilise the River Parrett through Bridgwater as part of his floating harbour. He proposed instead that a new floating harbour be built just north of Bridgwater at Crowpill, with access to it achieved by cutting a wide ship canal, a little over 3 miles in length, from Combwich, where a tidal basin would connect to the Parrett. The Bridgwater and Taunton Canal was to be diverted around Bridgwater to enter the new harbour at its western end.

The canal itself was to be 18ft deep with locks 163ft long and 36ft wide to 'accommodate the largest class steamers'. In order to achieve this depth without a massive amount of digging, Henry Price proposed that the spoil from the excavations be used to form raised banks. He estimated the cost of the shorter, western route to be £79,681, with a further £14,000 to extend the Bridgwater and Taunton Canal, again from Standards lock. He stated that 'he was convinced that a greater expenditure of capital is rendered necessary to make the old river available as a Dock'; an unfavourable reference to the 1829 scheme by Jessop.

Once more Bridgwater Corporation seemed unwilling to support either of Henry Price's alternative proposals, and, as had happened so many times before, nothing was done and the plans were laid aside.

However, 1835 was to be the year that the Bristol & Exeter Railway, with considerable public support, proposed a railway between the two cities that would pass close to both Bridgwater and Taunton. The following year, after submitting their proposal to Parliament, they obtained their Act and this, no doubt, put an entirely different complexion on the building of more canals. For many businessmen and investors, railways were not just seen as competitors but possibly the future means of quick and reliable transport.

The Bridgwater & Taunton Canal Co. would also have seen these developments in the same light but, in a shrewd move, they also saw merit in the concept of an up-to-date harbour at Bridgwater, for this would safeguard imports of coal upon which their canal depended. If they could finance and construct a floating harbour at Bridgwater and link it to their own canal, they could achieve a near monopoly of the sea-borne trade up the Parrett. It would give them a strong trading base for business on the canal as well as future dealings with a newly emerging railway, which would require considerable quantities of coal in its operations.

Accordingly they proposed a Bill to Parliament to build a floating harbour on the west bank of the River Parrett adjoining Crowpill House and to extend their canal from Huntworth to the western end of the new harbour, almost exactly as Price had proposed the year before. On 21 April 1837, the Bridgwater & Taunton Canal Co. received their Act.[10]

They engaged the services of the engineer, Thomas Maddicks, to design and oversee the construction of the canal from Huntworth and the new floating harbour. Bearing in mind the earlier scheme drawn up by Henry Price and the similarity of the company's present proposals to his own, it is rather surprising that they commissioned yet another engineer. Little is known of the work of Thomas Maddicks although it is possible that he had been an assistant to Brunel.

Not five years earlier, Brunel had completed a range of works at Bristol Docks that were very similar to those now suggested for Bridgwater and it is possible that the directors of the Canal Company, whose registered offices were in Bristol, were equally impressed by what they saw. With Brunel himself totally committed to a vast amount of railway work at the time, could it be that he put forward the name of Maddicks, as an engineer to handle the work whilst he, himself, would be in the background to offer engineering advice? Certainly the complexities of the tidal flushing systems proposed for Bridgwater Dock, which many think would have been beyond the abilities of an inexperienced engineer, owe much to Brunel's designs at Bristol. Thomas Maddicks, however, prudently engaged the surveying services of the ever-reliable John Easton and must have appreciated and welcomed his depth of experience in the matters involved in the canal at Bridgwater.

The cutting of the short length of the new canal to the dock would have presented the Canal Company with few engineering difficulties with which they were not already familiar, although the short tunnel at West Street and the 30ft-deep cutting between there and Albert Street would have absorbed much labour and money.[11] They did, however, encounter some problems over the initial purchase of the land, for unlike the open country between Huntworth and Taunton, this was urban land, upon which stood a number of riverside industries, chiefly brick and tile works. John Chapman, who had operated a brick and tile works in Bridgwater since the turn of the century from a site just south of the town on the west side of the Parrett, now found that his land, like that of other adjacent brickmakers, was on the route of the proposed canal and would be severed, requiring the demolition of some of his buildings.

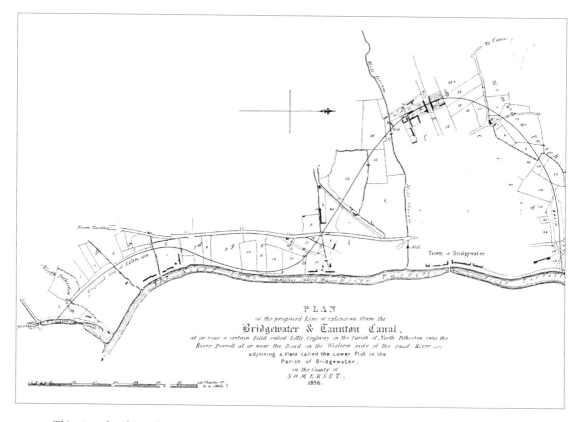

This 1836 plan shows the proposed line of the extension of the Bridgwater and Taunton Canal to the north side of Bridgwater.

Dissatisfied with the original offer of £390 5s from the Canal Company, he took the issue to an Inquiry by Adjournment at Wells in July 1838, where the jury awarded a total of £750 5s as being the appropriate figure to include purchase, damage to buildings and other lands, and severance damage.

Pending the inquiry decision, however, Mr Chapman had allowed the Canal Company 'access to his land so that they could proceed with their works, but they refused to pay more, and insisted that they were entitled to hold possession on these terms'. In August, not surprisingly, an injunction was served upon the Canal Company, who were also criticised for their conduct; attempting to hold possession of land without paying the owner the sum awarded by the Jury. This injunction was later dismissed upon the moneys, awarded by the Jury, being paid into Court, pending discussions and allowing the work to proceed.[12]

As the line of the canal also severed many roads around the outskirts of Bridgwater, the company had to build a number of brick bridges spanning both the canal and the towpath, a tunnel under West Street and some large culverts. As the excavated ground was prime brick-making clay, and in the manner in which they had operated during the cutting of the canal to Taunton, this spoil was put to use profitably by the local brickworks.

The cost of the dock, the tidal basin and the cut to Huntworth was estimated by Thomas Maddicks at £25,000. Unfortunately for the company, it was to cost almost exactly four times that amount, a financial burden from which the company never recovered!

BRIDGWATER AND TAUNTON CANAL.

THE Committee are willing to receive Tenders for Loans of money, for three years, in sums of not less than £200, upon the security of loan notes to be issued under the Company's seal, bearing interest at the rate of Six pounds Per centum, per annum, payable half yearly.

The whole of the Canal and the Company's Docks, at Bridgwater, are completed and in operation.

Tenders may be addressed, to Messrs. Isaac Cooke and Sons, Solicitors, Bristol.

22nd June, 1841.

Construction was completed in 1841. As required, 'when the new cut and works should, with the old canal, form a new navigation communicating between the River Parrett and the town of Taunton, the company should close the lock from the river to the canal at Huntworth',[13] the old spur and basin at Huntworth were closed and filled in. Today, it is still possible to see the site of the earlier canal basin at Huntworth, just east of Somerset Bridge, and to recall that short period in the history of the canal when barge traffic would come up the Parrett on the tide and enter this basin on its way to Taunton.

The new tidal basin and dock was to be far more convenient, both for the sailing vessels entering and leaving the Parrett and for the barges, some of which still used the Parrett and would need to enter the dock to take on freight. It was provided with its own barge lock, as was usual in basin designs at the time, which allowed barges through without the need to operate the large ship lock gates. The water area of the dock itself extended to over four acres with a number of deep-water berths around its perimeter.[14]

The Conservators of the River Tone would again have watched these developments with interest, if not bemusement. However mistakenly, many inhabitants, merchants, and traders still held the Conservators, in some degree, answerable for any shortcomings that arose on the navigations and for the operations of the Canal Company. Concern was not long in coming. No sooner had the dock been brought into operation than the Canal Company began to charge tolls for barges using the basin. In May 1841, the Conservators sought counsel's opinion. They were advised that the Canal Company could legally claim tolls in respect of barges trading from Taunton through the basin to the Parrett, 'and which do not rest, load, or unload therein'.[15] Understandably, the company wished to discourage barge traffic from Taunton passing directly through their dock to trade at the wharves on the Parrett. If the barges loaded up or unloaded within the dock or came into the dock from the Parrett to do so, then basin tolls would not be applicable.

Although much barge traffic now used the canal, there was still some that navigated the River Tone to Ham Mills, principally carrying coals and other freight for local distribution to Chard and Ilminster and to the villages in the area. By early 1840 the River Tone had fallen into 'a deplorable state' and the Conservators expressed their concern to the Canal Company that this was contrary to the assurances given by the company at the time it had bought out the Conservators' interests, a view not accepted by the Canal Company.

By 1842, a year after the Canal Company had opened its dock at Bridgwater, the Bristol and Exeter Railway linked Taunton to Bridgwater by rail, as part of its growing network of lines in the West Country.

BARGE TRAFFIC ON THE CANAL

In 1840, when the canal still terminated at Huntworth, it carried nearly 90,000 tons of goods and earned the company a net income of over £5,000; twice the figure the Conservators had managed to achieve on the river, only fifteen years earlier, during their best years!

The Canal Company enjoyed a short period of successful trading immediately after the dock opened, with nearly 120,000 tons being hauled to Taunton and with the net income increasing to over £8,200, but it was clear to the company that with the coming of a rail link to Taunton they would be engaged in a perpetual struggle to earn sufficient income to offset their costs. The heavy mortgages the company had been forced to take out to meet outstanding debts, of £10,000 on the canal construction and nearly £90,000 for the dock and its short connecting canal to Huntworth, meant that much of this income went on interest repayments.[16] Their projection of canal trade was now in jeopardy, but whilst its future may have seemed in doubt, the dock still represented a sound investment. The volume of shipping in Bridgwater was steadily growing, and by 1853 nearly 2,400 vessels used the port and dock facilities.[17]

1842 also marked the completion of the Chard Canal between Creech St Michael and Chard, a link that it hoped would enable the Bridgwater and Taunton Canal to earn additional toll income, by allowing barges to use their canal from Bridgwater to Creech St Michael. A similar source of extra income had already been achieved four years earlier, when the Grand Western Canal Co. finally completed their link from Holcombe Rogus to Taunton, at Firepool, where the main freight carried was coal and culm. Unfortunately, neither the Grand Western Canal,[18] nor the Chard Canal,[19] with their intriguing mechanical lifts and inclines, were to play any significant role in the fortunes of the Bridgwater and Taunton Canal. Their presence, however, on the canal scene is interesting and they certainly deserve a brief mention in the context of the other waterways that served Taunton. They never attracted the volume of trade envisaged when they were built and for which their shareholders had hoped, almost entirely because of the coming of the railways. The Bridgwater & Taunton Canal Co., facing up to this same competition, considered abandoning its canal altogether and using the land for the formation of a railway! They proposed that this would run from Stolford on the Bristol Channel, via Bridgwater, Taunton and Chard to the South Coast, a railway equivalent of the earlier inter-channel schemes which had thwarted successive generations of canal promoters! Despite vigorous opposition from the Conservators of the River Tone who threatened to invoke, yet again, the powers of the 1832 Act, the company presented a Bill to Parliament in 1845 which was passed the following year. Presumably because of the lack of available finance, no further action was taken on this proposal and the powers later lapsed.

By 1858, the Bridgwater & Taunton Canal Co. had lost more than half its toll income due to railway competition,[20] and the continuing demands for mortgage repayments, with an interest of 5 per cent, was a burden the company found hard to meet. Curiously, it was lent much of the money it required from the firm of Isaac Cooke, whose principal held the position of clerk to the company itself.[21]

The inevitable drop in trade, heightened by the reduction in coal prices from collieries in the North of England, led to lower receipts for coal from South Wales, and had the expected result.[22] Repayments on the mortgages were difficult to maintain, and shareholders received scant reward on their investment.

By the early 1850s the company was in the hands of Receivers.

THE MAIN CARGOES CARRIED

The Canal Company's income was almost exclusively derived from the levy of tolls upon the merchandise carried on the barges. These were laid down in the Act obtained by the company[23] and could only be altered at some later date by further reference to Parliament. A glance at these shows the range of goods specified for the canal and the rates for each, at the time the canal was authorised:

coals, culm, coke, cinders, charcoal, iron, stone, pig- iron, iron ore, copper ore, lead ore, lime, limestone, other stone, bricks, tiles and pipe clay, *2d* per ton per mile.
hay, straw, peat, chalk, clay, sand, *1½d*
corn, grain, flour, malt, meal, cider, timber, lead, kelp, pitch, tar and turpentine, *2½d*
persons, *1½d* per mile
cattle, sheep, swine and other beasts, *1½d* per head per mile

The firm of Messrs Sully & Co. were, perhaps, the largest importers of coal and culm into Bridgwater during the nineteenth century. The company occupied large premises adjacent to the dock at Crowpill, and owned a fleet of colliers. As the century progressed, these vessels changed from the smaller 50 ton sailing brigs to larger steamships, readily distinguishable by the ubiquitous emblem of a white cross on their funnels. The company also owned river and canal barges as it was the main supplier of coal and culm to the Bridgwater Gas Works, the Parrett and Tone Pumping Stations as well as markets at Langport and Taunton.

Most of the coal carried on the canal would be steam coal used in industrial boilers in factories, laundries, bakeries and tanneries as well as in the local hospitals and infirmaries. There would be a substantial tonnage supplied for delivery to the railways in addition to smaller amounts for the local foundries and for fire-engines, road-rollers and threshing machines. With the considerable numbers of horses used at the time for heavy haulage

At the dockside, late nineteenth century. (Courtesy of Mrs L.P. Woods, Goathurst)

An early photograph (1881) of a barge on the Bridgwater and Taunton Canal, at the dock entrance. (Courtesy of the National Rivers Authority)

and transport on the roads and in the fields, the work of the blacksmiths and farriers also relied on regular supplies of coal.

Stone coal, more commonly known as anthracite, was favoured by the maltsters and brewers while, for domestic heating, house coal was available, also used for kitchen ranges and ovens, and heating greenhouses and conservatories, a popular adjunct to many of the larger houses in and around Taunton in Victorian days.

Culm is a low-volatility coal slack and was used extensively in the retorts at both the Bridgwater and Taunton Gas Works, whilst local lime kilns would use culm laced within the limestone to produce the lime so necessary to the farmer and the builder. As a by-product from the gas works, coke was produced which was also used for heating domestic ranges.

By the 1840s there were over a dozen different coal merchants operating in the Taunton area alone,[24] giving some idea as to the heavy demand there was, at the time, for the fuel. The merchants became household names, like Goodland's, Kingsbury's, Davidge's, the Taunton Coal Co., and, a little later, Hammett's. Most of the coal that was delivered on the barges came from collieries around Newport, Cardiff and nearby Llantwithin as well as from Lydney and the Forest of Dean, a popular house coal being that from Bullo Wharf.

Salt was another commodity carried in large amounts in the barges and great care had to be taken to ensure that it was kept dry and clean during its handling and carriage. Many coal merchants stocked salt, such as Hammett's who had premises on the south-west corner of North Town Bridge. Much of it was brought down the River Severn from Cheshire to Bridgwater, coming in various qualities depending upon its use. Besides the fine salt for domestic use, there was agricultural salt which was spread on the land to improve its condition for cultivation, and, like lime, was essential in the days before fertilisers. Rock salt was used, amongst other purposes, as 'licks' for cattle, supplementing the often bland feed from the poor grasses. Dairy salt was used by butchers and butter and cheese makers, for, in the days before refrigeration, salting was the usual way to preserve some foods. Salt was also used by bakers in their bread-making and in water-softeners to be found in the larger houses and institutions.

Supplies of bricks and tiles and other clay products, were bought along the canal directly from the manufacturers' wharves at Bridgwater. These would be for the building firms, who from the mid-1850s were to be kept increasingly busy meeting the demand for houses to accommodate the growing numbers of people living in the Taunton area. Sand, building stone, and slate were also required, as the industrial products from the manufacturing areas of South Wales and the Midlands.

Timber, particularly softwoods from North America and the Baltic, formed a considerable tonnage of trade brought into Bridgwater Dock and a number of timber importers set up businesses there, and later, in Taunton. Edward Sealy & Son had premises in Bridgwater by 1824, and later, in Taunton, regularly receiving shipments from North America. By the middle of the nineteenth century, George Pollard and Bagehot Edwards & Co. had also established timber yards in Taunton, alongside the river, followed shortly afterwards, as the demand for house building rose, by Thomas Penny and Son, who had a yard just above the North Town Bridge. In 1866 Colthurst & Son set up their timber business with river-side wharves; a business that was to continue in Taunton until the early 1980s, whilst, at Bridgwater, both Snows and George Randle were to establish themselves as major timber importers towards the end of the century.

Fulling and shearing was carried out extensively in western parts of the county, it being almost a village industry in the Somerset of the mid-1800s. Centres such as Chard and Taunton had already developed important woollen industries by this time and the export of cloths and woollen garments provided the Canal Company with an income for the returning barges to Bridgwater.

By 1852 there were three firms in Taunton who, with their own barges, operated a daily carrier service to Bridgwater and back: John Westcombe, who operated from St James's Street, Henry Trood and Sons, from North Town Bridge, and Charles Goodland, from North Town.[25]

In the unfortunate absence of Canal Company records, it is still possible to glean a little of the extent of barge traffic during this time. A toll invoice, from the mortgagees of the Canal Company to Charles Goodland & Co., dated January 1851, gives considerable details of the movement of his barges during that month.

It shows that ten journeys were made by three of his barges (Nos 7, 18 and 19), bringing over 20 tons apiece of coal to his wharf at Taunton, whilst additional deliveries of other cargo were made to his wharf at Bathpool. Barge No.19, after delivering coal to Taunton, returned unladen to Bridgwater and was back at Taunton with another load of coal two days later! Alongside his coal wharf, Charles Goodland owned a lock-up, confusingly called the barge lock,[26] where goods destined for Bridgwater could be stored securely, as part of his business as a carrier. His wharf at Bathpool was useful for the local distribution of coal and other freight to the eastern area of the region.

As on most canals, it was the conveyance of coal that provided the canal companies with most of their income and the Bridgwater & Taunton Canal Co. was no exception. The invoice

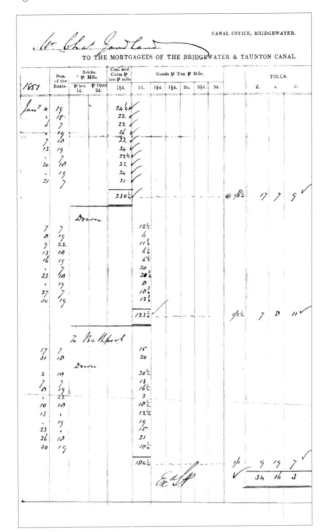

Toll invoice from the mortgagees of the Bridgwater and Taunton Canal Co.

shows that 230 tons were delivered to Charles Goodland during that month. With perhaps nearly a dozen other coal merchants in the Taunton area also receiving deliveries, it is possible to calculate that approximately 2,000 to 2,500 tons would be carried on the canal in a month, accepting that some of the merchants would be small concerns and Goodland's might act as carriers for those traders who did not own barges themselves. Each barge carrying around 18 to 20 tons apiece could mean 125 trips to Taunton being undertaken in a month. With no Sunday working and assuming an average of twenty-six working days a month this would mean about five trips per day, excluding the return trip!

Like the other general carriers, Charles Goodland made use of his empty returning barges to carry freight back to Bridgwater, and as the invoice shows, over 120 tons of general cargo were carried in this way, being largely agricultural produce, such as flour from the Taunton Town Mills, barley, rye, potatoes, apples and hay.

The boatmen would be under strict instructions that the cargoes they carried were to be delivered intact, for theft and pilfering presented a perpetual problem for both the traders

---

TONE BRIDGE COAL YARD.

TO BE LET,

With Immediate Possession,

THE Old-established COAL YARD, DWELLING HOUSE, LOFT, and PREMISES, on *Tone Bridge*, occupied by JOHN HANCOCK, wherein a considerable Business has been carried on for many years past. The Stock to be taken at a fair valuation.

☞ Apply on the Premises, or by Letter post-paid.

N. B.—A New Crane has been recently erected on the Premises.   May 8th, 1838.

Taunton Courier, 9 May 1838.

and the Canal Company. Coal was carried loose, as was sand, stone and gravel. Timber and other freight that might be damaged by water would often be sheeted down, as had been the custom on the rivers. Salt would be already bagged but kept dry and under cover.

Company bye-laws prevented the conveyance of passengers unless specifically sanctioned, although cattle and other livestock could be carried. The lock-keepers, as company employees, whose cottages were usually remote from any other convenient access, could reasonably expect a delivery of coal left for them as the barges went through, but care had to be taken that none fell into the lock chambers in so doing, a bye-law strictly enforced by the company.

The barges needed to be unloaded as quickly as possible and all available hands at the wharf would be summoned to assist the boatmen in their work. If the cargo was coal, this was both a dirty and tiring task; it entailed either lifting the heavy wicker baskets or shovel and barrowing out across narrow gangplanks, either method ensuring that those involved were covered in a fair measure of coal dust and grime that further added to the discomfort of their job. The coal would be taken to bays for loading into waggons, again in wicker baskets. For customers it would be bagged into ½ to 1 cwt bags in the merchant's yard for the hawking-cart trade.[27]

The work could be dangerous work as well:

… in November 1835, a William Woodland, while unloading corn from a barge in Mr Joyce's yard, slipped from the plank upon which he was standing and fell with a bag of barley upon him. On removing him to the Taunton and Somerset Hospital, his thigh was discovered to be broken.[28]

Some wharves possessed a crane to help in unloading bulky cargoes directly into waiting waggons, such as timber and bricks.

The Bridgwater & Taunton Canal Co. also needed to deliver coal to their engine house at Charlton. Particularly during the summer months, it was in frequent action to pump water from the river into the canal and probably consumed over 20 tons of coal a week, or the equivalent to one barge load. The engineer in charge lived in a cottage to one side of the engine house, whilst to the eastern side a low range of outbuildings were used for the storage of the coal and as a shelter and stables for the horses.

There was no limit to the range of cargoes carried, but it is unlikely that the Bridgwater and Taunton Canal ever witnessed a cargo such as was carried on the neighbouring Kennet and Avon Canal in 1829:

> A large barge passed … loaded with curious exotica; among which orange and lemon trees, some with their fruit ripe and others in bloom, besides a choice collection of valuable and scarce shrubs. They appeared as a moving forest of the most fragrant productions of the East, and were attended by a Native. They were going to the seat Marquis of Aylesbury, at Burbage.[29]

OTHER CANALS TO TAUNTON

No account of the Bridgwater and Taunton Canal, and the trade it brought to Taunton in those years immediately after its opening, should fail to make brief mention of the cutting of two other canals, both of which, in their own way, were intended to encourage even further waterborne traffic to Taunton.

THE GRAND WESTERN CANAL

The lucrative coal trade carried on the Bridgwater and Taunton Canal was sufficient inducement to the Directors and Shareholders of the Grand Western Canal Co. for them to reconsider in the late 1820s the possibility of constructing a link to Taunton themselves. Up to now they operated only a detached length between Tiverton and Holcombe Rogus and the concept of a link to Taunton, and achieving additional revenue from carrying coals from Bridgwater to Tiverton, was certainly attractive. For the Company of Proprietors of the Bridgwater and Taunton Canal such a move could only be encouraged for it would mean more traffic using their canal as well!

The Grand Western Canal Co. engaged James Green, an engineer from Devon who had already built up a reputation as a canal engineer with novel ideas for constructing waterways across hilly terrain. He had already proposed the inter-channel canal from Taunton to Beer in 1822 and again in 1828, and had just completed a tub boat canal at Bude which involved water-powered lifts and inclines. He was certainly the man of the moment, and here he was, in 1829, proposing a similar solution for the Grand Western Canal Co.

For the 11-mile canal, between Holcombe Rogus and Taunton, which would require seven lifts and one inclined plane, to lift it up over 270ft, he estimated the cost to be a little over £61,000. Compared with the £224,000 that the company had spent in constructing the level, 11-mile section between Tiverton and Holcombe Rogus some fifteen years earlier, this was cost-cutting with a vengeance, and probably just what the company directors and shareholders wished to hear!

The originally approved line for a link to Taunton in 1796 proposed a cut from French Weir to Silk Mills, making it necessary for barges to navigate about a mile or so of the River Tone before entering the Bridgwater and Taunton Canal at Firepool. But in 1829 the Conservators of the River Tone were already objecting to the Bridgwater & Taunton Canal Co. taking their barges on the river to the town centre and were likely to object to the Grand Western doing the same. Therefore Green, working with John Easton, amended the route of his canal to avoid the Tone altogether, connecting his canal directly to the Bridgwater and Taunton Canal at Firepool. Here a mechanical lift was constructed to raise the Grand Western Canal 29ft (8.84m) above the level of the Bridgwater and Taunton Canal, so that it could cross Kingston Road (now known as Station Road), and on to Silk Mills and Bradford on Tone.

By 1835, this initial length had been completed and was open to traffic. It was a great occasion for the company, who at last saw some potential for earning revenue to offset their costs. The *Taunton Courier* gave a fulsome account of the great day:

> Seven barges, laden with coals, attended by another barge, in which were a band of musicians and several spectators, yesterday passed through the Aqueduct which crosses Kingston road, having been brought into the higher level by the novel and efficacious process of lifting. The barges proceeded to BRADFORD, where a wharf, having been opened, the nuisance of the coal carts along Wellington Road – it may be expected – will, in a great measure, now cease, and entirely so when the navigation is further completed westward which it will be in a few months.[30]

Months, however, turned into years, and it was not until the end of June 1838, that 'The Grand Western Canal, at Tiverton, will be opened … this will complete the line to Taunton and Bridgwater, and must tend to enhance the ultimate interests of all those concerned in this unquestionably beneficial undertaking'.[31]

Unfortunately, it proved to be misplaced optimism. Despite all James Green's ingenuity, the lifts and inclines did not work efficiently 'due to the bad arrangement of the engines' and thorough modifications had to be made, replacing the water counter-balances with steam power:

> The chief obstacle to the Grand Western has been the Welsford plane, which is eighty feet in perpendicular height. The difficulty, which has so long prevailed, in this case … has been obviated by the scientific skill and industry of our townsman, Mr James Easton, senior, of Bradford. Mr Easton's engine was set to work on a boat and load weighing seven tons, and effected its object with ease, to the astonishment and admiration of all present, in five minutes.[32]

Within ten years of the canal's opening, the Bristol and Exeter Railway had constructed their branch line to Tiverton and future trading prospects for the canal seemed limited,

Creech St Michael. The aqueduct carries the Chard Canal over the River Tone. The fine wide arches and the cutwaters show this to be a structure built to the highest standards.

GRAND WESTERN CANAL.

BOATS FOR SALE.
TO BE SOLD BY PUBLIC AUCTION,

At the GLOBE INN, Sampford Peverell, on *Monday*, the 18th day of March next, at eleven o'clock in the forenoon, 40 BOATS, numerically marked from No. 9 to No. 48, both inclusive, now conveying part of the Trade on the Canal, between Taunton and Tiverton.

The Boats may be viewed on the Canal, and further particulars may be known on application to Captain TWISDEN, Halberton, or Mr. JOSIAH EASTON, Taunton.

By order,

FREDERICK LEIGH,

Principal Clerk.

Dated Feb. 14th, 1839.

Was this an indication of the receding fortunes of the Grand Western Canal? *Taunton Courier*, 27 February 1839.

certainly for the conveyance of coal which could now be brought to Tiverton by rail at a fraction of the time it would take by water.

At Wellington, the canal passed through the premises of Fox's Tonedale Works and the wharves there allowed the barges to bring large quantities of coal and coke, the latter a by-product of the Taunton Gas Works, to fuel the nine steam engines and two steam pumps which supplied power required for their woollen processes. Another by-product was ammoniacal liquor, again brought up on the barges from the Taunton Gas Works, which was then used as a detergent in the cleansing of woollens, 'pumped into barges fitted with proper tanks, which, being drawn up alongside our distillery at the Tone canal wharf, were easily emptied into the still'.[33]

THE CHARD CANAL

The idea of linking Chard to a canal system had seemed possible when the various inter-channel ship canals chose routes that passed close to the town. None of these had been pursued, and, even by the time the Bridgwater and Taunton Canal had been completed; Chard still remained isolated from any waterway.

In the early 1830s, all this was to change. A group of speculators and businessmen were prepared financially to back a canal, branching off from the Bridgwater and Taunton Canal, to link Ilminster, Ilton and Chard. A leading light in this promotion was Isaac Cooke, already involved in the Grand Western Canal venture and at the time principal clerk to the Bridgwater & Taunton Canal Co. It was to his Bristol firm of solicitors that the Bridgwater & Taunton Canal Co. was later to become mortgagors. He no doubt foresaw a lucrative trade in hauling coal and other freight along the Bridgwater and Taunton Canal to Chard, because, up to that time, most deliveries to Ilminster and Chard were chiefly by horse-drawn waggons taking their freight from the river barges at Ham Mills.

With the possibility, at long last, of a canal, and no railway proposal to Chard immediately in sight, it is scarcely surprising that the general public clamoured for the canal. What is surprising, however, is that speculators and businessmen were prepared to back financially such a canal when, in the late 1830s, a railway was already being laid between Bristol and Taunton. 'Perhaps one can say the Chard Canal was the victim of decisions taken under pressure; five years later it would probably not have been built at all, as the case for railways would have been immeasurably stronger.'[34]

The canal promoters were obviously convinced that a waterway between the Bridgwater and Taunton Canal and Chard would be economically feasible, and instructed James Green to draw up the necessary details. Twelve years earlier he had proposed a canal on much the same alignment for his English and Bristol Channels' Junction Canal, which was popularly received at the time, and he was already working on the Taunton link of the Grand Western Canal which, like the Chard Canal, involved taking a canal over very hilly countryside. Like the Grand Western, his Chard Canal was to be 'narrow', only 23ft wide, thereby minimising the amount of earthworks to be undertaken; a necessary consideration as his line contained four mechanical inclines to lift the canal over 230ft to Chard, together with two tunnels. It would be capable of taking tub-boats, also called 'shoes', carrying around five to six tons apiece with a train of six capable of being hauled by one horse.

Green completed his survey by 1833, estimating the cost of the canal to be £57,000. It would leave the Bridgwater and Taunton Canal at Creech St Michael, be 13½ miles long, and rise over 230ft throughout its length to Chard. After much enthusiasm at public meetings when the proposals were first shown, it was agreed that a Bill be presented to Parliament and by June 1834 an Act authorising the works was obtained.

There was obviously some public restlessness over the apparent delay in starting work on the ground, and the following report appeared in the *Taunton Courier* of 11 March 1835:

> Some have erroneously concluded that this undertaking is become a dead letter, because the preparation for putting it into actual progress seem to be delayed. The fact is, that by the agencies of Mr Summers, Surveyor for the Company, everything in a preliminary way, has been proceeded with throughout the winter. The valuation of the line of Canal, and the necessary negotiations for the purchase, have, of course, required time; and we have now the pleasure of announcing, from the best authority, that such is the state of treaties and arrangements in these respects, that operations for carrying the plan into effect will be shortly commenced.

Work at last got underway on 24 June, 1835, with a start being made on the two tunnels, one at Lillesdon, nearly 545 yards long, and the other at Crimson Hill, 1,989 yards long, 'with unceasing activity'.[35]

These were to take four years to complete and during this period James Green was experiencing continual troubles over his inclines and lifts on the Grand Western Canal, whose directors were growing increasingly impatient over the resultant delays. As the Chard Canal was to use similar inclines, its directors likewise became concerned to such an extent that halfway through the works Green was replaced as engineer for the project by a young man of twenty-two, Sydney Hall.[36]

CHARD CANAL.

NOTICE is Hereby Given, that this CANAL will be opened for traffic from the BRIDGWATER and TAUNTON CANAL to ILMINSTER, on THURSDAY the 15th of JULY instant.

By order of the Committee of Management,

ISAAC COOKE and SONS, Clerk.[1]

July 8th, 1841.

Isaac Cooke was clerk to both the Bridgwater & Taunton Canal Co. and the Chard Canal Co. (*Taunton Courier*, 14 July 1841)

It is evident that the 'unceasing activity' on cutting of the tunnels that was mentioned by the *Taunton Courier* was no exaggeration, for work was carried on virtually round the clock, possibly in shifts.

> One of the labourers employed on the Tunnel near Curry Mallett [Crimson Hill tunnel] was killed by the sudden fall of the superincumbent earth. This sad event happened at 12 o'clock at night, and it required 4 hours before the body could be dug out. Five other men, who had quit the spot a few minutes before for refreshment, would otherwise have shared the fate of their companion.[37]

The tunnels, hardly wider than 7ft, were almost complete by the end of 1839, by which time the 'navvies' were transferred to cutting the rest of the canal to Ilminster, from where they subsequently informed their superiors that:

> We are happy to be able to report that the workings in the long tunnel met, and an opening is now made entirely through the hill, so that a few weeks clearing of rubbish, etc, will render this formidable part of the undertaking complete. This tunnel is 1,800 yards, or more than a mile in length.[38]

By the summer of 1841, Messrs Summers and Slater, who were coal, culm and lime merchants, had opened up a wharf at Ilminster in anticipation of trade upon the canal, and had built a lime-kiln and wharf at Ilton, from which they would supply the neighbourhood.[39]

The great day came, and on 15 July 1841, after considerable time had been spent on forming the inclines at Thornfalcon and Wrantage, the canal was opened to Ilminster, when barges were ceremoniously led into the canal at Creech St Michael from the Bridgwater and Taunton Canal. The *Taunton Courier* reported that:

> The Directors … in a boat appropriately fitted up for the occasion, proceeded along the line towards Ilminster amidst the cheers of a large concourse of spectators. Several boats laden with coal and culm followed, belonging to Messrs. Summers and Slater, and other merchants who have taken wharves adjoining the canal. The advantages so long sought for by the inhabitants of Ilminster, Chard, Crewkerne, Yeovil, Axminster, Beaminster, Honiton and the numerous villages around in having a direct and uninterrupted communication between Bridgwater and Chard are now afforded by the opening of this canal to Ilminster … [and] the further opening of the line to Chard. We trust this canal will prove as beneficial to the proprietors as it undoubtedly will to the public.[40]

Work proceeded on the rest of the canal. A third tunnel at Herne Hill, Ilminster was constructed wide enough for barges to pass within and a further incline was necessary before the canal was opened to Chard in 1842, the same year that the Bristol and Exeter Railway reached Taunton; an ominous indication, if the canal promoters ever needed one, of the relentless pace of railway development in the region!

Most of the cargo carried was coal and culm, and whilst this amounted to an acceptable 30,000 tons annually in its first few years of operation, it slowly fell away and by 1855 accounted for no more than 17,000 tons. It did not produce the profits, nor realise the expectations, of its shareholders, and its operational life lasted barely more than twenty years.

Working this narrow, tub-boat canal would have been slow and at times difficult. Certainly the boatmen who were used to the wider Bridgwater and Taunton Canal could have found the experience of taking trains of six tub-boats up a mechanical incline, one by one, slow and tedious work, whilst the tomb-like effect they would have experienced when man-hauling their tubs through the dark mile-long tunnels, little larger than modern-day drainage culverts and lit with perhaps a single oil lamp, was alarming to say the least and challenges the imagination!

Some idea of the difficulties facing the boatmen in taking their barges through the tunnels on the Chard Canal, is contained in a letter written in 1934, from a Mr W.E. Curtis,[41] referring to the tunnel at Crimson Hill 'which is about a mile from Hatch Beauchamp, and emerged at the village of Beer Crocombe', he writes that:

> My Uncle, who was a coal merchant, had his wharf at Beer Crocombe, and got his coal down from Bridgwater by barges on this canal. At the entrance to the tunnel the horses were dispensed with and the bargeman propelled the barges for the half-mile or so, by means of hooked poles which engaged with iron rings fixed in the roof or sides of the tunnel.

Two years after the opening of the canal, six of the original twelve traders who were prepared to use the canal, abandoned it and sought other means.[42] By 1846, the Chard Canal Co. proposed to replace the canal with a railway, taking a branch from the recently constructed Bristol and Exeter line at Creech St Michael. It is, perhaps, no coincidence that the Bridgwater & Taunton Canal Co., as has already been mentioned, also decided that year to do a similar thing to their canal. Although both obtained their authorising Acts nothing became of either proposal.

The Bristol and Exeter Railway obtained powers themselves to construct a railway of their own to Chard, which effectively spelt the end of the canal. It was opened between Taunton and Chard in 1866 and the following year the railway, having purchased the Grand Western Canal in 1865 and closed it down, did the same to the Chard Canal in 1867, disposing of its machinery and leaving the waterway abandoned.

The subsequent dismantling of both the Grand Western and Chard Canals has removed much of the evidence of the visionary work of James Green. In many ways he was an engineer before his time, and many of his views on mechanising transport were more applicable to the following steam age. There is little doubt that the failures he experienced in relying upon water-power to operate his lifts and inclines were due mainly to his reliance 'with too much confidence on theoretical principles never subjected … to a full and fair trial, so that many practical difficulties were only gradually developed and detected.'[43] Despite his failures, however, he deserves a better memorial to his work than the derelict tunnels, earthworks and fragments of finely built stone walls that now remain. His ideas, whilst not followed with much conviction in this country, were developed with greater commercial success abroad.

THE RAILWAY TAKES OVER

Whilst the Bridgwater and Taunton Canal was in the hands of the receivers, there was little opportunity to undertake anything other than the most necessary maintenance and, as a consequence, the condition of both the canal and to a lesser degree, the dock, deteriorated. The canal continued operating in this manner for a number of years, and as traffic increasingly turned to the railways, the receivers found it harder to sustain their undertaking financially.

The next steps were taken, not surprisingly, by the Bristol and Exeter Railway. Prompted by the Corporation of Bridgwater, who themselves were concerned at the silting problems being experienced at the dock, the railway were prepared to consider the possibility of purchasing the Canal Company's interests. They would even construct a short railway line from the dock to their station at Bridgwater on the far side of the River Parrett. In June 1866, possibly attracted to the idea of owning the dock which daily received large shipments of coal, even if this meant the doubtful privilege of owning a canal, terms were agreed. The Act, authorising the sale for £64,000, was passed that same year.[44]

The Conservators of the River Tone agreed to the proposal, their treasurer reporting their:

> ... satisfaction at finding that the canal has been transferred into the hands of a company who have the means as well as the will of maintaining and keeping the navigation in thorough and complete repair and efficiency in all respects, so it may always afford a good and sufficient water communication between the towns of Bridgwater and Taunton.[45]

The railway undertook to operate and maintain the Bridgwater and Taunton Canal and its towpath, as well as the towpath alongside the River Tone to the Taunton Gas Works, an important customer and heavy user of barge hauled coal. There was, however, no provision for them to maintain the River Tone below Firepool, a matter which was to cause other problems later on.

Contrary to the popular belief that railways bought up and hastened the demise of the canals in the country, the Bristol and Exeter Railway were good custodians, anxious to keep the canal operating and in good condition, for they saw it as complementing their own transport system. The Conservators of the River Tone retained their right to inspect the canal once a year as before with the company rectifying any problems.

LIFE ON THE WATERWAYS: THE BOATMEN AND THEIR WORK ON THE RIVER

There are few records of the lifestyle of the boatmen who for more than 200 years, in fair weather and foul, in droughts and through floods, hauled their cargoes of fuel and merchandise regularly from Bridgwater to Taunton and back on the inland waterways. What research has been done shows what hard and monotonous work these skilled boatmen undertook.

> During the pre-railway age, little public notice was taken of the boatmen who had made industrial expansion possible. They were rough, sometimes dishonest, itinerant, but by no means poor. They may have troubled local land-owners and village constables, but they seldom oppressed the social conscience.[1]

The Goodland family have been well known in Taunton for many generations and have been closely involved with both the rivers and the canal for the last three centuries as boatmen and later as, traders and businessmen in the town. From records collected in 1938 by Roger Goodland, who was able to draw upon earlier material written by Charles Goodland, it is possible to piece together some aspects of the work of the boatmen during the preceding centuries.

He states that, like others, 'these boatmen also owned land alongside the river itself, from which they extracted a living to supplement their work on the river'. Edward Goodland, who died in 1769, and his brother, William, both worked for their father, who was a boatman.

> In the early days of the Bishop of Winchester and the Bishop of Bath and Wells, who then owned all the land, they [the boatmen] held their holdings on the duty of keeping the river banks in repair so as to prevent flooding. At the Reformation all these people, being so much out of the way, stuck to their holdings and there they remained to this day, clustered on the banks of the river for miles. This particular state of affairs produced a peculiar population of semi-aquatic habits, getting their living both on land and water. William, when a lad, accompanied his father on his trips up and down the Parrett and was soon able to hold his own against the might of the bore or tidal wave which is a feature of that muddy stream. It required great strength and skill to contend with the rapid tides of the Parrett and Tone. Many of them owned barges for navigating the tidal waters, as well as smaller boats for fishing and fowling on the Moors.
>
> In those days, the boatman had the monopoly, in that district, of the transportation trade, as the roads were very bad, owing to the land being undrained. All goods had to be either brought up the river from Bridgwater or down from Langport, and it will easily be seen how very useful the barges were.[2]

Many of the boatmen were in the employ of the larger merchants and carriers in Bridgwater and Taunton, whilst others owned, perhaps, one or two barges themselves and set up their own businesses as carters carrying general freight. By the early 1800s the largest mercantile traders in the South West of England, with extensive business interests in the region, was the firm of Messrs Stuckey and Bagehot; they employed a number of boatmen and owned a fleet of barges which worked upon the Parrett and Tone, carrying fuel, general freight and agricultural produce.

The life of the boatmen was hard and strenuous with long, lonely hours and labours governed by the seasons, the weather and most importantly, the tides. Their work attracted little attention from the commentators of the time since their efforts, however necessary and however many depended on them, were scarcely newsworthy compared with the social life and activities in the towns. The communities in which they lived were scattered, the lands prone to regular wintertime flooding and what little communication there was between them was achieved, if not by water, by foot or horseback along the droves and banks of the rivers. It was not until a network of rhynes were dug across the Moors, the river banks strengthened and mechanical pumping introduced, that the droves gave way to firmer roads and the area began to be opened up.

After a lifetime of experience of the rivers, the boatmen became adept and skilful at harnessing the rising and ebbing tides to their own advantage. With the growing tonnage of shipping attracted to Bridgwater from the 1820s onwards, their knowledge of handling these tidal conditions became invaluable, for the boatmen would now be required to transport considerable tonnages of cargoes up-river, as quickly and as efficiently as possible. Shipping agents such as Messrs Stuckey and Bagehot who operated from Bridgwater and Langport, Frederick Axford at Bridgwater and Henry Trood at Taunton, as well as many smaller suppliers and traders, could look forward to busy and, hopefully, lucrative years ahead!

An illustration accompanying H. Trood & Sons' notice in the *Taunton Courier*, 20 February 1828, advertising their daily courier service.

THE PORT OF BRIDGWATER

The arrival and departure of the sea-going vessels totally depended, as it did for the barges, upon the state of the tides. Access to the quayside moorings at both East and West Quay could only be safely achieved for the larger vessels at high water and it would be the responsibility of the ship's master to ensure that his vessel was moored on the tide. It was a tricky calculation, for the last mile or two into Bridgwater would be undertaken with sails furled; the ships being brought in towed on the rising tide, by harnessed horses and with assistance from hobblers, the local watermen.

Amongst the many types of vessels that would sail into the port of Bridgwater would be ketch-rigged trows (which plied the coastal ports and those of South Wales), schooners, brigantines and the larger brigs. They would occupy every available mooring, discharging their cargoes either into the barges alongside or into wagons on the quay, while other vessels would be loading up and making ready for sea. Every week the local newspaper would give the names of the vessels arriving and departing during that week, together with a description of their cargoes.

Besides the imports of coal and culm there was also a considerable trade in slate from Wales, timber from both North America and the Baltic and wines, sherries and madeira from the Mediterranean and Biscay ports. London was usually a fortnight or three weeks' sailing away and there were agents in both Bridgwater and London who could arrange the conveyance of passengers, general goods and personal effects between the two towns. In 1836, a new vessel, the *Taunton Packet*, made the journey from Bridgwater to Toppings Wharf London in an average of six to ten days.[3]

Bricks, tiles and other clay products were the main exports from Bridgwater, there being a number of brickyards in the town with their wharves alongside the river. From further afield, barges brought in much of the agricultural produce from the region, including flour, wheat, barley malt, apples, wool and flaxseed, with cloth and woollen garments, leather goods, including boots and shoes, gauntlets and gloves, from towns such as Shepton Mallet, Yeovil and Chard.

Advantage had to be taken of the limited hours of high water for loading and unloading. If high tide occurred during the hours of darkness, nighttime working by the porters and quayside labourers would be necessary.

When the vessels were berthed, precautions had to be taken to ensure they remained upright during the 'reflux of the tides'; stout ropes would be attached to their chain plates and made off to suitable anchorages and mooring bollards, so that they could settle upright on the soft mud when the tide ebbed. Warps would be attached to further secure them while cargoes were trans-shipped, allowing this work to continue during the periods of low water. Then the ship's master would use all available weights, such as ballast and anchor chains, to help keep his vessel upright against the quay wall.

The coal and culm brought over from South Wales would be carried loose in the open holds of the trows, between 50 and 90 tons at a time, although on the larger vessels there would be side decks and the holds would be covered. Casual dockside labour would be recruited to shovel the cargo into sacks for hoisting ashore using the vessel's own gear or chuted into the waiting barges lying alongside. The men would be used to carrying loads of up to 1½ cwt on their backs using wicker baskets. The unavoidable double-handling of the coal, each basketful accompanied by clouds of coal dust, would have made this unpleasant and dirty work and, for the boatman, there was still the unloading at the other end!

The loading of bricks and tiles would often be carried out using cranes at the brickyard wharves themselves. Heavy or bulky goods, such as iron products and baulks of timber, would be moved by cranes on the quayside or the vessel's own gear. Even with cranes to help them, accidents still happened. In June 1829, a 'newly-erected cast-iron crane on the quayside was being used to lift oak timbers of about 5 tons weight into the hatchway of a vessel, but, being overloaded, it sheared, and fell with its load into the vessels hold crushing the legs of its Master'.[4]

On the quayside, where the offices of the Port Officer shipping agents were situated, their representatives would be checking the goods loaded into the barges or taken ashore, against the manifests and bills of lading. Traders, buyers and merchants would also be waiting to conclude the purchase of goods and contracts of carriage, whilst arranging the dispatch of the newly arrived freight.

Like any dock of the day, it was the scene of great activity carried out within the cramped confines of the quay. Waggons, already harnessed to their horses and waiting to be loaded up, would jostle for space amongst stores, crates and stacked goods and the usual plethora of side fixtures; cranes, hoists, capstans bollards, and mooring lines. The hobblers, whose main task was to work the vessels to their moorings, would be available to assist in the loading and unloading of the vessels for the few extra pence they could earn.

Working conditions were not without their dangers, particularly during night-time working. The limited number of oil lamps on the quayside provided poor light whilst there were few mechanical aids to help with the tasks and safety considerations were minimal. Whilst loading a barge, it is recorded that on a dark evening in November 1822, William Hoare, a bargemen in the employ of Messrs Stuckey and Bagehot, fell out of his boat at Bridgwater and was drowned, 'leaving a wife and several children'.[5]

There were doubtless many such incidents and most would have gone unrecorded unless it became a fatality or required treatment at the local Infirmary. Robert Thorne 'was engaged in making fast a rope for the purposes of checking a trow, which was running rapidly down the river, when, by some means, the rope got twisted round the poor fellow's leg. It was severely lacerated, and he was taken to the Infirmary'.[6] Thirty years later in another incident, a hobbler, James Creedy of Bridgwater, was discharging a vessel at the quayside, when the rope of the windlass 'to which was attached a heavy weight, became entangled round his right leg and he was thrown down with the sinews of his leg twisted.'[7]

Time ashore between sailings was important for the ships' crews and there were enough ale-houses and cider rooms in the town to meet the demand! For some the journey back to their boat may not have been as clear as when they went:

> A sailor from the ketch, *William the Fourth*, fell into the river; the tide was running rapidly at the time, and he would have been swept away had not John Griffiths, a boatman, caught him by his hair and dragged him aboard his barge. This is the thirteenth life Griffiths has saved from drowning![8]

This page: Although these photographs were taken in the early 1920s, the scene they depict at Bridgwater Dock would have changed little from that of the mid-nineteenth century. (Courtesy of The Colin Wilkins collection)

Above: The ketch *Fanny Jane*, built by John Gough, Crowpill, in 1858, preparing to unload coal. These vessels differed from the trows in that they had closed decks and hatches.

Right: A closer view of the side decks and aft hatch.

Below: The *Severn* – a Severn trow, built in Bridgwater in 1867 at the Grain Wharf.

The quayside at Bridgwater, below the Tone Bridge. An open-decked trow lies at the East Quay, while the *Emma*, built in 1865, is moored with her sails drying. Beyond the bridge the barges wait to load up. (Courtesy of the Colin Wilkins Collection)

Bridgwater Dock around 1890. A coal barge manoeuvring alongside a collier to take on board further cargo. In this busy dockyard view the dredger can be seen and, amongst the far sailing vessels, a barge unloading hay and chaff for delivery to the pit ponies in the South Wales collieries. (Courtesy of the Douglas Allen Photography Collection)

It was a pity that John Griffiths was not around later that same day when 'a Thomas Clarke, aged 19, slipped as he walked across the gangplank to his trow in Bridgwater Basin and was drowned'.[9]

In 1857, Bridgwater experienced two bores in the space of four months, each causing considerable damage. 'A freak bore, aided by strong winds produced a "clash of waters" and caused considerable damage to a number of vessels on the river, and barges were broken away from their moorings,[10] whilst in July, 'another freak bore severely damaged the *Venus* and *Guardside*, both being driven on to the bank. A barge loaded with scouring bricks, the property of Messrs Browne and Co. was destroyed'.[11]

Although the distance between South Wales and Bridgwater was not great, any sea passage can be difficult in bad weather conditions and some colliers foundered on the journey. During a 'dreadful storm, on the night of 20 June 1839, the 60 ton Somerset Brig, with coals from Newport to Bridgwater, struck on a sand bank between the Steep Holms and Bridgwater and sank with all her passengers and crew of eight'.[12] Not such a tragic outcome befell the brigantine *Polly*, belonging to Messrs Sully & Co. 'She was on a voyage from Swansea to Bridgwater, laden with culm, when she sprang a leak and foundered off Swansea, the crew escaping in boats.'[13] Storms at sea could badly affect the expected arrival of vessels, with the consequent adjustment of sailing times for craft already berthed in the port, and waiting to leave.

After the neap tides there were periods of low water when it would be difficult to get the vessels either into port or out to sea. In good conditions though, a collier could sail from Bridgwater to Newport, and back again, in 24 hours, but it was more likely to be two or three days, again depending upon the state of the tide. Boats could be detained for several days, four or five days in a fortnight, which could seriously affect the deliveries of merchandise further up-river.[14]

An experienced master would certainly be able to handle the capricious currents and eddies of the Parrett but the Parrett bore was altogether something different.

By 1841 Bridgwater had its floating harbour[15] which provided the town with facilities that were vastly superior to those on the river. The vessels, once in the dock and in permanently high water, could now be loaded and unloaded irrespective of the state of the tide, a great saving in time both for the ships' masters and the town's merchants. The design of the tidal basin provided for a barge lock allowing the boatmen to enter and leave the dock with their barges without interrupting the shipping traffic. From now on barge traffic to Taunton could use the newly extended canal from Huntworth, while others would continue to take their barges up the River Parrett to supply the gas works and, later, the pumping stations with fuel as well as taking goods to Langport and Ham Mills.

Navigating the Parrett and Tone

By leaving Bridgwater on the rising tide, the boatmen were able to use the current of the river to take them, quite frequently, as far as Burrowbridge, before a horse and tow-line would be required. The distance between Bridgwater and Burrowbridge is around 6 miles and they could expect to cover this distance in about 45 minutes on a tide running at about 10 miles an hour. However, it was the long periods of slack water and the fast currents of the ebbing tide that made the Parrett such a difficult river to navigate. There

The River Parrett at Bridgwater, looking down-river at Binford Place, where the barges are moored alongside the quay.

were two large shoals just up-river of Bridgwater called 'the coals' and 'the stones', which represented a considerable navigational difficulty, and caused constant complaint.

In 1836 Edward Winstall and his employer, William Goodland, both boatmen, said that these obstructions often meant that they were unable to proceed down on the ebb-tide from the canal basin at Huntworth to the quayside at Bridgwater, a length of just under a mile, unless there was sufficient water in the river to carry them over the shoals. 'A loaded barge could get down the river between Huntworth and the Port of Bridgwater only for two hours after high tide, and an unloaded barge six hours.'[16]

Thomas Maddicks, the engineer to the Bridgwater & Taunton Canal Co., and designer of the floating harbour at Bridgwater, stated that:

> … the barges going down to Bridgwater from the canal basin usually did so on the ebbing tide, but needed to judge this so that there was sufficient depth of water to get them over the shoals … it was important for a barge to be at the Port of Bridgwater in time for them to put cargoes aboard … it would be injurious for those cargoes to have to wait until the next tide, for it could well be ten days before a vessel returned.[17]

There was also a shoal 'of rocks and stones' a short distance down-river of the old bridge at Burrowbridge – a shoal which William Armstrong had commented upon in his report to the Conservators of the River Tone in 1824. Clearly nothing had been done about it, but nevertheless it was a particularly difficult obstruction for the boatmen to avoid, being so close to the narrow arches of the bridge.

Each barge could carry around twenty-five tons of cargo apiece, and would carry a crew of two, one at the tiller and one at the prow. With the tide propelling the barge and both travelling at the same speed, the tiller became virtually useless for steering until it came under tow. In these cases, the forward boatman would use a 'sculling oar', some 25ft long fixed to the front of the barge and projecting forward. By means of grips either side of the handle, he was able to steer the barge by twisting the blade from side to side as it went up the river. Once the effect of the tide had been spent, and on spring tides this might not happen until New Bridge half-lock had been reached, the forward boatman would no longer be required to steer from the front and would harness a horse and towline to haul the barge further up-river.

These barge horses quickly became accustomed to their repetitive routine and knew instinctively when to stop at the locks or when to slacken or pull harder. The bridges on the rivers, unlike those on a canal, did not have towpaths under them, and so a horse had to pull harder, and even 'break into a gallop' when approaching a bridge in order to give the barge sufficient momentum to pass under after the tow-line had been slipped, and then wait on the far side to be reattached!

Burrowbridge, as well as being the junction of the Tone and the Parrett, was almost exactly halfway between Bridgwater and Ham Mills. It became an important point on the navigation for boatmen to meet, waiting either for horses or suitable tides to take them up to Langport or Ham, or down to Bridgwater. There was also a wharf, certainly up to the mid-nineteenth century, which would have been used by boatmen to deliver coal and other freight for distribution locally.[18]

When the depth of water was particularly low in the river, the half-lock at Curry Moor would be opened, and a large amount of water released called a 'flash', which increased the depth and allowed the boatmen to proceed further, at least until the next half-lock! Edward Winstall stated that he often had to wait at Burrowbridge before New Bridge half-lock was opened in order to get sufficient water 'sometimes walking there to do it'.[19]

Such delays led to frustration as many boatmen were paid on delivery and were anxious to get their cargoes unloaded. There is no doubt that this also gave rise to arguments and the rising of tempers. In May 1826, Robert Woolland, of 'Borough Bridge', described as a boatman on the River Tone, wilfully damaged a boat belonging to Henry Trood & Son. He subsequently made a public apology 'signed with the mark of Robert Woolland' and agreed to pay for the damage.[20]

On occasions it would be necessary for a boatman, if he considered the water too shallow to continue, to 'hove-to' and wait for a more favourable tide. A glimpse of the river banks of the Parrett today is enough to emphasise the wisdom of this, for otherwise he faced the risk of 'taking the ground' on the ebbing tide. Another problem he had to contend with was navigating his barge during the hours of darkness for although such working was expressly forbidden on the canals, the times of the tides on the river made it unavoidable. Even with the poor light given out by the oil lamps, the boatman would still have to keep a watch out for shoals and mudbanks if he was to avoid the risk of grounding and possibly damaging his barge or losing his cargo when the tide turned.

With a number of barges all taking the opportunity of running up on the same tide, the boatmen had to be skilful to avoid colliding with each other. At places like Burrowbridge where they tended to congregate before taking the River Tone to Taunton, much care was needed. 'James Sweet, a bargeman in the employ of Messrs Stuckey and Bagehot, whilst steering his boat laden with baulks of timber came in contact with another, which, violently forcing the timber, rolled upon his leg, and so severely injured it that amputation was deemed necessary, which was performed by Mr Merchant, of North Curry.'[21]

Very shortly after this unfortunate incident 'a little boy, about thirteen years of age, belonging to Borough Bridge, fell out of one of the barges on the Tone, and was drowned'.[22]

THE NEW BRIDGE AT BURROWBRIDGE

Before 1826, as William Armstrong had pointed out, the old three-arched bridge not only caused problems for the boatmen since its arches were only a few inches wider than the barges, but it presented a massive constriction to the free flow of the river in time of flood. In 1824, commissioners were appointed and an Act 'for taking down Burrow Bridge over the River Parrett, in the County of Somerset, and erecting another in lieu thereof', was passed later the same year.[23] Their clerk, at the time, was J.S. Warren, a Conservator of the River Tone.

The proposed bridge was to be sited immediately north of the old bridge (see page 31) which would remain until the new structure had been built. The first design was for a slender and graceful cast-iron bridge with a single span of 70ft. It had been drawn up by a Taunton surveyor, Philip Bawler Ilett, with assistance from R. Darby of the Coalbrookdale Co. However, because of the high cost of cast iron at the time, Philip Ilett amended his design and submitted one in stone which was accepted by the Commissioners. It was built and opened in 1826.[24]

Very soon after its opening the Commissioners appointed Thomas Bathe as their Collector of Duties and John Hoare as their Water Bailiff, whose duty it would be to 'inspect the loadings of the barges and boats at Bridgwater'. Every barge that passed under the bridge paid a toll (or tonnage duty as it was called) based upon the type of cargo carried: 1s 6d (7½p) for stone and coal and 1s for culm. It is interesting to note that 'for the convenience of both the toll collector and the boatman, the bailiff could give the boatman a ticket at Bridgwater denoting that the loading had been inspected and the duty paid, whereupon the boatman only had to hand such ticket to the collector at the bridge. Not only would this arrangement allow the boatman to take his barge through without the need to stop, but it avoided him carrying sums of money about with him.'[25]

The opportunities to avoid payment were often too tempting. 'Four boatmen appeared before magistrates at Bridgwater … for evading the payment of the tonnage duties payable for passing under the bridge with coals.'

[James Kitch] passed under the bridge without either paying duty or delivering a ticket denoting payment, and was fined £2. William Meade and Henry Sanly were fined £4 each for passing under the bridge with nine tons and nine hundredweight of coal, whilst paying for only nine tons … and for want of sufficient witnesses, the fourth defendant, William Fry, was acquitted.[26]

TO IRONFOUNDERS.

BURROW BRIDGE.

THE Commissioners for taking down and rebuilding BURROW BRIDGE over the River Parrett, within the parish of Lyng, in the county of Somerset, having made an order that the Bridge to be erected shall be of Cast Iron, and of one arch, with abutments of stone ; I am directed to give Notice, that all persons wishing to contract for the erection thereof, (70 feet in the span,) may see the plan and specifications, at the office of Mr. Armstrong, Engineer, near the Post-Office in Bristol, and at the office of Mr. Ilett, Land Surveyor, Taunton : and all further particulars may be had of the said Mr. Ilett, or me (on application by letter post-paid.)

All persons who wish to make Tenders for the erection of such Bridge (before Michaelmas, 1825,) and keeping the same in complete repair for five years, are to send them (free of postage) to me, before the first day of March next.

I. S. WARREN,
Clerk to the said Commissioners.

Langport, 14th January, 1825

Taunton Courier, 26 January 1825.

BURROW BRIDGE.

TOLLS TO BE LET.

NOTICE IS HEREBY GIVEN, that a GENERAL MEETING of the COMMISSIONERS will be holden at the King Alfred Inn, at Burrow, within the parish of Lyng, in the county of Somerset, on Friday, the Twenty-ninth Day of December instant, at Eleven o'Clock in the Forenoon, at which a general statement will be made of the monies received and paid by the said Commissioners, or by their order

And also, that a PUBLIC MEETING of the said COMMISSIONERS will be holden at the same place, on Friday, the Nineteenth Day of January next, at Eleven o'Clock in the Forenoon, for the purpose of LETTING TO FARM, for One Year, the TOLLS of the GATE to be erected on the said Bridge ; and that the said Commissioners will let such Tolls by Auction, to the best Bidder, on his producing sufficient sureties for payment of the Rent monthly.

The Tolls are payable once a day, and are as follows :—

	D.
For every Horse, Mule, or Ass, drawing	3
For every Horse, Mule, or Ass, not drawing	1
For every Ox, Cow, or Neat Cattle, drawing	1½
For every Ox, Cow, or Neat Cattle, not drawing	0½
For every Calf, Swine, Sheep, or Lamb	0¼

But with exemptions for Horses accompanying, or going to, for the purpose of accompanying, or returning from, after accompanying, any Barge, Boat, or Vessel, on the River Parrett, and for Horses, Mules, Asses, or other Cattle, or for any Carriages which are now exempted from Toll for passing through any Turnpike Gate or Gates erected or set up on any part of the Taunton Turnpike Road ; but the exemption for not passing one hundred yards is not to be allowed.

J. S. WARREN,

Dated 11th Dec. 1826.   Clerk to the said Commissioners.

Taunton Courier, 20 December 1826.

Measuring the cargoes carried in order to assess the appropriate toll was important, for the tolls provided the income to defray costs of waterway maintenance. Few records have survived of the checks that were made on the passing barges, but it is recorded that, in January 1855, the Parrett Navigation Co. hired Benjamin Gillet to carry out the inspection of a load of timber at Langport, where he charged £1 10s 0d for both himself and his assistant to measure the loading of a barge, containing 10½ tons of 'elm timber'. In May 1857, he charged only 10s for measuring 11½ tons of ash timber, no explanation being given as to why the charge was so much less than two years earlier![27]

THE FLOODING OF THE RIVERS PARRETT AND TONE AND THE PUMPING STATIONS

James Dugdale wrote in 1819, that the Parrett:

> … has no barrier and the tide flows up as far as Langport, filling its banks, and … floods over the moors and meadows adjoining, so that nearly thirty thousand acres [12,100 ha] of fine land are frequently overflown for a considerable time together, rendering the herbage unwholesome for the cattle and the air unhealthy to the inhabitants.[28]

Josiah Easton, the Somerset engineer and surveyor, had already been considering the problems presented by these regular inundations and prepared a plan 'for draining all the low lands between Polden Hill and Langport, and supplying them with fresh water for cattle in a dry season',[29] although this appears not to have been carried out. In 1824 and again in 1828, the whole area suffered from severe flooding which caused great distress and loss to 'the many agricultural interests and residents'. After incessant rain for many days, it was reported that 'the whole country for miles around Langport presents one unbroken lake'.[30]

Edward Winstall, who frequently took his barge up the Parrett, said that when the floods came, 'plenty of horses were needed to draw the barges up' and with the tow path often totally submerged below the expanse of water, the horses had to wade through, 'even having to swim at times, this being very dangerous to both horses and boatmen'.[31] In 1860, there was a particularly damaging flood which alerted many to the urgency of undertaking some remedial measures to prevent such floods causing so much damage. So bad was the flooding on that occasion that it was reported that:

> … corn, cut and uncut, stood up to its ears in water for a considerable time; one half, if not two thirds, of the hay crop was destroyed as fodder, and rendered fit for litter only; the arable low-lands so long retained the surface water that they were unfitted to receive the seed wheat at the proper season, and the pasturage of the grass lands was lost for the whole season … such is the unhealthy state of the land that cases have come under observation where fields of five acres have been sown to wheat three times in one season, and the produce did not amount to one sack in the whole field.[32]

In 1861 the Land Drainage Act was passed, which authorised the setting up of Local Drainage Boards with power to collect rates in order to finance works in each Board area. In Somerset, the lands adjacent to the Parrett were divided up into five districts; Chedzoy, Aller Moor, Stanmoor, Curry Moor and North Moor. The overall authority at the time, and until 1877, was the Commissioners of Sewers.

Heavy repair to a breach being undertaken on the banks of the River Parrett around 1890. (Courtesy of Brian Denman, Yeovil)

Burrowbridge, erected in 1826, seen here in 1994.

Above: The Steam Pumping Station at Curry Moor, 1938. (Courtesy of the National Rivers Authority)

Left: 3067, Curry Moor Steam Engine which was demolished in February 1955. Easton, Amos and Appold contifugal pump, installed 1864. (Courtesy of the National Rivers Authority)

Besides strengthening the riverbanks, the respective drainage boards investigated the possibilities of pumping water mechanically from the Moors into the Parrett, in order to return the fields to cultivation as soon as possible after inundation. This was feasible because of the developments that had taken place in perfecting a reliable steam pump. As early as 1822, in Nottinghamshire a 'steam engine had been brought into operation, of 40 horse-power, in a novel purpose of draining land, in which uses it had exceeded all the calculations of the parties combining to give it a trial'.[33] Earlier scoop-wheel pumps were probably reliable enough but were so inefficient that the water pumped was not considered worth the cost of the coal consumed. The first in Somerset was a 27hp beam engine installed in 1830 which powered a scoop-wheel, and served over 1,600 acres at Westonzoyland, but it soon fell out of use.[34]

It was the construction of the centrifugal pump, a device evolved and developed by John Appold in the mid-1840s, that gave the local drainage boards the opportunity of undertaking large-scale pumping schemes. These pumps could raise sizeable volumes of water to a moderate height, and were therefore particularly appropriate for dealing with flood waters. Between 1861 and 1869, eight large pumping stations were erected alongside the Parrett and Tone. Those at Chedzoy and Westonzoyland were the first to be built in 1861, followed by Curry Moor and Stanmoor in 1864, North Moor and Saltmoor in 1867, and Southlake and Aller Moor in 1869.[35] All were individually designed and financed. Although involving large capital outlay, they illustrated the total confidence and reliance the new drainage boards had in this new form of steam-driven pump. The designers themselves were working at the forefront of the technology for this type of large volume pump and their creations remain today as examples of outstanding mechanical engineering.

The boilers that provided the steam power consumed around four tons of coal a day when in operation! This was brought up-river on barges and laboriously taken ashore in wicker baskets containing nearly a hundredweight of coal apiece (50–60kg), the boatmen carrying these upon their backs or shoulders. It would take most of the day to deliver a week's supply to a pumping station, and there would be another seven still to serve! The labour involved in this work by the boatmen is quite staggering.

Aller Moor Pumping Station at Burrowbridge still survives with its boilers and steam-driven pump, although they have not operated since 1957. Whilst the distinctive tall chimney has long been removed, the engine house now accommodates a collection of other historic pumping machinery. For those with an interest in the subject, the Westonzoyland Engine Trust has restored the Easton and Amos engines and Appold pumps at the Westonzoyland Pumping Station, and 'steam days' for the public are held.

TIME FOR REFRESHMENT

In most accounts of canals and river navigations, the term 'boatman' is commonly used to describe the person in charge of a barge; indeed in the various Acts of Parliament relating to canals, this is the word most often used. Occasionally the word 'bargeman' will be found, particularly in newspaper reporting of the day. The former term clearly relates to the days when the navigation of rivers was seen as an extension of the seaman's skills with his boat and the term continued well into the days of canals. Amongst themselves the boatmen referred to each other as 'bargees'.

The boatmen worked long hours, frequently as many as twelve a day, many of which today would be termed 'unsocial hours'. They were spent outdoors throughout the year with little protection from inclement weather. Their day would start with ensuring that their barges were properly loaded and balanced, the cargo weighed and the necessary toll charges recorded; then, relying both on the tides and their navigating skills, they would embark on the long haul up the river. At the wharves at the end of the journey they would unload their cargoes generally by hand, in wicker baskets or by barrow if it was coal or culm, although some wharves had simple hoists to handle bricks and timber.

It is not surprising, therefore, that at intervals along the riverside, there were places where they could rest awhile and take refreshment. Most inns would also have some outbuilding where the boatman could bed down for the night if it was necessary to wait until a following high tide, before continuing his journey. There were a few beer and cider-houses conveniently situated near the banks of the River Parrett, like the Thatchers Arms, near Moorland, the King Alfred at Burrowbridge and the King William, now a private residence, just upstream of Stanmoor Bridge.

Further up the Parrett near Staithe, there is the well-known Black Smock Inn. Acquiring this name officially only after the Second World War, it was originally called the George Inn, although it had been known as the Black Smock Inn locally since the early 1870s. Emrhys Coate, from Stoke St Gregory, recounting stories of the days of the river barges, adds that when his great-grandfather was the landlord at the Black Smock Inn he would put out his black smock on a pole on the river bank when he wanted the boatman to call for further supplies or messages passed to his suppliers down-river. As they knew they could get good food and drink there, the inn became popular and the name stuck.

Some inns had facilities near at hand where horses used for hauling the barges further up-river could be stabled. Along the River Tone, there were further inns such as the Kings Head and the Cottage Inn, both at Athelney; the New Bridge Inn near North Curry and the White Horse Inn at Ham, many of which are now private houses. Again facilities for the boatman would be available there whilst some private houses and farms close to the river also provided drinking parlours and cider rooms.

Mrs Nora Meade, whose father was the landlord of the former Kings Head, recalls his stories of the boatmen coming into his inn at Athelney in the early years of this century. Many of the riverside properties had their front entrances facing the river, for it was from that side that the barges delivered their fuel and daily provisions and the customers came. The boatmen would moor their barges in the river and use gangplanks to reach the river bank and the steps to the cider room. At the Kings Head, and at many others, this room had a low stone platform on one side, known as a 'jibbin', on which the cider barrels were laid. Boatmen with time to take a few hours' rest would be able to bed down on sacks in a corner of an adjacent room. If the barge had been left with its cargo aboard a colleague would keep watch to see that no petty pilfering took place.

Thieving from barges was a continuing problem for the carriers and haulage companies. Where the cargoes were coal, sand or of a bulky nature generally, the risk was not too great but on some navigations quite valuable freight was carried, including wines and spirits, food and clothing and it was necessary to take precautions by the provision of lock-up compartments in the barges themselves. Referring specifically to canals but nevertheless, appropriate for rivers as well, Harry Hanson, in his book, *The Canal Boatmen, 1760–1914*, states, 'The increasing number of valuable goods carried, and the need for casual labour, brought unsatisfactory characters to loiter on the canal banks, in public houses and in the beer shops.'[36]

Cargoes were mostly carried uncovered although canvas covers could be used if wet weather was likely to damage the goods. Foodstuffs and agricultural produce, such as wheat and barley for the mills, were in sacks, but would be covered, as would be skins, hides, timber and salt, which were already bagged for their journey down the River Severn to Bridgwater. All of these goods needed to be kept dry.

Sometimes barges carried ball clay from Bridgwater, a fine pipe-clay which was unloaded at various landing places and taken to private houses where it was moulded and fired into the familiar white clay smoking pipes so popular in the rural areas at the time. It was, in a sense, a 'cottage industry', providing a small additional income for those in the vicinity. The fashioned pipes would be laid out to dry in the cross-ventilated roof spaces of a number of houses before being packaged and taken to Bridgwater, again by barge, for distribution further afield.

Around the farms and cottages there were often apple orchards. The production of home-made cider was popular and used within the household, although there was always enough for visitors and guests. 'The cider house provided the social focal point ... where labourers came to collect their daily ration of cider, and where the ordinary visitor was entertained. On Sunday mornings some cider houses were local meeting places like pubs.'[37]

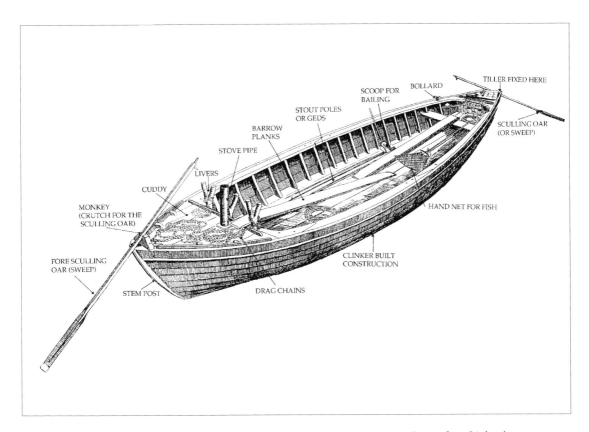

River Parrett barge. (Reproduced by kind permission of Edward Paget-Tomlinson from his book, *Britain's Canal and River Craft*)

As Mrs Meade recounted, the cider room provided a centre where the boatman, many of whom could not read, were able to hear the latest local news read to them by the landlord and from others who happened to be around; the inns and cider parlours were, indeed, the meeting place of the village where stories abounded, some true, others suffering some exaggeration in the retelling!

Some boatmen rented or owned cottages alongside the river, at places like Athelney and Curload, conveniently situated for their work. Some who owned perhaps a small coalyard and a couple of barges, were able to build their own cottages, on the earth banks bordering the Tone itself, using rejected bricks from the brickyards in Bridgwater which they could acquire quite cheaply.

THE BARGES

The design of the river barges evolved over many years and were ideally suited to the purpose of carrying heavy loads in shallow waters. They were distinctive in that they were pointed at both ends. Those that operated on the River Parrett were over 66ft long with a beam of 13ft. Whilst the same size barges would have operated upon the Tone, it was generally the smaller barge of 53ft length that was manoeuvrable enough to reach Taunton. These larger barges would carry up to 25 tons apiece, although smaller barges were also constructed for less bulky goods, carrying no more than 15 tons.

Being of shallow draught and flat-bottomed, they were ideal for operating over the shallow lengths of river between Ham Mills and Taunton and could safely take the ground when being used in the Parrett estuary. They were clinker-built, and had open holds with a small decked area at fore and aft under which was provided a small storage space called a cuddy. It was in these that ropes and hooks, oil lamps and tools would be kept as well as canvas cloths, waterproof covers and provisions for the boatmen. There would also be a stove and space for the boatmen to sit. The barges had a large tiller which was essential when under tow on the river above the tidal limit, although in tidal waters it would be detached and steering achieved by using the 'sweep' or sculling oar.

Manoeuvring and stopping the barge, particularly when it was under the momentum of the tidal currents, required much strength and skill and drag chains would be thrown over to 'ride the bottom', in addition to tow-lines. The three naturally-forked timbers, called 'livers', fixed to the forward bulkhead as shown in the illustration, were used by the boatman to shorten the drag chains as necessary. The fore-timbers would carry a number and the name of the carrier. If the barge was carrying a heavy load of coal or culm, slack boards would be inserted to keep the cargo from spilling into the steering well. Barrow planks were carried as well as stout poles, called 'geds', which would be used to moor the barge off from the bank or if it became grounded.[38]

Besides the two boatmen on the barge, a third was occasionally taken on, usually a youngster acting as a 'barge-boy' whose duties would be to attend to the various time-consuming jobs such as attaching tow-lines after passing bridges, ensuring the towpath was free and gates open and attending to the horse.

A Tone barge around 1910 on the River Tone, near Athelney. . This photograph, lent by Sid Palmer, Stoke St Gregory, shows his grandfather, who was a general agricultural carter, on one of his barges. This was obviously a weekend outing, with a chance for duck-shooting not to be missed.

Henry Palmer, the last lock-keeper at the New Bridge lock on the Tone near Curry Moor, abandoned in the 1930s, used to recount the days when he went with his father on the barges. When he was a lad in the 1880s, he would accompany his father and when work was slack they would, with other boatmen, take a barge down past Bridgwater to the estuary of the River Parrett. Here his father, carefully selecting the right spot in the shallow water, would anchor the barge and wait for the tide to ebb further so that, ultimately, it settled upon the pebbles. Then they would get out, and load up with large pebbles, placing them carefully in the barge in order to get the correct 'trim'.

He remembered this as surprisingly heavy work, and after the loading had been completed, they would all drop back into the barge 'to have a blow and some cider' and wait for the incoming tide. It would be some hours before the tide returned, and when the water began to surround the barge, the stronger members would get out and rock it from side to side to release the suction that had built up. For a lad, he explained, it was all quite frightening, not only seeing the water getting higher and higher around them, but realising that they were in the middle of the wide estuary, entirely at the mercy of the incoming tide! With a clearly audible crack, the barge would break free and they would be propelled upon the tide towards the river and home! The pebbles were put to many uses: for backing walls; when halved, for cobbles; and when broken up, filling pot holes in the road.[39]

Barges would also settle upon the areas of sand in the estuary and take on sea sand which was used in large quantities, both in the manufacture of bricks in Bridgwater and as ship's ballast. The esturial silt, which was an important trade for the barges, was also collected and after baking in brick ovens formed bricks used for cleaning and scouring.

The building of the barges, as well as other small river craft, was generally carried out at the boatyards in Bridgwater. Messrs Stuckey and Bagehot, amongst their other interests in banking and business, had extensive shipping interests in the South West area and they were able to build and repair their own fleet of barges, whilst Sully & Co., the large coal importers in Bridgwater, also had their own barges. The main ship building yard, where the occasional barge was constructed, was Messrs Carver & Son at East Quay, Bridgwater. The many brick and tile manufacturers who had premises in the town, alongside both banks of the Parrett, generally owned their barges which were capable of working on either the river or the canal. Their repair and maintenance was carried out at the boatyards in the town and brought in good income.

By the beginning of the twentieth century the amount of shipping coming up the river had declined and barges were no longer required to carry freight from the docks to the various riverside wharves. A few continued to navigate the Parrett and Tone until the late 1920s. Edmund Porter states that two barges still used the Bridgwater and Taunton Canal until 1930, 'conveying clay for approximately half-a-mile to a brick and tile works in Old Taunton Road, Bridgwater'.[40]

THE HALF-LOCKS

The waters of the Tone were slow moving and for the most part shallow, so when they were required for navigation, measures had to be taken to enable the barges to have enough depth of water to reach Ham and Taunton. As had been necessary on the upper reaches of many other navigable rivers in the country, half-locks were constructed, being a development of the opening weir or 'flash lock'. They consisted of a single pair of gates across the river at intervals of perhaps a couple of miles along its course.

By the mid-1820s there were five between Burrowbridge and Taunton; at New Bridge, Knapp, Ham, Bathpool and Obridge. There were a further four-pound locks (i.e. a lock with a double pair of gates at either end of a barge-length chamber, more familiarly seen on canals) at the mills at Ham, Creech, Bathpool and Firepool Weir at Taunton.

The principle was simple enough; by holding back the flow down the river behind gates, it was possible to provide a 'reservoir' of water which could be released into the stretch below the half-lock, called the pounding, adding depth for a barge to move forward. The process would be repeated at each half-lock. The flash would generally last for an hour or so, the down-river traffic descending first, helped over the shallows below by the flood of water, whilst those barges coming up-river, had to wait until the upper and lower reaches were approximately level before they were hauled through the gap between the lock gates and could progress up-river towards Taunton. It was a slow and time consuming operation, particularly when there were a number of barges needing to come up-river at the same time.

The two pounds between New Bridge and Knapp, and Knapp and Ham Mills were, at times, tidal, which helped the boatmen get up-river, the influx of the tide throwing open the gates in the process. When the tide ebbed, the gates which faced up-river would shut, retaining the water which could be used for the next 'swell', a term the boatmen

The half-locks on the river slowed down the progress of the barges considerably; frequently three or four would be kept waiting until it was possible to 'flash' the lock and let more water through.

used to describe the additional water brought down the river. The gates were very similar in design to those to be seen on canal locks today, except that their construction was probably a little rougher and they were of no great depth. They had a sluice, known as a 'lasher', which was operated by a lever and allowed the water to flow through. When this was level on both sides, the gates could be opened by pushing against the long arms called 'sway-trees'. The usual practice seems to have been to shut the half-lock gates about 2 hours before high tide, in order to retain a sufficient head of fresh water from the river and then to release it half an hour before the tide arrived. In this way the two sources of water would swell sufficiently for the barges to proceed.[41] The release of water through the half-locks also provided an increased 'swell' to carry the boatmen over the notorious 'shoals' in the Parrett on their journey down to Bridgwater. The barges would draw between 10 and 12in when travelling light, and about 36in when fully loaded with 25 tons of cargo.[42]

In summer months the flow of water in the Tone was often insufficient to support regular use by the boatmen, for the mill owners also had a right to the water which they penned back for their mill ponds. The Conservators of the River Tone found it was necessary to issue instructions to boatmen and traders to ensure no water was wasted, and in 1826 it was reported that several boatmen were summoned for a breach of instructions because they had opened a half-lock less than half an hour after the preceding boat had passed through. Apparently the preceding boat was waiting for additional water from 'the next pound above, when boatmen, by opening the hall-lock, had drawn the water and stranded the barge'.[43]

The New Bridge half-lock, also known as Curry Moor half-lock, in the 1930s. (Courtesy of the Somerset Archaeological and Natural History Society)

The Ham half-lock. (Courtesy of the National Rivers Authority)

COAL HARBOUR

Records show that as early as 1559 there was a landing place at Coal Harbour, known then as Colehouse, for coal and probably other heavy goods as well.[44] Later, in the seventeenth century, the extensive grounds around Coal Harbour Farm, conveniently set within the sharp bend of the river and at the limit of its tidal reach, were used for distributing much of the freight carried up the Tone. In 1684 Richard Bobbett took a lease on the 'back-river' and a moor at Ham with the right to land coal there.

Until the Conservators of the River Tone undertook to improve the navigation of the river, particularly from Ham Mills to Taunton in the early eighteenth century, Coal Harbour was the terminus for virtually all the river-borne traffic. Here the barges would draw up on either side of the river. Those on the north side brought their cargoes of coal to be discharged into the waiting horse-drawn waggons and distributed in the neighbourhood, taking a trackway alongside the river to Bull Lane and Creech St Michael, a route still discernible today. Those drawing up to the landing places on the south side would bring other freight, such as sand, bricks, stones and grain and take away agricultural produce, feed and flour produced at the mill. In the summer months when the water level in the Tone was low, it was often possible to ford the river at Coal Harbour at a place close to the mill, and so avoid a circuitous route to reach Ham, Stoke St Gregory and North Curry.

As the river trade grew so did the importance of both Coal Harbour and Ham Mills and many boatmen had contracts permitting them to trade between Bridgwater and the wharves there. The Conservators installed their own Inspector at Ham Wharf, whose duties were not only to oversee the condition of the navigation on their behalf but to collect tolls from the boatmen, delivering to Coal Harbour and continuing onwards to Taunton. By 1839 only three of the many wharf-side businesses remained, victims of the fierce competition in the coal trade brought about by the opening of the Bridgwater and Taunton Canal.[45]

HAM MILLS

There were water mills at Ham from medieval times, but the present building, although much altered, largely dates from the middle of the last century. It is situated on an 'island' formed by the River Tone on its north side and a communication canal, bypassing the weir and mill pond, on its south. The mills occupied the entire width of the island and a mill race, fed from the upper reaches of the river, passed through the centre of the site and drove two large mill wheels, long since removed. (See photograph on page 125.)

The mills received their supplies from a landing stage alongside the bypass cut below the pound lock, and it was undoubtedly a very busy place, with barges jostling for space at the wharf. Amidst this activity were horses with carts and waggons waiting while mill hands and carters helped the boatmen get the barges unloaded and the sacks of grain and flour taken on board. The barge horses were unharnessed for a short but well-earned rest and led to stables, while those that needed to be re-shod would be taken to the local smithy. The presence of the toll-keeper ensured that order prevailed and that all monies due from the boatmen were paid! However, in such conjested space and often working in darkness, accidents were bound to happen.

In March 1826, a boatman:

> … Richard Dibble, aged thirty, got out of the boat to open the gates of the lock at Ham, at ten o'clock at night, and, after he had opened the two upper gates … and, in opening the lower gates, he fell into the River Tone and was drowned, leaving a widow and three children.

The coroner at the inquest stated that, 'as such a number of boats were passing at all hours of the night, a lamp was quite necessary there', directing the Conservators of the River Tone to provide a lamp 'to prevent any future accident'.[46]

In 1832, Ham Mills were described as Linseed Oil Mills:

> The Mills have an abundant supply of water driving two large wheels, and with a commodious warehouse, conveniently situated in the centre of the market for English seed, on the River Tone, navigable to Bridgwater, from where oil, linseed cake, etc, can be sent to London, Bristol, Gloucester and Liverpool.[47]

At that time the owner, Thomas Davidge, lived at the mill. He was still in occupation in 1855, for it is recorded that he chartered a sea-going trow to take his produce down-river, but it sank on the journey![48]

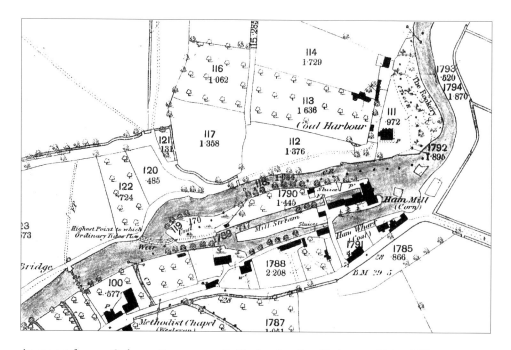

An extract from an Ordnance Survey map of 1889 showing Coat Harbour and Ham Mills.

Ham Mills: the waterwheel before its removal, around 1930. (Courtesy of Mrs M. Adams, Creech St Michael)

As demand for water from the River Tone increased during the last quarter of the nineteenth century, particularly at Taunton, the quantity reaching the mills at Bathpool, Creech and Ham was badly reduced. At Ham, for instance, the head of water that could be achieved in the mill race was rarely more than 4ft which was never to be sufficient for the effective working of the mill. During the 1890s, George Coombe, the owner, found that it was necessary to install a steam-driven turbine to supplement the inadequacies of the waterwheels. He built an engine house alongside the mills to accommodate both the machinery and boilers, the latter requiring regular deliveries of coal. At this time the mill employed seven men.

The mills were last used for milling flour in 1914, shortly after the outbreak of the First World War. At that time, the War Department requisitioned the steam boiler which powered the turbine for Admiralty use. Amid much local interest and probable amazement from the villagers, a team of horses arrived drawing a large six-wheeled bogie, upon which the boiler was ultimately loaded and hauled to Taunton station. From here it was sent to Lowestoft to be fitted into a trawler, which was being converted for use as a minesweeper for operations in the North Sea.[49]

Since then the mill has been a private house; there was little need to produce flour at Ham, and the barge traffic through to Taunton had ceased. The pound lock lost its gates and within the last thirty years, has been converted into a weir. Until recently, the tall brick chimney of the boiler house still stood, a local landmark, but after it was considered unsafe it too was removed.

Top: Impression of how Coal Harbour and Ham Mills might have looked around the middle of the nineteenth century.

Above: Ham Mills around 1890. The barges to Taunton used the cut in the foreground. (Courtesy of Mrs M. Adams, Creech St Michael).

Left: Ham. Some of the original buildings at Ham Mills still survive, such as this one, adjacent to the Manager's House.

At Creech St Michael, the Creech Paper Works was built in 1875, within a few hundred yards of the older Creech Flour Mill. The paper works did not require water power but used large quantities of coal for its boilers in the manufacturing processes. The company owned some river barges which brought coal up to Coal Harbour where it was discharged into their own waggons and brought by horse to their premises.

Murder Most Foul!

The work of cutting the new canals required large numbers of labourers. Most were recruited locally, usually from the ranks of the unemployed agricultural workers who saw permanent work for two or three years as preferable to intermittent seasonal employment on the farm. The contractors also brought with them their key workers, as they moved from town to town and job to job.

The presence of these labourers could, on occasion, disturb the rural calm. They had a somewhat unenviable reputation as tough, hard working and hard drinking men, often involved in disturbances at the ale and cider houses in the villages. The disturbances were mostly confined to drunken brawls and petty thieving, although some incidents were considered serious enough to warrant mention in the local newspapers. In April 1831, for instance, a house in Stoke St Mary was broken into and robbed by two men, described as 'navigators', who had lodged in the house the night before the robbery. They were later traced and apprehended at Wellington on their way to seek work on the cutting of the Grand Western Canal.[50]

Ham Mills, from Coal Harbour, 1897, from a painting by H. Frier. (Courtesy of Somerset County Council)

During 1838 when the Chard Canal was being cut, a robbery on the night of 11 June, was to turn to murder. A farmer, Henry Derham of Knapp, on his way from North Curry, was 'assailed by four men who knocked him down, beat and kicked him, and kneeled on him and rifled his pockets'. He died as a result of his injuries, and the four, James Andrews, John Andrews, James Shumack and John Dare, who were all residents of North Curry, and 'labourers on the navigation now proceeding at Thorne and Creech', were charged, found guilty of wilful murder and sentenced to death.[51]

In the summer of 1829, at the lock on the River Tone at Creech St Michael grave suspicions centred around the story of an eleven-year-old boy, Joseph Honeyball. He had been seen by boatmen and others collecting mussels with another lad, Joseph Percey. When the latter failed to come home late at night, Joseph Honeyball was interrogated as to the whereabouts of Percey, for it appeared from witnesses that the two had had a quarrel. Later Joseph Honeyball admitted he had heard him fall into the lock where he was later found. Despite the fact that 'no mussels were found on the deceased, but the other had a great amount in his possession', no evidence incriminated Honeyball, and a verdict of 'Found Drowned' was returned.[52]

THE WITHY INDUSTRY AND THE RIVER

The growing and harvesting of withies for basketmaking had been carried out in a small way on the riverside Moors for many years but production increased during the middle of the nineteenth century to meet local needs. One family firm still flourishing at Stoke St Gregory, P.H. Coate, was founded as long ago as 1819 and others shortly followed. As demand grew, particularly for agricultural and household goods, and the means of conveying and distributing the finished products by river was possible, the willow industry evolved as one of great importance in this essentially agricultural region.

Round the turn of the century new uses for this lightweight and flexible material were found and within a few years both withy growing and basketmaking were further developed as a vital 'war industry' when it was appreciated that the finished product was a resilient and versatile packaging material, ideal for providing the baskets and panniers used for carrying provisions and equipment. Local growers were encouraged, with financial assistance from the Government, to expand their production. After the war, there were over 2,000 acres under withies, and many family businesses had been established to meet the demand. Together with the basket industry, withy growing in the region employed about 200 men and 150 women.[53]

In Bridgwater, at least eight basket and wicker furniture-making firms were set up, meeting an upsurge in the domestic market for products such as wicker garden furniture and linen and laundry baskets, whilst a number of local growers produced other wicker-work items, including sheep hurdles, pet baskets, hampers, eel-traps, coal and log baskets and skeps for bee keepers, a popular hobby in the area.

The process of preparing withies for basket making required them to be 'stripped', for which they would need to be boiled in large vats for many hours. The coal used in heating these boilers was usually delivered by river barge. The brick chimneys of these

Above: Stripping willow around 1900, near Athelney. (Courtesy of Mrs N. Meade, Athelney)

Right: The River Tone, looking towards Athelney with, in the distance, the Curry Moor Pumping Station. A couple of bundles of withies are placed outside to indicate to the passing boatmen that they have more inside ready for collection to take down to Bridgwater. (Courtesy of D. House, Stoke St Gregory).

boilerhouses can still be seen, and although most are no longer used, they remain as interesting historical features in this lowland landscape and reminders of an industry that once relied heavily upon this regular delivery of coal. The barges on their return journeys took back quantities of ready bundled withies for the furniture makers in Bridgwater and for destinations further afield.

Hay and chaff (the chopped stalks of hay) were also bundled up and dispatched by barge to Bridgwater, destined for South Wales, as feed for the pit ponies.

The barge trade carried on until the end of the 1920s, when the motor vehicle began to offer quicker, countrywide distribution to further markets. Although the willow industry suffered a slight decline in the 1930s and 1940s, due to a fall-off in demand following the introduction of cane and other substitute materials, many of the original firms on the moors are still producing wickerwork and today, with the re-awakened interest in the material and the range of products available, there is little doubt that they can count on a successful future.

LIFE ON THE WATERWAYS: THE BOATMEN AND THEIR WORK ON THE CANAL

It is said that when the great James Brindley was asked about the use of rivers, he replied, 'to feed canals!'[1]

As more and more canals were built across the country, they offered a means of transport which was both reliable and economic and when working in unison with some river navigations, formed a transport network that was to suffice until the coming of the railways. As the *Taunton Courier* was to remark in 1822, the year a start was made on cutting the Bridgwater and Taunton Canal:

> … the number of navigable canals in the United Kingdom was over 100, mostly in England, covering a distance between them of over 2,500 miles! Yet, barely seventy years earlier, not a yard existed – the idea of canals was ridiculed as superfluous and absurd in a country like England, enjoying favourable lines of coast, and provided with numerous navigable rivers.[2]

By the time the railways entered the scene, the cost of providing the network of canals represented a considerable financial investment for by 1830, 'over £20 million had already been invested in inland waterways.'[3] The Bridgwater & Taunton Canal Co. had invested heavily but, like so many other canals, they were never to achieve the degree of financial success of which they no doubt dreamed.

When the canal was opened in 1827 it provided a far more efficient and faster means of water transport between Bridgwater and Taunton than the Conservators had been able to achieve on the River Tone. For the boatmen it was a challenge requiring different navigation skills. No longer would their work be largely controlled by the state of the tide and their working hours restricted to daylight. There would be no more delays due to shallow water, half-locks or obstructive millers and as for the periodic flooding of the rivers, whatever other difficulties the canal boatmen might face, this would not be one of them.

It is almost certain that the boatmen who worked their craft upon the rivers were drawn from the seafaring families of earlier years. For the canals, it is likely that the boatmen were recruited from itinerant workers, accustomed to working with horses, attracted to the possibilities of a traveller's life in the open air, whilst receiving a regular wage. Others worked for local hauliers, starting their working life as small boys guiding the horses. Some became more successful, able to acquire their own barge and set up business on their own account as carters and hauliers. Michael Ware suggests that even the local coach drivers and waggoners, driven out of their work on the roads by the arrival of the canals, turned to them for continued employment.[4]

The boatmen on the Bridgwater and Taunton Canal were most likely to have come either from among carters and waggoners employed by the local coal merchants and brick and tile makers in the area, or from agricultural labourers dissatisfied with the low wages of seasonal work on the farms. Some of the merchants and carriers who had earlier traded upon the river now turned their attentions to the canal, familiar names, such as William Axford, Henry Trood, Charles Goodland and John Westcombe.

The canal barges they used were similar to those that operated upon the river, except that they were slightly shorter, at 53ft and carried around 25 tons. The Canal Company was unlikely to have owned many barges itself, save those required for canal maintenance. They would look to the traders to provide their own. But sea-going boats, of a size that could be accommodated in their locks, might be another matter, thus eliminating the need for double handling of cargoes at Bridgwater. In 1826, whilst the canal was still in building, the company gave consideration to ordering 'boats from 30 to 35 tons burden, so constructed as to navigate the Bristol Channel, and bring coals direct from Newport to Taunton.'[5]

Shortly after the opening of the canal:

> … the inhabitants of this town [Taunton] were gratified with the novel sight of a vessel, direct from Newport, with coals for Messrs Cox and Townsend, lying at their wharf, close to North Town Bridge. The vessel is the property of the Canal Company, and is to be let for freight or charter from this town to any of the ports on the Bristol Channel … she was immediately engaged to return with coals and iron from Newport and that other vessels of a similar construction are now fitting out by the merchants of that port for the same trade.[6]

Another observer at the time, Harry Hanson, writes:

> The early canal boatmen were not timid men. It was inevitable that lock-keepers and toll collectors should become their natural enemies, just as they had been, and were, to the river boatmen. These canal guardians were exhorted to save water and to preserve the fabric of the canal, and to collect the just dues of the Canal Company on pain of dismissal. On the other hand, the boatmen, being paid by results, were eager to proceed on their way as quickly as possible, and were often careless of wasting water.[7]

William Goodland, who had been a boatman on the river and by 1830 had set up his own coal business in Taunton, indicates the wages of the boatmen. 'The wages given to the boatmen on the Tone for some years past, have not averaged more than 2/4*d* per ton … whilst those for the canal are given as 1/8*d* per ton.'[8]

The canal boatman, no longer reliant upon the tides to give momentum, would need a horse and tow-line for the whole journey which now averaged around 6 hours – this represented a benefit to the boatman, a financial advantage to the traders, and, hopefully, a profit to the company.

One difficulty that the canal boatmen faced were delays during hard winters, when the slow moving waters of the canal were likely to freeze over. The sluices and paddles were unable to be worked, the gates became unopenable and the towpath too icy for the horses to get a firm grip. There was an ice-breaker on the canal which had:

An iron ice-boat, similar to that which would have been used on the Bridgwater and Taunton Canal. The boats were cleverly designed: the punt-like prow allowed it to ride upon the ice whilst the hull, which swelled in size towards the rear, helped in breaking it up with the assistance of men rocking the boat from side to side, whilst slowly hauled along by horses. (Courtesy of Edward Paget-Tomlinson and Richard Dear)

Local skaters enjoying the icy conditions on the canal in the early 1920s. (Courtesy of J.E. Cole)

… a semi-circular hull, and was fitted on deck with a bar about 3ft high, running its full length, by which eight men, standing four on each side were able to rock the boat as it was slowly drawn forward by two horses. On those occasions when the company could not provide personnel to rock the boat, men from the brick and tile works volunteered to do so when their day's work depended on the barge transport.[9]

In January 1837 the editor of the *Taunton Courier* had to apologise to his readers. 'Only one, out of several cases of type, which ought to have arrived a fortnight ago from BOWER and BACON, Typefounders, of Sheffield, has yet reached us … the frost on the canal has most probably occasioned this delay.'[10] A year later, such inconvenience was put to good use, for 'after severe frosts during the second week of January, the Tone and canal throughout its line from Bridgwater to Holcombe are frozen over, affording a fine opportunity for healthful recreation on the ice, both in sliding and skating, of which thousands are daily availing themselves'.[11] Again 1850 'the canal and pounds near Taunton, being firmly frozen, opportunity has been given to the skaters for indulging in that animating recreation.'[12] While the canal offered such a wonderful playground for the skaters during these wintry periods, it is doubtful whether either the Canal Company or the merchants in Taunton were too delighted at the enforced idleness of their barges and consequent loss of trade in Taunton.

As was the case with the river barges, thieving was always a problem, particularly as the waterside areas of a town usually attracted undesirable characters and those looking for casual work, while the boatmen would have little security in the more remote rural stretches of the canal. Shortly after the canal had opened, the inhabitants of the town were informed by the London & Bridgwater Shipping Co. that as part of their service of conveying goods between London, Bridgwater and Taunton, their agents, Henry Trood

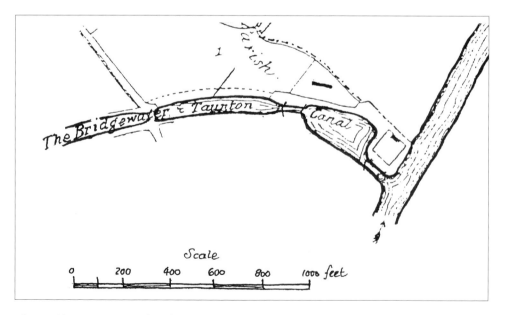

The canal basin at Huntworth as shown on the plan of 1836 prepared by John Easton when an extension to the canal was being prepared to the north side of Bridgwater.

& Son were building a barge, constructed to lock up '... for the greater security of the goods entrusted to their care'. [13]

Even the short length of the Bridgwater and Taunton Canal was no deterrent, for it was reported that '... some thieves broke open the cabin of a barge on the canal belonging to Mr W. Trump, of Durston, and stole ten pounds worth of half-pence.' [14]

THE CANAL BASIN AT HUNTWORTH

The original line of the canal included a tidal basin at Huntworth, where it entered the River Parrett. There were two sets of pound locks either side of the basin which was some 1½ acres in extent. The lock chamber to the Parrett contained strong gates, deep enough to withstand the high tides of the river, while the second lock chamber enabled the barges to be lifted up to the level of the canal and would have provided an effective means of shutting off the canal if repairs needed to be carried out to either the basin or the river gates. Built around the north side of the basin was a terrace of cottages which were the homes of many boatmen and their families. A larger dwelling near the river gates was occupied by the basin inspector whilst nearby were the stables and workshops.

The basin would act as a holding bay for the barges awaiting the ebbing tide before passing through the river gates and making their way down to Bridgwater. With the rigid timetable of day-to-day working on the canal and the varying times of the tides, the Inspector would need the utmost diligence in ensuring that the barges were passed through as quickly as possible and those that were waiting to enter from the river were not put in any unnecessary danger.

In October 1837 a mishap did occur, which must have further convinced the Canal Company of the wisdom of building the new dock at Bridgwater:

> At seven o'clock in the evening, after it had become dark, the tide in the Parrett rose so suddenly, between the Town Bridge and the Basin, that seven or eight heavily laden barges, which were about to enter the canal, were driven from their moorings, and, being forced against each other, were much damaged; one belonging to Messrs Stuckey and Co. with a valuable cargo aboard, was driven underneath another boat, and immediately sank. Such a sudden and boisterous influx of the tide has not been known before in that river for the last thirty years. [15]

THE CANAL COMPANY'S OPERATING REGULATIONS

By 1841, the Canal Company had a dock to administer in addition to a canal, and it was necessary to issue strict regulations to all masters of vessels as well as to the boatmen. Some of the regulations concerned the procedures to be followed in taking vessels and barges through the locks to the river, so as to avoid losing too much water, whilst others related to working hours, loading and unloading at the dock and navigation on the canal. One of the regulations required that between 25 March and 29 September no boatman would be

A drawing of Kings lock.

permitted to navigate a barge on the canal earlier than four o'clock in the morning and not later than nine o'clock in the evening. For the rest of the year it would be 1 hour later in the morning and 1 hour earlier in the evening. No Sunday working was permitted.

The competence of boatmen was also considered. Those 'having the care or command' of a barge on the canal 'shall be duly qualified to steer and manage such barge, and also a competent person attending to drive the horse'. No barge was to travel faster than 3 mph and the boatman was to take the greatest care not to damage the lock-gates while entering or leaving, otherwise he would incur a heavy fine. The regulations required that barges going towards Taunton kept to the towing-path side of the canal, so that Bridgwater-bound barges could pass on the far side. Empty barges had to give way to loaded ones, and loaded barges going down the canal to Bridgwater had to give way to loaded barges coming towards Taunton where the canal was of restricted width, such as at swingbridges and locks.[16]

THE CANAL BOATMEN'S FAMILIES

As the canal was only 14½ miles long, the barges did not contain living accommodation as was usual on the longer, cross-country canals. They were day boats, built purely to carry cargo and with minimal space for the comforts of the boatmen. Almost without exception they lived or shared accommodation in cottages close to the waterways, not only at Taunton and Bridgwater but in the villages as well, such as Bathpool, Creech St Michael and Huntworth.

The swingbridge at North Newton, 1902. (Courtesy of Mrs C.W. Coate, North Newton)

The 1841 census shows that thirteen boatmen and seven 'excavators' lived at Creech; the mention of the excavators presumably referred to those who were working at the time on the cutting of the Chard Canal. The census ten years later shows that more than forty boatmen's families lived at Moorland and along the canal between Fordgate and the old basin at Huntworth, these locations being particularly convenient for those working on both the river and the canal. There were a number of families who, for generations, had been involved with the waterways, such as the Meades, who occupied cottages, then called Meades Buildings, on the site of the present Boat and Anchor Inn, known today as Meades Crossing. Many members of the Goodland family lived and worked in the area around Moorland.[17]

THE ATTRACTION OF WATER

It was perhaps inevitable that the canals possessed an attraction for children who lived near them. Most were fascinated by the presence, not only of the water, and the activity upon it, but by the variety of cargoes that the barges carried, goods from far and wide. Above all, most of the boatmen who lived locally would be known to them. It became their playground and despite rigorous regulations set down by the canal owners, the children still found ways of enjoying themselves around the waterside.

Some boys worked both on the river and the canal as boat-boys from the age of eight upwards with few requirements over safety or the employment of child labour. It is not surprising that accidents and fatalities occurred. A year after the canal was opened to traffic a boat-boy, called Joseph Davey, aged fifteen, was employed in driving a boat-horse from Bridgwater to Creech. The boat was laden with 37 tons of coal, and did not arrive at Creech until six o'clock on Sunday morning. Shortly afterwards the boy was sent back with the horse, which, it is conjectured, he was riding under the bridge at Buckland Farm – a not unusual practice, but extremely dangerous; the towing path under the bridges never having been intended for riding upon. In this manner, it is supposed he must have fallen off the horse into the canal where, about seven o'clock that morning, he was found drowned by the side of the towing path. Attached to the verdict of 'accidentally drowned' was a word of censure to all boatmen, reminding them of the restrictions placed upon the working of barges in the dark. Whilst no criticism seems to have been made over the excessive hours worked by the youngster, it was stated that 'it is not improbable that the poor boy may have fallen asleep from fatigue, and that he might, in this way, have come into contact with the arch of the bridge, there being a slight contusion on his forehead'.[18] It is interesting that no mention was made of either Sunday working or working during the night!

A verdict of accidental death was recorded on another boat-boy, Henry Farrence, aged eight. 'He had been seen by another boy on the canal towing path, going to feed his horse near to the Firepool lock … it is supposed that he must have lain down to sleep – a very common custom for boat-boys at this time of the year – and that he fell into the canal and was drowned.'[19]

Understandably, when youngsters, who often worked unaccompanied and had no schooling whatsoever, were hurt or drowned there was considerable sympathy. They obviously provided cheap labour and worked extremely long hours; their tiredness was often a contributory cause of the accidents. The Canal Company would come in for criticism if it was proved that their works were in any way unsafe or defective. For adults, accidents were usually the result of plain carelessness and poor judgement although drunkenness claimed its toll as well.

… AND THE SWINGBRIDGES

The 1811 Act stipulated the way the swingbridges were to be operated. The Canal Company were required to 'affix a chain to each swivel bridge which shall be laid over or across the canal so as to extend across the bottom of the canal to the opposite bank, and to be affixed to such opposite bank to enable persons to shut such swivel bridge when necessary'.

Experience on other canals had shown how vulnerable swingbridges were to abuse. They could be left open which meant that anyone on the far side could not get across. As most of these swingbridges provided crossing points for farmers with land on either side of the canal, the failure to close a bridge could cause considerable frustration. In practice, it is likely that even with safeguards, the boatmen would find a willing young lad along the towpath to open and close the bridges for them, for they were as attractive to the youngsters of those days as they are today! Unfortunately they could also be places of danger. In January, 1836, a swingbridge claimed the life of Thomas Virgin, a boatman. He had been admitted 'to the Taunton and Somerset Hospital with concussion of the

Right: Bridgwater & Taunton Canal sign. Recently found fixed to a farm outbuilding on the Devon/Somerset border. (Courtesy of Gerry Hollington)

Below: The swingbridge at Bathpool, 1960. Although fixed when this photograph was taken, the iron arms of the earlier swingbridge, installed after a fatality in 1856, are clearly visible.

brain caused by his foot slipping when pushing a canal bridge open ... he fell, and the bridge swinging open, crushed his head between it and the earth'.[20] Bearing in mind this accident happened in January, it is possible that the ground was icy and slippery at this time.

Two years later, and within a month of each other, two further accidents claimed young lives. At Creech St Michael, a verdict of 'accidentally drowned' was passed on William Drew, aged six, who was drowned when he fell off a swingbridge over the canal, near the church. In evidence, it was stated that the church path led over this bridge and that 'it is frequently left not closed, and that it is not unusual to see twenty children swinging the bridge backwards and forwards.' In this case, the jury were unanimous in declaring that the bridge was dangerous, the Canal Company being fined 'one sovereign'.[21] Shortly afterwards, a ten-year-old boy, John Bartlett, was playing with other children and 'while amusing themselves by riding on a swingbridge at a place called Copse Bridge, on the Bridgwater and Taunton Canal, and in the act of jumping off the bridge, he fell into the canal and was drowned'.[22] The name, Copse Bridge, is not familiar, but as the inquest was held at Moorland, it is possible that it refers to the bridge at Fordgate.

A further fatality was recorded in 1856. William Howard, of Brownes Farm, West Monkton, who, it was assumed, was walking home, fell into the canal at midnight and was drowned, because the swingbridge had been left open. The incident so concerned the jury that they considered:

> ... that the swingbridge over the canal leading from Bathpool to West Monkton ought to be locked in consequence of the quantity of traffic which takes place at all times of the day and night – especially at night, and that the lock-keeper should have special instructions to that effect, and that iron arms should project from the bridge to meet the guard rail on the towing path ... we also consider that hooks and drags ought to be kept at the different stations.[23]

The Canal Company appears to have taken these instructions to heart, for up to the time of the reconstruction of the Bathpool swingbridge in 1992, the projecting 'iron arms', mentioned by the jury, were still in place.

LOCAL INTEREST

Apart from these unfortunate and distressing instances, there were pleasant occasions as well when the public enjoyed the presence of the new waterway. As the years went by, not only did the new construction begin to mellow and the raw, clay earthworks of the cut blend into the countryside, but the canal itself began to be assimilated into the pattern of local life. Many of those who worked upon the canal lived nearby and took pride in working upon it.

The canal passed through the estate of General Sir John and Lady Slade at Maunsel House. At certain festive times of the year, custom demanded that those 'in the big house' helped to make it a day to remember.

> Lady Slade, always alive to the wants of the poor, gave, at Easter, 200 weight of beef, with bread in proportion, to those immediately around Maunsel; and on Easter Monday, according to custom, twenty of the labourers were regaled with roast beef and plum pudding, with plenty of strong beer and punch in the servants hall.[24]

Another large house alongside the canal also figured in the news that year. Court Barton at Creech St Michael came up for sale. The estate was described in the *Taunton Courier* as 'situated 3 miles from Taunton...the Taunton and Bridgwater Canal passes near the premises'. It is interesting to note that the canal, which had been open barely ten years by this time, was now considered an important selling point! Indeed, in Slaters Directory of 1852, Taunton is stated as '... situated in the lovely vale of Taunton Dean, on the banks of the River Tone and the Bridgwater and Taunton Canal'.

The River Through Taunton

Apart from its use as a navigable waterway, the River Tone was also a popular and well-used recreational asset in the town. Taunton, even in the 1830s, was still a compact town and its northern outskirts did not extend much further than Firepool. Beyond this the river flowed through pleasant countryside, itself contributing to Taunton's reputation as an attractive country town. Between Firepool and Bathpool the river banks, including the walks through the Priory Fields and the locks and weirs at Obridge, were popular venues for the townspeople to spend their limited leisure hours.

Whether the water of the river was as attractive as the countryside to either side is doubtful, for it received not only all the trade effluent from the factories, tanneries and mills on its course, but also much of the sewage and waste water from the town as well; a situation that was not to improve until a sewage treatment works was built at Obridge at the end of the 1860s. It would appear, however, that there was little concern for pollution, especially during the long, hot summer weeks, when the river attracted swimmers and bathers. At Obridge, which was particularly popular, there was deep and turbulent water below the weir for swimmers, whilst the springy arms of the lock gates provided a fine substitute for a diving board!

Aware that Bristol in the mid-1830s already had 'a good bathing establishment', the editor of the *Taunton Courier* argued in August 1835 for the establishment of a similar facility in Taunton. He wrote that:

> … the extraordinary heat of the present summer has induced a very general regret amongst those who delight in bathing, that Taunton, which above all other towns has such a desirable 'locale' for the construction of a bath, should be without so enviable an appliance to health and recreation. The River Tone, running so adjacently to the Town, has on its banks, within 2 minutes walk of the Parade, many spots, at very small expense.'

He urged that 'one, amongst the many respectable coal merchants and wharfingers who reside in that vicinity' should be prepared to provide such a facility, pointing out that French Weir was too far from the centre, and public decency was offended because a footpath ran close by.

This plea, however, appears to have fallen on deaf ears, for nothing came of it. The Priory Fields and Obridge remained as the popular bathing places for years to come, although Edward Jeboult, a local tradesman and early photographer of the town, was instrumental in establishing a bathing station at French Weir in 1862.[25]

Thomas Hugo, a London antiquarian who visited Taunton in 1860 and 1861, recorded his impressions of the River Tone, after walking from the town to Bathpool in the company of William Goodland. Starting at Firepool, he remarked that there was once a mill there, but that this had been demolished, after having been purchased by the Conservators of the River Tone some fifty years earlier as it had fallen into such a derelict state that it impeded the navigation on the river. He added that 'Firepool Weir is a truly picturesque bit of river scenery, especially as approached from the canal bank, where there are pollarded willows, blackberry bushes and purple loosestrife'.

Obridge, Taunton *c*.1865. The footbridge over the Tone with five passers-by intently watching the photographer. (Courtesy of Robin Bush, Jeboult's, Taunton)

Hugo, obviously relying upon William Goodland's extensive knowledge of the river, gained when he was a boatman and later Inspector for the Conservators of the River Tone, states that:

> Priory lock is of no great age, but was constructed when the Tone was made navigable from Ham Mills to Taunton in the earlier part of the last century… at Priory Weir, there is another set of flood gates connecting to Obridge Weir, whilst, at both, with their high flood gates, the rushing and sparkling water is a most charming object; in winter, when the flood is more than ordinarily abundant, the scene is often times awfully grand.

Whether the boatmen, when they had to haul their heavy cargoes of coal up this river in the depths of winter, would have described this scene in exactly the same way is doubtful.

Hugo continues describing the river downstream of Obridge as a favourite spot for fishermen, 'where it flowed through orchards'. At Bathpool:

> … the lock dates from the formation of the Tone navigation … the river was, in fact, a series of levels, caused by the obstructing mills which kept back the water. Until the making of the Navigation, when these impediments were neutralised by means of locks, it was impossible, under ordinary circumstances for boats to travel either up or down river further than from mill to mill.

Two years before Hugo wrote these lines, a complaint was voiced in the columns of the *Taunton Courier* that 'some of our finest rural walks, such as Priory Fields, are practically closed to the "fair sex" during summer months in consequence of the number of men and boys bathing in the nude.'[26] The Local Board of Health was urged to provide public baths and wash-houses.

A 'Taunton Traveller' was moved to comment in 1865 that:

> We love our noble river. In summer, its banks have afforded the coolest and most pleasant walks; in winter we have occasionally seen many parties of men and boys skating and sliding on its frozen and slippery face. We have dived under it, swum through it, skated over it, rowed upon it, enjoyed many a pleasant walk upon its banks; we have strained every nerve in a regatta, have hunted the otter and moor-hen in all excitement, we have fished and angled in its waters, have sailed in barge, boat and steamer upon its face; out of it we have pulled the drowning, and last but not least, we have ourselves been drawn out when cramp had rendered our limbs useless.[27]

This picture of rural bliss was not to last. Edward Goldsworthy, in his *Recollections of Old Taunton*, stated that, at Obridge, 'the low-lying fields were undrained and produced little besides bullrushes and prickly plants'. Pollution was reaching unacceptable levels, with effluent piling up at the Firepool and Bathpool weirs. Captain George Beadon, at Creech Barrow House, complained bitterly at the nuisance, as did many others of the public concerned at the neglected state of the river. Many complaints were unfairly directed towards the Conservators of the River Tone whose responsibilities for this stretch of the river had been removed some thirty years earlier. It was not until 1868 that the Local Board of Health bought land alongside the river at Obridge on which to build a temporary sewage treatment works.

THE CONSERVATORS STRUGGLE TO KEEP THE CANAL NAVIGABLE

After 1832, relieved of their responsibilities on the River Tone, the Conservators were able to carry out their new duties of inspecting the canal once a year, no doubt with a degree of relief. No longer would they feel the burden of financial responsibility upon their shoulders as they had done when inspecting their river in earlier years, for their new role was now to ensure that it was the Canal Company that maintained its own waterway. As the Conservators were able to bring guests along on these inspections they were able to mix business with pleasure!

The format of these inspections was to change little throughout the century. They would hire a barge from a local trader in Taunton for perhaps two or three days and arrange to have it cleaned and carpenters erect an awning and provide seats the day before the inspection.

On the day of the inspection, which was usually arranged for a public holiday during July each year, the vessel would be victualled by a local inn or hotel, and at around 9 a.m. the Conservators and their guests would embark at the Conservators' steps at the North Town Bridge, as they had done many times before when inspecting the river, and proceed through Firepool lock to Huntworth, before returning late in the evening. In later years the awning was replaced by a quickly constructed 'upper deck', which afforded the Conservators and their guests not only fine views during their journey but gave under-cover accommodation for those who preferred to enjoy the food and drink!

Records of these inspections each year were kept by the Conservators and some details are worth giving as they throw an interesting light not only on the way 'al fresco' occasions were arranged, but also the costs involved. For example, in 1849, the account they charged the Canal Company showed:

Conveying Conservators up and down canal,	£2.0.0d
Tobacco pipes	1.0d
½lb tobacco	2.6d
refreshments for men	3.8d
potatoes	4.0d
Total	£2.11.2d

No mention is made of guests on this occasion nor is there any mention of ale or spirits, although it is too much to imagine the conservators ran a 'dry' ship in those days.

The next year, the account shows a further 8/8d was spent on 'an extra horse and boy', while, in 1851, there is mention of 'one gallon of beer at Bathpool for 1/4d'.

Twelve years later, in 1863, the accounts are more detailed; eleven Conservators took part, each bringing a guest.

Hire of Boat and men from Goodlands	£2.11.0d
Refreshments, from Wickendens	4.10.6d
Beer, Ale, Porter, Spirits, from Taylors	2.1.6d
Pipes and tobacco	4.0d
Sugar and lemons	5.6d
Ale (for the men)	6.0d
Cider from Musgraves	3.0d
Corkscrews, spoons, lemon squeezer	8.9d
Waiters	7.0d
Total	£10.17.3d

Following that particular inspection, the treasurer to the Conservators, King Meade-King wrote to Mr C.W. Loveridge, the canal manager, stating that, 'The Conservators of the River Tone, having, in the course of their annual inspection of the canal yesterday, remarked at the existence of an unusual quantity of weed, which, if not speedily removed, would, in their opinion, seriously impede the navigation', and asking that 'you give the necessary direction to obviate this contemplated evil'. Needless to say, the work was carried out without delay.

These, however, were the years when the Canal Company was in the hands of Receivers. Money for canal maintenance was limited and, as a consequence, the quality of the navigation suffered. When the Bristol and Exeter Railway finally purchased the canal from the Receivers in 1866, they tried, with commendable determination, to retain its barge traffic, accepting that this performed a useful adjunct to their own railway business.

The Act authorising the purchase of the Bridgwater & Taunton Canal Co. stipulated that tolls could be charged at a ratio of 5:3 between the railway and the canal 'for the conveyance of coal, culm, brickyard goods, timber, deals, slates, potatoes, salt and grain'.[1]

Although the railway would need to be reminded of this clause within the next eight years, they found they had inherited an immediate and more pressing problem: that of water shortage in the canal. It was to be a continuing headache and despite carrying out necessary maintenance, they were increasingly having to face up to the fact that there was simply not enough water coming from the River Tone to supply their canal, especially in the summer months.

The fortnightly scouring out of the dock at Bridgwater, necessary if it was to be freed of the clogging mud and silt that accumulated there, took a lot of water from the canal. Similarly, the needs of the railway station and locomotive sheds at Taunton required water with the inevitable result that the canal often became starved and barge traffic was seriously affected as a consequence. As the years went by this problem worsened, and with diminishing trade and therefore diminishing returns, maintenance was further neglected. The result was a waterway partially blocked by weed growth, despite the many concerns expressed by the Conservators during their annual inspections.

During January 1866, and again during January and March 1867, the centre of Taunton suffered particularly badly from flooding and the Local Board of Health was requested to review:

> ... the water courses – mainly the River Tone – within Taunton St James, West Monkton, Ruishton and Creech St Michael, which had not been regularly viewed since the Bridgwater & Taunton Canal Co. took over the navigation of the River Tone in 1832.[2]

They appointed an engineer, Thomes Howard, to look into the matter, and he subsequently recommended to the Board a number of proposals which he considered would safeguard the town from much of its troubles from flooding.

He suggested the raising of river banks and walls, as well as the conversion of the 'old lock at Obridge' into a weir, with the half-lock at Bathpool being removed altogether; they both caused unacceptable constrictions to the free flowing of the water in times of flood. He observed that, 'at Creech, where the river and the canal are close', the canal could be used for running-off surplus water from the river. His comments reinforced the view of many that much of the river, and particularly the length between Taunton and Creech, had become sadly neglected once the canal had opened.

During the hot summer of 1874, the Conservators of the River Tone, a body of Trustees now relieved of their previous responsibilities for maintaining the River Tone, received a complaint from the Local Board of Health, requesting that, 'their attention be called to the state of the River Tone from French Weir to Obridge, and to the fact of the waterway being silted up with offensive deposit likely to be prejudicial to the health of the Town'. The treasurer to the Conservators replied to this somewhat unfair criticism quite correctly, if not a little disdainfully, by saying that, 'he was not aware of any power beyond that possessed by the Inhabitants of the town generally, to remove the evil – or even if they have the powers, they certainly do not have the means of giving effect to it'.[3]

However, during that summer of 1874, there was growing concern at the deteriorating state of the canal as well, and again the Conservators were held to be responsible. They received complaints from Taunton businessmen and traders, concerned at the difficulties being experienced by their boatmen. In one complaint it was stated that several coal merchants remarked at 'the state of the river and also the canal ... the latter is so choked with weed that it takes 14 hours to bring boats from Bridgwater – 6 hours are to be the average time – and that only 18 tons, instead of 25 tons of coal can be brought in consequence of shallow water'.[4]

'Taunton Men of Commerce', comprising, in the main, owners and occupiers of waterside premises in Taunton, made similar comments, drawing attention to the state of the canal and reminding the Conservators of the original undertaking by the railway in which they 'covenanted to keep the Navigation open in an effective manner from Bridgwater to Taunton Gas Works'. They complained that 'water was being constantly drained from the canal by the Pumping Engine erected at Taunton by the Bristol and Exeter Railway' and also at the:

> ... foul state of the canal, which, having not been cleared out for many years, a process of silting up is going on ... formerly we were able to get our barges from Bridgwater to

Taunton in 6 hours, now it takes, more frequently, 14 hours. When the canal was purchased, there was a rest-house midway on the canal bank, for horses and men, this has been destroyed and there is no place of shelter between Bridgwater and Taunton so that the horses and men have to endure great suffering, more especially in the winter season.[5]

The Pumping Engine referred to, was, in fact, a 'hot air' engine, situated some 200 yards west of the Firepool lock. It was to be replaced by a more efficient pumping station in 1889, a building of two storeys, erected above two disused lime kilns, alongside Firepool lock itself. It drew water from a small reservoir built alongside, which was connected to the canal by a metered conduit.[6]

With these complaints from both the Local Board of Health and the Taunton traders, the Conservators found themselves at the receiving end of embarrassing and unwanted criticism. They were in an impossible position. Whilst they were held by many in the town to be accountable and indeed, had powers to ensure that the condition of the canal was maintained to a navigational standard, they were not its owners, preferring to exert pressure by persuasion, following their annual inspections, rather than instigate litigation.

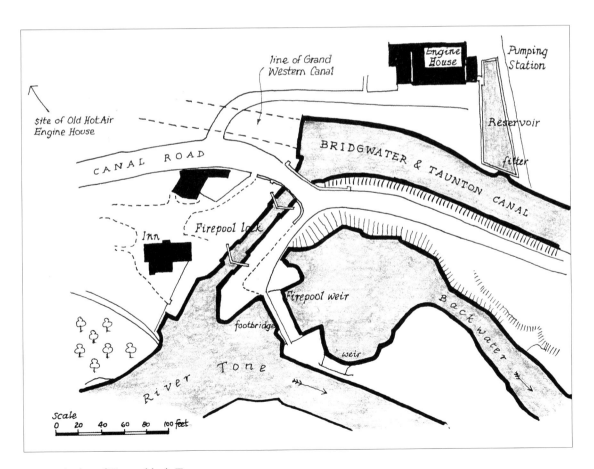

A plan of Firepool lock, Taunton.

Clearing reeds from the River Tone at Creech St Michael in around 1910. (Courtesy of J.E. Cole, Creech St Michael)

In July 1874, the Conservators held a meeting on site at Firepool. This was the year that the new sewerage works were being built at Obridge by the Local Board of Health and water was being 'run-off' from the Tone to facilitate these works. The Conservators noted the low state of water in the canal which 'was silted up and choked with weed'. They informed the Directors of the Bristol and Exeter Railway of their 'great concern', and that they were failing to meet their maintenance obligations.

Patience was wearing a little thin with the Conservators' gentlemanly approaches to the canal owners and by November, the traders themselves wrote to the directors, complaining at the deteriorating state of the canal. The directors' response, rather defensively, was 'that they were not prepared to admit that the complaints of the traders are well founded, and … that the main channels were sufficiently free from deposit.' They went further, stating that 'a great deal of objectionable refuse is allowed by the Board of Health to be thrown into the river'.[7]

In October that year, William Pritchard, representing 'the Canal Traders and Wharfingers', wrote to the treasurer of the Conservators of the River Tone, King Meade-King, pointing out that the railway was 'now reducing the charge for coal carried from Bridgwater to Taunton from 3/2d to 2/6d a ton', and he wanted the tolls reduced proportionately on the canal. 'The charge', he said, 'at the present is 1/9¾d and this should be reduced to 1/6d in accordance with the agreed ratio of 5:3 as set out in S.24 of the Act authorising the sale of the canal to the Bristol and Exeter Railway.'[8] It is unlikely that the Conservators were successful in persuading the Railway to act quickly in reducing their tolls, for at that time they, themselves, were involved in discussions with the Great Western Railway over impending amalgamation, and it would have been in their interests to demonstrate the attractive terms they could offer for rail freight.[9]

Bridgwater and Taunton Canal, *c*.1905. Outriggers fixed to a canal barge to carry a cargo of hay. (Courtesy of Kodak Museum and the Boat Museum)

Steam-powered weed-cutter *c*.1865. This is probably the craft designed by Captain George Beadon, who was known to be working on such vessel about this time. (Courtesy of Robin Bush, Jeboult's, Taunton).

Not surprisingly, with uncompetitive levels of tolls on the canal, and the declining state of the navigation, its trade dropped and by the end of that year, 1874, income to the Bristol and Exeter Railway had been reduced to only £1,700, compared to over £2,500 only four years earlier. This was no better than the Conservators had achieved way back in 1825! There was no doubt that the presence of the railway between Bridgwater and Taunton, which was now carrying an increasing amount of freight, was slowly depriving the canal of its own traffic, and it is not really surprising that the railway was unwilling to do more than was absolutely necessary to meet its statutory maintenance obligations.

By 1877, with the amalgamation of the Bristol and Exeter Railway with the Great Western Railway, 'line management' effectively passed from Bristol to Paddington. For the Great Western Railway, the canal would be maintained primarily as a source of water for their operations at Taunton station and Bridgwater Dock. As the next chapter shows, from now on the new railway company would have very decided views as to where their true interests lay and the continuation of canal traffic would not be one of them.

The Conservators' dinner bill, July 1850, at the Giles's Hotel. This Taunton Hotel is nowadays known as the Castle Hotel.

Against this background of apparent indifference by the Great Western Railway towards the canal, the Conservators continued to exercise their statutory duty to inspect the navigation annually. Their inspections were rarely newsworthy, but in 1881, the *Taunton Courier*, with its reporter unfortunately confused between the river and the canal, stated:

> … the River Conservators made their annual inspection of the River Tone … at 9 o'clock the gentlemen … started from Messrs Goodlands' wharf in the barge, covered with an awning. It went down the river as far as Huntworth. The object of the visit was to ascertain whether the navigation has been kept open and in good order, and we believe this was found to be the case. During the day, the party partook of luncheon on board the barge; the spread, a most RECHERCHE one, being supplied by Mr Wickenden, of this town. The Company returned home about 8 o'clock. [10]

It was the presence of reeds and weed that was again the main problem. If not cut regularly, their uncontrolled growth could affect not only the flow of water, but hinder the passage of the barges. In those days and well into the present century, the task of cutting the reed was slow and labour intensive. Those reeds that could not be removed with long-handled rakes from the maintenance barge or from the towpath, needed to be 'sawn'. The thick stalks in the water presented a problem that only sharp scythe-like blades could manage. These blades were each about 2 to 3ft long and were bolted loosely together like links in a chain. With stout ropes at each end, two men on each side of the canal would literally 'saw' their way slowly through the stalks.

The Conservators on the Bridgwater and Taunton Canal. From a painting by H. Frier based on an earlier print from around 1860. (Courtesy of Taunton Deane Borough Council)

An idyllic pastoral scene at Standards lock between the wars. (Courtesy of Somerset Archaeological and Natural History Society)

The Conservators returning after a canal inspection. (Courtesy of J.E. Cole, Creech St Michael)

Captain George Beadon, the owner of Creechbarrow House, Bathpool, was a naval man with an inventive mind. In 1865, he designed and built a steam-driven boat with twin screws on either side to cut the weed on the canal. It was an astonishing looking craft, which was provided with its own towing carriage so that it could be easily taken to parts of the canal that needed attention. The twin weed cutters were placed at the front of the craft, turning in opposite directions to throw the cut weed to the side of the canal. The whole contraption, which was possibly horse-drawn, was of shallow draft, around 2ft, suitable for both the canal and the river. How effective Captain Beadon's invention was and how much it was used is not recorded, but it was doubtless the precursor of many later attempts to adapt boats with cutters in order to keep the weeds down.

CANAL VERSUS RAILWAY: THE GREAT WESTERN RAILWAY TAKES CONTROL

Until the Great Western Railway completed the Severn Tunnel in 1886, its dock at Bridgwater handled most of the imports of coal and slate from South Wales, as well as considerable quantities of merchandise from Europe and overseas. Alongside any structural repairs to the dock that were necessary from time to time, such as the replacement of the massive river gates carried out in 1886, the company had continuous maintenance problems largely because of the heavy silting up caused by the large deposits of mud and silt brought in from the Parrett, which had to be 'scoured' out once a fortnight.

In the summer months this scouring consumed vast quantities of water, brought into the dock from the canal. When the canal was cut, the Canal Company constructed, in 1826, the Charlton Pumping Station at Creech, also known as Creech Engine House. This three-storey building housed a Cornish-type Boulton and Watt beam pumping engine which abstracted water from the nearby River Tone to replenish the canal above its highest lock. The single engine is said to have met the Canal Company's demands for water, even when it was operating the dock, indeed:

> In 1840, the water in the canal was used only for navigation purposes, but shortly after the dock was opened in 1841, the canal water was used for flushing. It has always since been used for flushing because the basin could not be kept clean without'.[1]

The dock would need to be out of commission for a day or two during these times, which must have represented a considerable loss of income to the owners.

In winter months, when water was more plentiful in the canal, scouring was carried out 'sometimes as often as three times a week'.[2]

After the purchase of the canal by the Bristol and Exeter Railway and later, when under the control of the Great Western Railway, there was increased demand for water from the canal. Growing shipping activity in the dock brought with it the need for additional scouring, whilst the expanding railway network again added to the demands. The Great Western Railway had to provide water for their steam locomotives shedded at Taunton, and for Taunton and Durston stations, the latter having been built in 1853 to serve the Yeovil branch. The pumping station at Firepool was enlarged to cope with this increased demand, new pumps being installed which were able to supply 140,000 gallons a day.[3]

This water had to be obtained from the canal which, in effect, meant the River Tone. Considering the severe lack of water in the Tone that the Conservators experienced back in the 1820s, even before the arrival of the canal, it is difficult to see how the same source

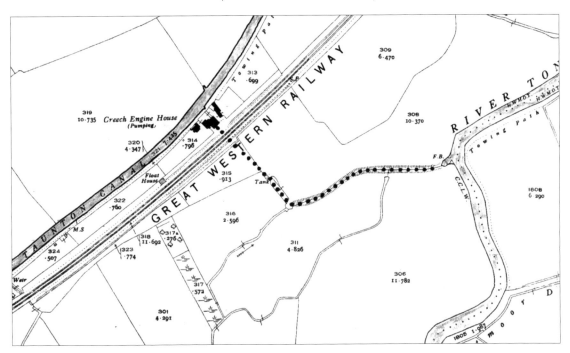

Extract from an Ordnance Survey map of 1889 which shows the proximity of Charlton Pumping Station at Creech to the River Tone from which it abstracted water for the canal.

could be expected to supply the considerable quantities now needed for the canal, the dock and the railway at Taunton.

There still remained a need for continued barge traffic on the canal. Demand for coal in Taunton continued to rise as the town expanded during the late nineteenth century and new businesses and factories opened. The Taunton Gas Light and Coke Co. was still a large consumer of coal and culm brought up the canal and through Taunton by barge to its premises in Castle Street, alongside the river where it had a wharf. An extension to the premises in 1874, to accommodate a further six benches of retorts, greatly increased the company's needs for fuel,[4] and the company still found it convenient to receive their supplies by barge.

The condition of the canal, however, continued to deteriorate to such an extent that not only the boatmen, but the traders and merchants in the town, were increasingly frustrated. In normal conditions, when the canal was in good condition, the boatmen could haul their barges through in about 6 hours, but with the neglect they now encountered including, at times, a severe lack of water, it was taking far longer. If traders could not rely upon the barges, there was always the railway to turn to!

By midsummer 1881, when there had been very little rain and the level of water in the Tone and the canal was low, Thomas Penny & Co., timber stockists and importers in Taunton, complained directly to the Great Western Railway suggesting that they might have to transfer their trade to the railway. The reply was not encouraging, '… unless a sudden change takes place in the weather, there is no prospect of the canal being better supplied with water. We are now, and have been for a long time past, pumping night and day and Sundays included'.[5]

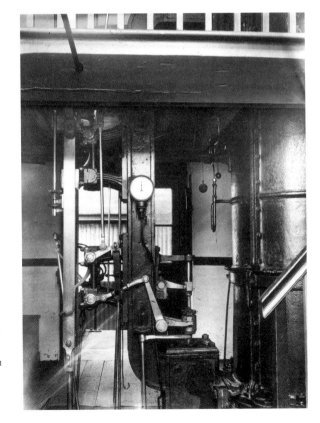

This page and opposite: The Charlton Pumping Station at Creech. Four interior views showing the machinery before its removal.

This Cornish-type Boulton and Watt beam pumping engine had a steam cylinder 2ft 9½in in diameter with a 7ft stroke; the steam being supplied by two Lancashire boilers at very low pressure. There are two pumps, one with a cylinder of 28in diameter, with a 7ft stroke and a smaller one of 12in diameter by 3ft stroke, operating at fourteen strokes per minute. The operating head was 24ft and these pumps could raise water at a rate of 120,000 gallons an hour when working to full capacity. The boilers consumed nearly 4 tons of coal a day on these occasions. (Courtesy of the Royal Commission on the Historical Monuments of England – George Watkins Collection)

A fortnight later, the Great Western Railway wrote again:

… the canal is now in as good an order as it is possible to have it in such dry seasons as of late. We are getting little or no water from the River Tone, as all the water which now passes, goes to the mill at Bathpool, and that is not sufficient to keep the mill at work half time. The miller keeps watchmen at Firepool locks night and day to see that no water is taken by us for use on the canal … and owing to the drought … sufficient water cannot be obtained to make the canal thoroughly navigable.[6]

The letter contains some interesting comments on the barge traffic on the canal at this time:

The traffic on the canal, up to now, has not been positively blocked, but the larger boats have to reduce their cargoes to some extent. On the 20th July, 1881, Messrs Showers and Company's boat, [coal merchants in Taunton] brought through from Bridgwater 16½ tons; they have no loaded boats now on the canal nor at Bridgwater. On the 23rd, Mr J. Hammett [another coal merchant] brought through four shoes and one boat loaded in all 43½ tons, and on the 25th Messrs Goodland and Sons passed two boats equalling eighteen tons each. Yesterday these boats returned empty to Bridgwater and are now lying at the docks idle, as the vessel is discharging their cargo into trucks. On Monday last, Mr Denman sent six small boats from Taunton to Bridgwater, these were left by the boatmen at Maltshovel Bridge, which is about half a mile from Bridgwater Docks, and the boatmen have returned to Taunton by train. The Captain of the coal vessel had the boats taken alongside, and loaded them with thirty-six tons of coal, and

The Charlton Pumping Station built in 1826 to pump water from the adjacent River Tone into the canal. In 1901 it was converted by the GWR to pump water from the canal to feed the railway troughs. Note the water tower alongside the railway line. (Courtesy of British Rail Western Region and the Boat Museum, Ellesmere Port, Cheshire)

they left Bridgwater at 12.40 p.m. yesterday, but from the appearance of the water in the canal, it is doubtful whether they will reach Taunton tonight.

Hardly the description of a business-like operation, and if matters were to continue like this for many more years, then the future of canal traffic was most certainly in doubt. And continue they did. The summer of 1890 was very dry, and with the consequent lack of water in the Tone, the problems of the railway and the canal users were repeated.

> In dry seasons, the canal gets very low, as we can only take a small quantity of water at the Taunton end, from the River Tone on Sundays, when the Mills are not working, and have to resort to continual pumping at Creech.[7]

The Great Western Railway revealed that in 1900, when water was again scarce, a barge had actually grounded and stopped due to shortage of water in the canal, and in 1901 the company predicted that, based on past experience, the summer would 'find them in a worse position than ever; there appeared to be every prospect that not only would the canal be closed but Bridgwater Dock as well'. From the Engineer's Office at Taunton it was mentioned that 'the amount of water now pumped at Creech every twenty-four hours is equal to the area of both the inner and outer basins at Bridgwater Dock, at 4ft 4ins deep'.

It was evident that the single beam engine at Charlton Pumping Station could no longer either cope with the heavy demands placed upon it or, due to its age, be relied upon. It was over seventy years old and there was a need to supplement it. In 1901, George J. Churchward, the Chief Mechanical Engineer to the Great Western Railway, personally agreed to the request from his Regional Manager that two compound steam engines be provided, driving Tangye centrifugal pumps. It was no doubt the proposal to install water troughs in the railway track adjacent to the pumping station the following year that persuaded him to take this action. These troughs would provide water for the steam locomotives on the non-stop run between Paddington and Cornwall. They 'consumed' over 100,000 gallons a day[8] and although the canal was virtually defunct by this time, this placed yet further demands on water from the river.

The increasing rate of abstraction of water from the River Tone not only affected the canal and its users, but also the millers, whose premises on the Tone had long enjoyed a supply of water to their mill-ponds. In 1903, Thomas John Redler, owner and miller at Bathpool Mill and George Coombe, the owner of the mill at Ham Mills, brought an action against the Great Western Railway, alleging that the company was 'wrongfully and injuriously … diverting and drawing off large quantities of water'[9] from the Tone to supply the canal, and thence their own operations, whilst leaving the Tone low in water, such that they had difficulties in effectively running their businesses.

The subsequent judgement found that the railway had substantially interfered with the use and enjoyment of water to the mills and that its abstraction for 'general railway purposes and for the locomotives interfered with such use and enjoyment.' Apart from compensation being awarded to the plaintiffs, an injunction was served restraining the railway from drawing off water from the River Tone or diminishing the flow of the river below that which the mills had previously enjoyed.

Bridgwater and Taunton Canal, 1906 – the only known photograph of commercial activity upon the canal: a barge loaded with timber from the yards of George Randle & Son, Bridgwater Docks, passing below Lyndale Avenue, Bridgwater. (Courtesy of Mrs C.P. Woods, Goathurst)

Staff at W. & F. Wills Engineers, Bridgwater, around 1900. W. & F. Wills was a large engineering firm in Bridgwater and played a leading role in designing and building craft that would help to remove the constant accummulation of mud and silt from the River Parrett. They used a powerful water jet to dislodge the silt but this method was only moderately successful. (Courtesy of the Colin Wilkins Collection)

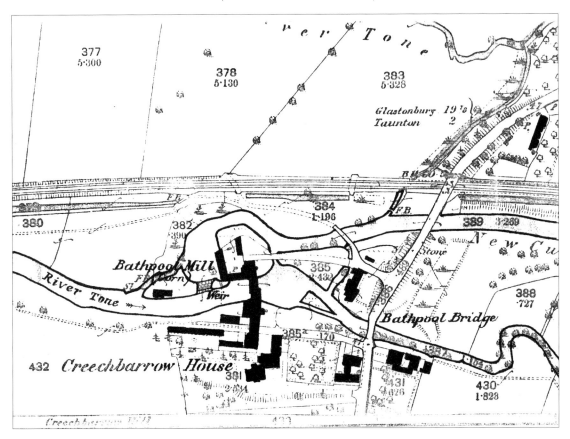

Bathpool Mill reproduced from an Ordnance Survey map of 1889.

It must have been clear to all those who traded upon the canal that the problem of insufficient water was never going to be satisfactorily resolved whilst the railway demanded so much from the river for their own purposes. The Great Western Railway, if it was serious in retaining traffic on the canal, would need to improve considerably its level of canal maintenance. This would include cutting back the encroaching reeds if the canal was to continue operating. The Great Western Railway stated at the time that:

> … it had procured a special weed cutter for cutting down the weeds close to their roots, and experiments are being made with a dredger which has been tried successfully in the Bridgwater Dock — and if these experiments prove to be satisfactory, it is intended to incur the further expense of purchasing the dredger, so that it can be used permanently for the purpose.[10]

It is more than likely that this was a vessel either adapted or designed by W. & F. Willis of Bridgwater, who were busy at this time providing dredging and pumping machinery for the River Parrett. Whether this particular solution was successful is not recorded but in any event, it was really all too late; traders had discovered that railway transport was more convenient and far quicker. Traffic inevitably diminished on the canal, and by 1907 commercial operations to Taunton ceased.

BATHPOOL MILL

Once the commercial barges had stopped coming to Taunton, the canal remained of value to the Great Western Railway solely as a source of supplying water to their own operations at Taunton station and replenishing that used in the scouring of the dock at Bridgwater. However, they had to ensure that the water levels in the River Tone were maintained at a sufficient height to benefit the mills, particularly those at Bathpool and Ham.

But the requirements of both mills were to be short-lived. The production of flour at Ham Mills continued, with some difficulty, for another few years until milling ceased altogether in 1914, when some of the machinery was removed. Bathpool Mill, which would appear to have been a more profitable undertaking, continued for only one year more. Its end was, perhaps, even more inglorious.

There had been a mill at Bathpool for many centuries, the earlier structures undoubtedly being made of timber. Over the years they were either adapted or rebuilt entirely. During the nineteenth century, the mill suffered two devastating fires which totally destroyed the buildings. At midnight, on 21 March 1812:

> Bathpool Mill was the melancholy scene of a tremendous conflagration, occasioned, it is said, by the excessive friction excited in the stones used in the process of shelling clover seed. These extensive premises, which have been built but a few years, were soon reduced to a heap of ashes together with property, consisting of flour, grain and a quantity of flax, to the amount of £2,500. Mr Hitchcock, the miller, resided on the spot.[11]

In 1861, Captain George Beadon, then owner of Bathpool Mill, purchased the Aerating Bread and Flour Co. of Taunton for £500, thus providing an additional outlet for the flour produced from his mill. By the mid-1880s, Thomas John Redler was already leasing the mill from Captain Beadon, and in 1889, upon the death of the owner, the opportunity presented itself for him to purchase the mill outright. In what condition the building was at this time is not recorded, but photographs of the Miller's House show a fine brick building with a pleasant garden surrounded by the various water courses. In 1891, however, disaster struck again; the mill caught fire and was badly damaged. John Redler, in rebuilding the mill, took precautions in the layout and method of construction to guard against future outbreaks of fire. For example, electric lights were installed, to be used when work in the evenings was necessary, and the boiler house was situated in the northern wing 'so as to be of the least possible danger.'[12]

The mill was rebuilt in stone and brick, and as well as fire precautions, incorporated other novel features. It had four pairs of stones which enabled the mill to produce over 130 sacks of flour a week and there were facilities to store a further 1,000 sacks of flour for local distribution. It was a large complex of buildings with the mill itself set astride the river above three, brick-arched mill-races. Alongside to the east, was attached the Miller's House, now rebuilt, but shorter than the elegant earlier house, which had been badly affected by the fire. Access to the house was down a wide drive to the Taunton–Bridgwater Road and a timber footbridge connected the house to the river-side path on

Above: The Miller's House at Bathpool Mill around 1885, before the 1891 fire which seriously damaged this building. Note the canoeist in the mill race.

Right: Thomas John Redler, owner and miller at Bathpool Mill around 1895.

Bathpool Mill after the fire of 1891.

the far northern side. The mill was also connected, on the southern side, to Creechbarrow House, by a covered timber walkway at first floor level, a feature which remained even after the two buildings came into separate ownerships. Each of the mill races contained a waterwheel, comprising both breast and undershot arrangements, running in masonry chases.[13]

There was a large mill-pond on the Taunton side of the mill, penning water from the river and providing the power for the waterwheels. So that the river barges could pass this mill-pond on their way to and from Taunton, a pound lock had been provided but, by the 1850s, when barges no longer used this stretch of the river this lock fell into disuse and was converted into a weir, thereby providing improved control of the river water in times of flood. Near to the mill-pond there was a salmon trap for, over the years, the occasional salmon had been known to venture this far up the river. 'A salmon, of 12lbs weight, and 2ft 10ins in length, was taken in an eel tub at Bathpool Mill, it was 'a very unusual occurrence for this fish to be found so high up this river the distance from the mouth of the Parrett, in the Bristol Channel, being upward of twenty-two miles'[14] although a year earlier, it was reported that a salmon of similar weight had been caught at Firepool Weir 'and sold for 15/6d'.[15]

Shortly after the rebuilding, Thomas Redler found it necessary, because of the unreliable level of water in the river, to install a steam-driven turbine, and this was followed, four years later, by a second turbine after which the original waterwheels were removed. Following the

The River Tone at Bathpool Mill around 1920, when barges used the river to reach Taunton. There was a lock here – evidence of which can still be seen in this view, but by the mid-nineteenth century it had been replaced by the weir. (Courtesy of The Boat Museum, Ellesmere Port, Cheshire)

success of these turbines a third was put in which 'matched the output of the two original waterwheels'.[16] With steam power now driving his main machinery, it is not surprising that towards the end of the 1890s, Thomas Redler decided to modify the original bread ovens that had been installed and convert them to steam heating thus, reputedly, providing the first such ovens in the county. There were four ovens and the loaves produced were delivered over a wide area around Taunton. There were also stables for the horses that were necessary for the deliveries, together with an extensive shed for the carts.

Despite the many precautions taken in the 1892 rebuilding, fire was again to break out at the mill. Flour, like malt dust, is highly explosive and can easily be ignited by a spark. It was in the late evening of 15 September 1915, that the fire was first noticed in the southern wing of the mill and within half an hour, the entire building was engulfed. There had been just enough time to take the horses to safety along with some waggons, but:

> … 500 sacks of flour and over 100 sacks of corn, having been carted from Taunton on the day of the outbreak, were destroyed together with many hundred pounds worth of machinery … ricks nearby, with the aid of soldiers, were draped with tarpaulins which had previously been saturated with water, and were thus prevented from being ignited by the sparks which showered upon them.[17]

Bathpool Mill as rebuilt after the 1891 fire. Notice the rebuilt and shortened Miller's House. The barges to Taunton used the cut under the footbridge and alongside the northern side of the mill. The view is taken from the Bridgwater Road, in around 1895.

The mill was totally destroyed with only the gaunt outside walls remaining, 'The interior was a mass of charred roofs, and windows had fallen in, while iron, twisted and bent, demonstrated the fierceness of the fire.'[18] It was never rebuilt and remained a ruin until the 1920s when much of it was demolished, leaving only a part to give some idea today of the quality of the stonework used.

RIVERSIDE CHARACTERS

While the canal slowly sank into a state of gentle dereliction soon after the turn of the twentieth century, the River Tone continued to carry an intermittent trade, with coal barges still delivering to Athelney and Ham and withies being taken back to Bridgwater.

Clearly the trade was a fraction of that carried in the days when the Conservators controlled the navigation but it did, however, provide a valuable source of work for some and a life-line for the many who lived alongside the river. The barges continued to use the river until shortly before 1930, and fortunately there are still some who remember those days and can recount stories and happenings of canal life at the time.

From time to time the boatmen would be able to call upon other people to lend a helping hand in tasks, such as loading and unloading the barges, bringing up waggons to the landings, and bringing the horses themselves to the riverbank when a barge needed a tow. There were always a number of men around looking for occasional work. Drovers, who herded the sheep and cattle from the moors, often helped alongside those who

The bread delivery. Bathpool Mill had its own bakery and delivered locally – a common village sight at the turn of the twentieth century. (Courtesy of June Small)

occupied themselves with a number of labouring jobs in the area, such as fruit gathering, ditching and hedging, with a little rabbit catching and fowling thrown in. In autumn time their work was usually directed towards helping with the harvest. They were real characters and often had colourful names to match, such as Busky Miller, Libbets Frowe, the Oaten brothers and Tommy Duke, one of the many Dukes in the neighbourhood.

Tommy Duke cut withies and generally helped the local farmers with any odd jobs that needed to be done. Unable to read or write, roughly dressed and continually smoking his clay pipe, he 'lived' in a tin shed in the middle of West Moor, around which was a small patch of ground, with an apple tree and some fowls and ducks. When the annual flooding of West Moor occurred, he would sleep amidst straw in his old withy boat with his few possessions, while the fowls perched on the roof and his ducks enjoyed the freedom of their new watery expanses. George Beck, who owned a small coal yard at Hook Bridge at Curload and had a contract to deliver coal to both Ham and Athelney, would hire Tommy Duke to bring the horses to the river at New Bridge, in time to meet him and his barge from Bridgwater and affix the towing line.

Another local coal merchant who owned a number of barges was Edward Watts. Before the turn of the century he established himself at Athelney, and under contract from Sully & Co. supplied coal to the local industries as far as Langport, to the pumping stations on the River Parrett and to Curry Moor Pumping Station on the Tone, almost opposite his wharf. He employed a number of men, and his plot of land at Athelney contained sufficient space down to the water's edge for him to beach a barge during high water if it needed recaulking or minor repairs.

After the fire in September 1915, a view from the west of Bathpool Mill, looking over the mill-pond, showing the extent of fire damage and the melancholy site that greeted the owner the following morning. The mill was never rebuilt.

Such repairs were often necessary. With the manoeuvring of the barges against the sides of the colliers in the dock, the lock chambers and the wharves, and the collisions with debris on the tidal waters, it was inevitable that minor damage was sustained and needed to be attended to quickly. Those barges owned by the bigger companies or those needing major repairs would be taken to the boatyards in Bridgwater but with the smaller concerns, where the boatmen themselves owned their barge, the work would be done on the spot, possibly involving the smithy and the local carpenter. With few mechanical aids, other than a set of sheerlegs and block and tackle, the boatmen became adept at using the fluctuating tides to help them, allowing the craft to be beached at low tide if work was to be undertaken on the hull.

Emrhys Coate of Stoke St Gregory well recalls a story that was related to him by Ernest Pocock, who owned a small number of coal barges around 1900. In 1912, just before the First World War, one of his barges was holed and sank in the River Parrett, a short distance above Burrowbridge. The total loss of a barge, with or without its cargo, to a small trader, could greatly affect his means of earning a livelihood, quite apart from the obstruction it caused to other river users.

On this occasion, ingenuity was called for. After the sunken barge had been located, Ernest Pocock positioned another empty barge of his immediately over it whilst the river was at high water. Later that day when the tide had ebbed and with the empty barge now settled firmly upon the sunken barge, they were lashed together to await the next high tide which would float them off and enable the holed barge to be beached on a nearby sandbank. Salvaging the cargo and carrying out emergency repairs would then wait until the waters dropped once more.

Bridgwater Dock in the early years of the twentieth century. Steam and sail fill the dock, but freight for the canal was declining.

Another member of the extensive Pocock family, Sydney Pocock, took over some of the work of Edward Watts in the early 1900s: he was affectionately known as Pumblefoot Pocock on account of his club foot. Arthur Stuckey, the last lock-keeper at Langport lock, recalls Sydney Pocock's barges being hauled up to Langport and discharging their cargoes of coal at the large wharves just down-river of Bow Bridge, in the town. Gangplanks or skids, as they were known, which would be carried on board, would be placed between the barges and the yard for the boatmen and other coal-porters to carry the coal across in wicker butts.

At the larger coal depots, wharves were provided which meant that gangplanks were not needed; the barge could tie up alongside and it would be possible for a number of men to work at the same time in unloading. Often it was possible to use wheelbarrows for this work, but occasionally the men might still have to resort to the laborious and dirty work of carrying the coal ashore in wicker baskets. These baskets, being made locally, were plentiful and relatively cheap for the purpose; Richard Goodland Hyde recollects how, in his early days with the firm of Goodland, he was required to cycle to workshops at Creech St Michael to place orders for more of the two-handled butts that his firm used, both on the barges and on the horse-drawn delivery waggons.

Many children from Langport and Burrowbridge have good reason to recall Sydney Pocock, for he endeared himself to them by giving free trips in his barges to Bridgwater, so that, once a year, they could enjoy a day on the sands at Burnham. During the four days of the Bridgwater Fair, and in the days before the arrival of the motor car, many people living in the villages alongside the river would use the barges to get to Bridgwater, a journey down-river that most would well remember, even if the return was a little hazy!

In wintertime, the River Tone was allowed to overflow into the Moors attracting large flocks of duck and geese. Wild-fowling had always been popular and many locals had their own long-barrelled shotguns ready for the shoot, drifting noiselessly into the thick reed beds in their camouflaged withy-boats. It was a centuries'-old 'sport' which supplemented both the dinner table and the pocket. In 1830 it was reported that the severe January weather had 'brought over to this neighbourhood vast flocks of wild geese, many of which fell to the guns of the numerous fowlers who were on the watch for them … three men at Lyng shot no less than fifty geese, all of which were sold at one shilling each'.[19]

When the hard frosts came, and the river froze over, skating was another popular sport, it being often possible to skate many miles without getting off the ice.

Mrs Nellie Exton, who earlier lived at Athelney, remembers her father, George Beck, hauling coal to Athelney for the railway station there and to Curload and Ham. Sometimes, when he was returning to Bridgwater, he would take her with him 'to run some shopping errands for Mother'. She recalls being told to sit still on the coiled ropes at the front of the barge. On occasions, she said, he would have to leave his barge at the dock after it had been loaded up with coal because the state of the tide was not right for him to get up the Parrett. This would then mean that he would either have to stop the night lodging locally or walk home. Then it would be necessary to leave in the middle of the night and walk back from Athelney to Bridgwater to reach his barge in time for the right tide.

Charles Clifford of Bridgwater recollects that many years ago, an old gentleman told him that, when he was a young lad of fourteen years of age, about 1910, he had a job during the summer, pulling the barges along the river when horses were not available, being hired out to local farmers during harvesting. The boys were required to wear thick leather belts around their waists to which was fastened the towing line of the barge. For this fatiguing work, they were paid 2s 6d a week!

In the early 1920s there was encouragement for many young men returning from the war, or who were unemployed, to emigrate to America and Canada to seek work, repeating the trend set in the 1870s and 1880s by earlier emigrants. Michigan was a popular destination for many from Somerset joining families that had gone there earlier and many boatmen, who felt there was little future at home, took advantage of this chance. Roy Beck recounts that two of his uncles went to America, starting their journey by hitching a lift on their father's barge from Ham to Bridgwater. Others were able to take a barge from Langport, booking their passage at a shipping office there, which adjoined the old gas works.

Wallace Musgrave, who, before retirement, was responsible for operating the Aller Moor pumps at Burrowbridge for the Aller Moor Internal Drainage Board, recalls the day when, as a boy, he watched as a steam traction engine brought in a new boiler for the pumping station in 1912.

It took all day to manoeuvre the giant boiler on its trailer into the cramped confines of the premises and although there was scarcely any traffic on the road in those days, it was still a difficult task that took a lot of skill and effort.

The Conservators' barge returning to Taunton after an inspection around 1910. The branch to the Chard Canal was in front of the two cottages – one of which was the lock-keeper's (demolished in the late 1950s), and the other was the White Lion Inn, used by boatmen on both canals.

Bridgwater and Taunton Canal in the 1920s looking towards Hyde Bridge and Taunton. This rural scene has now been replaced by a motorway bridge.

The lock-keeper's cottage on the Bridgwater and Taunton Canal, at the junction of the now abandoned Chard Canal. (All photographs courtesy of J.E. Cole, Creech St Michael)

Angling on the river was always a popular sport, as well as providing for the dinner table. It was possible to hide away amidst the rushes and also do some wild-fowling.

London. Pub.ᵈ May 1 1822. by R. Ackermann, 101 Strand.

Nearer Taunton, the townsfolk were able to walk to the riverside, and fish from the footbridges and weirs, such as at Firepool and Obridge.

He also remembers the coal barges coming up the river and the two boatmen shovelling the coal into the wicker baskets. One would hoist the filled basket on to the shoulders of the other for him to carry across the gangplank and up to the coal yard.

It was unimaginably hard and tiring work, shovelling up and delivering that coal, particularly when you bear in mind that they had probably started the day loading up the barge at Bridgwater in the first place!

A steam suction dredger, in the canal outside Bridgwater Dock in the early 1920s.

Perchance to Dream

With the demise of canal traffic, an important chapter in the story of waterways to Taunton ended, and, with it, an industry that had played an important part in the developing prosperity of the county for over 200 years. The enterprise of those 'thirty-four gentlemen from Taunton' who had petitioned Parliament to allow them to improve the river to Taunton, had now been replaced by a more modern and efficient competitor, the railway and, shortly after, the motor vehicle.

No longer would the dock at Bridgwater witness the canal barges coming alongside the colliers to be supplied with coal; no longer would the locks echo to the sound of swirling water as the keeper watched the barges through the chamber; no longer would the towpath resound to the slow and methodical tread of the horses as they trudged their

Some found the approach to Bridgwater Dock a little difficult. The *Martha* is shown here aground in the Parrett in November 1921. She was later re-floated and enabled to discharge her cargo of timber. (Courtesy of the Douglas Allen Photography Collection)

The *Anna* in Bridgwater Dock around 1900.

way along the canal, hauling their heavy cargoes to Taunton and back. All would now be quiet. The riverside wharves, once a scene of great activity, would shortly fall empty and derelict. As for the boatmen and their families, many of whom lived close to the canal which had been their livelihood for generations, they were no longer needed and their skills would soon be forgotten.

The Conservators of the River Tone, however, certainly had no intention of abandoning their responsibilities and continued to carry out their annual inspections. The Great Western Railway maintained the canal as before, but now with an obvious reluctance. For the five years 1908–12, they stated that 'the excess of expenditure over receipts was as much as £11,182 … this being the amount mainly involved in dredging the mud and vegetable fibre from the decaying weeds – a task carried out three times a year'.[20]

In 1911, the treasurer to the Conservators reported that there had been no barge traffic on the canal now for four years. It was suggested that in future, their inspections should include Bridgwater Dock as well, but it was two years before the matter was considered again, the difficulty being that their double deck barge was too high to pass under the Huntworth Road Bridge! Before anything further could be done it was 1914 and the country was at war. Little was done on the canal for the next four years; the war effort absorbed a number of local railwaymen, called up for military service, many of whom had previously worked on the dock and canal.

The Conservators Resume their Canal Inspections

At the end of hostilities, attention was once again given to the state of the canal, the Great Western Railway being keen to ensure it was in a condition good enough to keep them supplied with water for their own purposes. The Conservators resumed their duties; their first meeting after the war was held in the offices of their treasurer, Mr C.H. Goodland in Taunton, when it was agreed that the next annual inspection that year would go through to Bridgwater Dock, 'with luncheon at the Clarence Hotel in Bridgwater, and return by rail.'[21]

Despite the fact that the canal had now been closed for nearly fifteen years, there were still matters that needed the Conservators' attention. In 1922, they passed under the new Priory Road bridge in Taunton and stated that 'the headroom was found to be ample, in fact far greater than necessary – the distance from the lowest girders of the bridge to the platform of the barge being no less than 5ft!'[22] All through the 1920s and the early 1930s a professional photographer travelled with the Conservators on their inspections and the record he made has since been invaluable in the subsequent restoration work, capturing views of many features of the canal that no longer exist.

Although there were no traders in Taunton using canal barges, the Conservators hired one from the Great Western Railway at the dock. Messrs Goodlands were able to supply the horses for in those days they were still used to draw the coal carts around Taunton. A day or so before the inspection would take place, two horses would be relieved of their regular duties on the streets and be taken along the towpath to Bridgwater to collect the barge. This gave the horses a 'dry-run' giving them an opportunity of getting accustomed to hauling a barge, and at the same time enabling the towpath to be checked to see it was in passable condition. During the early 1930s, this was a duty entrusted to Tom Milton, a foreman, in charge of horses at Goodlands.

The barge, after being collected from Bridgwater Dock, would be drawn down to Taunton, to be cleaned and prepared ready for the Conservators' inspection, with seating added and an upper deck assembled.

The inspection day was similar in most respects to those of the previous century; the Conservators and their guests would embark at the Conservators' Steps at the North Town Bridge and proceed down the river to Firepool and thence to Huntworth. A record of one such trip was kept by the foreman in 1924:

	OUT	BACK
Firepool	9.08	21.20
Bathpool	9.48	
Creech St Michael	10.10	
Durston	11.07	
Higher Maunsel Lock	11.19–11.27	
Lower Maunsel Lock	11.30–11.35	
Kings Lock	12.00–12.04	
Standards Lock	12.21–12.26	
Huntworth Bridge	13.07	17.07

The Conservators carrying out their inspection at Maunsel, 1921.

The Conservators carrying out their inspection, 1924.

An interesting account appeared in the local newspaper at this time, recounting a Conservators' inspection:

> The Money Boat's a'comin! That is the cry which is heard in the villages along the Bridgwater Canal on the July day when the Canal Commissioners [sic] make their voyage of inspection. The hey-day of the canal is gone, but one memory of it is brought to life again when the Commissioners' double-decked barge goes ceremoniously along the river from Taunton to Bridgwater in the morning and back in the evening. As the great decorated barge is drawn steadily along by splendid horses, decked in equine finery, its passengers throw copper largesse to the children who run in small crowds along the banks. Some of the children make quite a harvest, and the writer was told of one determined small boy who was said to have kept up with the boat all day, and at the end of which he was the possessor of what was to him a small fortune.

The accounts of the Conservators for 1928 show that the work of assembling and dismantling the 'upper deck' was carried out by H.J. Manley & Son, Coach Builders and Wheelwrights, at Belvedere Road, Taunton, for £2 10s 0d.

The annual inspection by the Conservators of the River Tone, 1921. (Courtesy of the Conservators of the River Tone)

Children following the 'money boat', 1924.

The Conservators of the River Tone at Firepool, Taunton, 1925, at the start of their annual inspection. While the horses and the towing ropes are being prepared, bets are being placed on how long the journey to Huntworth will take! (Courtesy of the Conservators of the River Tone)

After 1932, it was decided that the old GWR barge that the Conservators had used every year since they resumed their inspections after the First World War, was no longer serviceable, and they looked for another from the few remaining Bridgwater firms that still possessed them. In 1933 they used a barge belonging to the Somerset Trading Co. in Bridgwater, but experienced difficulties as '… it was too wide to be squeezed through the locks'. The following year Mr C.H. Goodland approached Messrs H.J. and C. Major of Bridgwater, for it was known the firm possessed a 'small' barge that might be suitable. The barge, however, was not so small as the Conservators probably imagined, for it had a beam of 13ft 3ins, whereas the locks were 13ft 4ins at their narrowest! It was going to be a tight fit, but the boatman was confident all would be well. And so it was to prove, and the barge was hired annually for subsequent inspections, the last being in July 1938.

Fortunately a written account of this last canal inspection carried out before the Second World War was made by Sam Stagg, one of the carters employed by Messrs Goodlands at the time, and who was present on the occasion. There were four men involved in 'looking after everything for the barge'. As well as himself, there were other carters, including Titch Rowsell and Snowball Stowells, a nickname the latter enjoyed on account of his white hair.

There would be two Horsemen to lead the horses, and slip the ropes at certain bridges and at all the locks, a Prowman – who rode at the prow of the barge as the ropeman, seeing

Bathpool, 1925. The horse-drawn inspection barge of the Conservators of the River Tone, passing the opened swingbridge. (Courtesy of the Conservators of the River Tone).

The Conservators of the River Tone at play! Their annual canal inspections, here in 1923, usually ended with an outdoor skittle match at Huntworth before the return journey. (Courtesy of Somerset Record Office)

to the ropes – and a Bridgeman – who was responsible for the opening and closing of the several swingbridges.

The barge was a sixty-tonner, used by a Brick and Tile Works at Bridgwater to transport sand up from Burnham. The empty barge would be put into the canal on the Monday's high tide, ready to be brought to Taunton the following day.

The two horsemen would walk their horses – on this occasion, a mare called *Smart*, and another called *Prince* – down the towpath to the harbour gates, and return with the empty barge to Firepool lock, where it would be let through into the River Tone. Here, the bargee would pole it upriver to Messrs Colthurst, where it would be moored for the night.

The next day, the barge would be prepared for the journey by employees of Messrs Colthurst, erecting the upper deck, and turning the lower part into a neat saloon, complete with tables and chairs, whilst a number of folding chairs were placed on the upper deck for use during the trip, having to be laid flat when the barge was approaching a bridge! The two horsemen would stay in the yard and stables all that day cleaning the special 'trace' harnesses, kept specially for towing the barges. Polishing all the brasswork took a lot of time, alongside the other items which had to be prepared and cleaned, such as face pieces, martingales [leather straps running from the reins to the girth of the horse to prevent it raising its head too high] rib pieces and loin straps. Rosettes and leading reins were then attached to both sets of harnesses, the whole being 'all well-ribboned in red, white and blue braids'. Lastly, two feeds had to be prepared for the horses, to be put on board the barge for their midday meal next day!

On the day of the inspection everything is ready. The horses are fed early and taken down to Firepool lock, to meet the barge which had been poled down-river to join them with the Conservators and their invited guests already aboard. Once the barge has been taken into Firepool lock, not only are the food and drinks put aboard by Messrs Maynards, but the Conservators' Treasurer brings aboard two bags containing £10-worth of pennies. This is the moment for the horsemen to get the towing ropes ready; they are laid out along the towing path, one longer than the other, in readiness for attaching to the harnesses of the horses.

It is 9 a.m. and now follows one of those quaint traditions that has been enacted since the Conservators were first empowered to inspect the canal; their commodore, Harold Goodland, resplendent in his admiral's cap and white lanyard and whistle, demands entry into the canal in the name of the King, the National Anthem is sung and he strikes the outer lock gate three times before it is opened. The inspection is now under way. Meanwhile, down in the saloon, their treasurer lays out his green baize table cover, opens his ledger that has been used for the purpose for countless years, and takes bets on how long the journey will take this time.

The average speed of a good horse, walking, is 4 miles an hour. From Taunton to Bathpool, handfuls of the pennies were thrown to groups of children on the canal bank, and, if a man or woman was there with a babe in arms, the bargee would be told to point into the bank, the baby having some pennies put into its hand. The first stop was at the old Durston Boat Repair Yard, where after a short break the trip would continue 'at a fair pace' before coming to the first lock.

After we had passed through the last of the five sets of locks, and going nicely, we would hear the shout, 'stop, stop', followed by others yelling, 'go on, go on, keep going', being the shouts of members who had laid their various bets on the time to be taken. Eventually we

The canal on the outskirts of Bridgwater, 1938. (Both photographs courtesy of the National Rivers Authority)

Lower Maunsel lock, 1938. Even though the canal had been disused for over thirty years by this time, the lock has been kept in fine condition.

reached Huntworth Bridge, which was as far as the party went …That year was the fastest time recorded … 4 hours 1 minute, after such endeavours. The tables in the saloon would be laid out for lunch, the vegetables having been cooked by the people in the house by the bank at boat stop. The horses would be led into a little paddock, unharnessed and fed, while the four of us would carry the drinks across the bridge into a field where a portable skittle alley had been fixed up.

Later in the afternoon, around five o'clock, the horses would be harnessed up, the barge turned and tea taken in the saloon. At 6 p.m. the return journey would commence, a very pleasant trip, with plenty of songs.

At the end of the journey, the barge would be tied up alongside Messrs Colthurst's premises, the Bargee sleeping on board in the small cabin which the barge possessed at the prow. The next day the timber structures would be dismantled and the barge returned to Bridgwater, the horses coming back to Taunton, this time by rail in a cattle truck. The two horsemen, the prowman and the bridgeman received thirty shillings extra pay for their duties, a lot of money in those pre-war days![23]

Maintaining the Canal – GWR Style

Photographs taken during those inter-war years show how well the canal was maintained. No doubt as a result of the Conservators' annual inspections, the lock gates and chambers, the sluices and ground paddles were all kept in working condition, a fine testimony to a canal which had closed to navigation nearly thirty years earlier.

The canal had now become an important land drainage channel and the railway was obliged to ensure that it was free-flowing. To control the flow of water through the canal from the Tone, the canal lengthsmen could be called up through an internal telephone system, installed by the railway and much the same as they used on their rail network, and advised as to the adjustments to be made to water levels. The telephones were installed at Firepool, in the familiar 'black huts' at Durston (which was the main centre for operations on the canal), Lower Maunsel, Standards lock and at the Dock Office at Bridgwater. At Firepool there was also a small building adjacent to the lock, housing a water meter which recorded the amount abstracted from the canal to the company's pumping station there. This attractive instrument can now be seen at the British Waterways Museum at Gloucester Docks.

During the early 1930s, in response to an increase in traffic and the growth in holiday excursions, the Great Western Railway quadrupled its main line between Cogload and Norton Fitzwarren. This required additional water troughs to be provided at Charlton, where there were already troughs for two of the lines, and an extension to their pumping station to accommodate the necessary pumps.

The canal, as well as the river, had always attracted bathers, and the local youngsters no doubt found the water irresistible during the long hot summers, particularly when few had the means to get to the public baths in Taunton. The half-locks on the river were particularly popular, for the long arms of the lock-gates were sufficiently 'springy' to make excellent spring boards for diving and jumping in. The half-lock just down-river

Creech St Michael School *c.*1930. Swimming lessons in the canal (changing hut on the right), at North End swingbridge. (Courtesy of F. Thatcher and J.E. Cole)

of Ham Mills was a favourite place, where, on a summer evening, the local youths would congregate and enjoy swimming in the river until dusk.

At Creech St Michael through the 1930s, the children were able to use the canal for swimming, for there was a section near the North End swing bridge where a wider section had been fenced off to form a small, and relatively safe, bathing area. It was quite popular at the time, and many residents in Creech still recall how, as schoolchildren, they were taken there for swimming lessons.

Whilst there are no records that the children, or indeed their parents, found this arrangement anything other than satisfactory, these days it is emphasised that swimming in canals is strongly discouraged, for not only are there hazards of jagged debris and weeds to catch the unwary swimmer but there is a considerable risk of disease from contaminated water. It is inevitable that farm effluent and drainage from the fields ultimately ends up in the canal, quite apart from the effects of rodents and other wildlife along the canal banks. Whilst the waters might seem attractive in hot weather, they are certainly far from safe for swimming.

THE CANAL IN WARTIME, 1939–45

With the luxury of hindsight, it seems faintly incongruous that the Bridgwater and Taunton Canal could ever have been seriously considered as an important line of defence for this country during the Second World War. However, it must be remembered that during the early stages of that war, this country had witnessed invasions of other countries in Europe carried out so swiftly that the defenders were left stunned. In the early 1940s a sea-borne landing in England was a distinct possibility, and experience in France at that time had shown that even relatively strong defences and barricades were no deterrent to the heavy armour and tanks of an invading force.

Along with the south coast, it was soon recognised that the south-west peninsula of England was particularly vulnerable to invasion. It was necessary to defend this corner of England, with its important deep-sea harbours, naval port and airfields, all of which were crucial in protecting the Western Approaches. It was necessary to construct, as quickly as possible, a defensive 'box' from the Bristol Channel to the English Channel, with natural features being used wherever possible, in order to hasten the work.

One part was to be known as the 'Taunton Stop Line'. It commenced at Pawlett Hams, on the eastern side of the River Parrett, and continued round Bridgwater and along the Bridgwater and Taunton Canal to Creech St Michael, where it followed the line of the Chard Canal, via Wrantage and Ilton to Axminster and, ultimately, the South Coast.

> Almost the entire length of the Line is built on canals or railway embankments, so it formed a very effective anti-tank barrier … on the stretches of the Line where the Chard Canal was in tunnel, a deep anti-tank ditch was cut.[24]

The whole line, a little over 44 miles long, contained over 350 pill-boxes and, to achieve some deception, a few were disguised as cottages and half-timbered lodges. Those along the canal were spaced at roughly a fifth of a mile apart. Nearly all were octagonal, some built in 3ft thick mass concrete, while others were in rendered brickwork, and would have been proof against the artillery pieces of an initial enemy invasion force. They were built to accommodate men using nothing heavier than Lewis guns and rifles.

The construction of the pill-boxes, as well as the other obstructions, was carried out by private contractors and at a time when most building materials were in short supply. Naturally this work took precedence due to the war-time situation. Early in June 1940, representatives of a number of local building contractors assembled in Taunton, under the chairmanship of William Stansell, at that time a Conservator of the River Tone, and were told of the arrangements that would have to be made to build the pill-boxes and remove the swingbridges.[25] The work of building this Stop Line assumed top priority, and the contractors were expected to work a seven-day week to get the structures completed. In a little over five weeks the task was mainly accomplished, but the situations of the pill-boxes were determined solely on military requirements and not on the convenience of the contractors. Some pill-boxes were situated in the most inaccessible locations along the towpath, where the contractors' workmen had to barrow the concrete along lengthy barrow runs; a scene that would have been reminiscent of the days when the navvies first cut the canal.

The approaches to the bridges over the canal carrying main roads, such as those at Bathpool, Creech St Michael, and Taunton Road, Bridgwater, were provided

Standards lock, 1951. Note the concrete 'crocodile teeth' installed at the lock chamber as part of the Taunton Stop Line precautions. These have now been removed, as also, unfortunately, has the lock-keeper's cottage. (Courtesy Roger Sellick)

with anti-tank obstacles, whilst the low-level swingbridges across the canal were quickly dismantled to deny any convenient crossing from the adjacent fields. This last precaution was, however, ill considered, for many farmers either owned or tenanted land on both sides of the canal, and this precipitate action provoked a minor crisis, especially when farmers were being urged to cultivate all their land to the maximum. The Army were hastily called in to throw across inexpensive, fixed, timber bridges at towpath level for twelve of the locations, though the others remain severed to this day, stark reminders of those war-time years. Forty years later, those twelve bridges were to create many more headaches and problems for the teams restoring the canal.

Although the decks and swinging mechanisms of the swingbridges were entirely removed at the time, one, at Crossways, near Hamp, unaccountably retained its original cast-iron central trunnion. It shows a design similar to those used by John Rennie on his swingbridges on the Kennet and Avon Canal, strengthening the view that some of his assistants worked on the Bridgwater and Taunton Canal. When this bridge was restored in 1986–87, this relic, although rusty and unusable in the replacement bridge, was carefully taken out and is presently at the British Waterways Museum at Gloucester Docks, awaiting restoration and display.

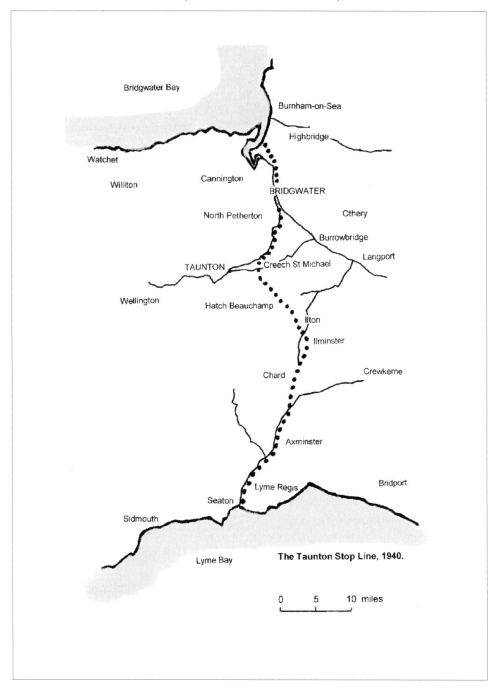

The Taunton Stop Line, 1940. A wartime defensive line between the English and Bristol Channels. Most of the line followed watercourses: the Rivers Parrett and Axe, and the Bridgwater and Taunton Canal.

Pill box at Charlton Pumping Station, Creech St Michael, August 2006.

The canal received little maintenance throughout those war years, save for ensuring that it remained 'watertight', particularly for fire-fighting and land drainage purposes, but some major works were occasionally necessary. The Great Western Railway was required to rebuild 'part of the retaining wall at the site of the children's school between West Street and Albert Street, Bridgwater, which had collapsed into the canal in 1940'.[26]

Bridge Street, Taunton, 1923. Showing the Conservators' Steps on the south-west side of the bridge – since removed when the adjoining site was redeveloped in the 1960s. (Courtesy of the Francis Frith Collection)

POST-WAR: A TIME OF AUSTERITY

At the end of the Second World War in 1945, the Conservators considered the possibility of resuming their annual inspections of a canal which still retained fixed swingbridges and pill-boxes along the towpath, but not until September 1947 was the inspection carried out, using a car and walking short lengths of the towpath, as this was still a time of petrol rationing.

Afterwards the Conservators wrote to the Great Western Railway:

> The condition of the canal at the Bridgwater end is deplorable; it resembles an open ditch more than a canal, and refuse is being dumped into it … the canal is not of good navigable condition, and owing to the swingbridges being fixed, the canal is not open for the passage of boats and other vessels laden with merchandise, as laid down by the Act of Parliament.

What it was exactly that brought about this seemingly uncalled for broadside from the Conservators is unclear, particularly since the railway itself had just emerged from five war-time years that had caused damage and wear to its own railway network. A canal that carried no traffic could hardly be seen as a priority!

The Great Western Railway engineers had already agreed with the Conservators that there were twelve swingbridges that needed to be attended to and the Conservators certainly intended to remind the Company that they had an obligation under their Act of Parliament to ensure the canal was navigable, whatever the circumstances. In October 1947 the Great Western Railway replied to the Conservators, pointing out that:

> … the twelve swingbridges were demolished by the Military during the war, and replaced by temporary, fixed timber bridges, which had the effect of closing the canal … correspondence has taken place with the Ministry in regard to the replacement of the temporary structures by permanent bridges, and the preparation of a design for the suggested new type of structure is now in hand by the company.[1]

At the end of the war, the inland waterways throughout the country were in a state of 'mouldering decay'. Some members of the public were concerned that, as an irreplaceable part of our industrial heritage and as a recreational asset, they should not be allowed to deteriorate further. The Inland Waterways Association was founded to campaign for the retention, development and restoration of waterways in Britain for the fullest recreational and commercial use and the legitimate enjoyment of all. During the last forty years or more it has played an increasingly important role in working to save and restore a number of canals that might otherwise have become permanently closed and abandoned. The Bridgwater and Taunton Canal would possibly have been one of them.

The Canal is Brought Under Public Ownership

As part of the Labour Government's programme of public ownership, the Transport Act 1947 created the British Transport Commission and established the four regions of a national railway network within a British Railway Executive. Many railway companies, at the time of this change, owned docks and canals and in the following year the operation and maintenance of these were transferred to the docks and Inland Waterways Executive. In the case of Bridgwater Dock and the Bridgwater and Taunton Canal, responsibility for the general upkeep was, from now on, to be carried out by the Western Region of British Railways which, in reality, meant much of the same personnel who were earlier working with the Great Western Railway.

By July 1950, a representative of the local branch of the Inland Waterways Association, Mr C.F. Clements, wrote to the Railway Executive, Western Region, reminding them that after two years the swingbridges were yet to be reinstated, only to be told that the executive was in no position to inspect the canal. It then added, in what must have been a bombshell to the Association and to Conservators for that matter:

> … in case you are not aware of the fact, I gather that the Somerset Rivers Catchment Board have suggested that consideration should be given to the transfer of this canal to them, for use as a flood drainage channel, and this matter is presently receiving consideration by the Railway Executive and the Docks and Inland Waterways Executive.[2]

The Somerset Rivers Catchment Board were successors to the Somerset Drainage Commission. At this time, the Conservators also wrote to British Railways reminding them that there was still no progress over the reinstatement of the swingbridges, only to be told that there were no developments in discussions with the War Department and, indeed, they saw little point in the Conservators, 'making an inspection of the Canal which cannot yet be used for navigable purposes'.[3]

Nothing developed from the suggestion that the canal be transferred to the Somerset Rivers Catchment Board, and by 1951 the Conservators were again demanding to know from British Railways 'when the canal can be used for navigational purposes, so that an inspection can be made, as laid down by Act of Parliament'. The continuing procrastination by both the Railway Executive and the War Department was no doubt largely due to disinterest by the parties to get this matter resolved, particularly as the time to have done this was soon after the war ended when the canal was still in the ownership of the Great Western Railway.

The deteriorating condition of the canal throughout the 1950s and '60s can be attributed directly to the lack of action over the 'fixed' swingbridges which made any form of economic maintenance and weed clearance quite impossible. The canal was quickly sliding into a condition of total disuse and abandonment, watched over by a seemingly disinterested Whitehall. It was faintly ironic that up to the outbreak of the war in 1939, the Bridgwater and Taunton Canal had remained perfectly navigable between the two towns. Now that it was in public ownership, was it to succumb finally to closure due to a petty squabble over a dozen swingbridges? The Inland Waterways Association and the Conservators were to have other ideas. With the one armed with growing public support and the other with an Act of Parliament, they began their fight for a future for the canal.

In 1952, through the efforts of a number of concerned people in the South West, the Inland Waterways Association established a West of England Branch, to start promoting the canal as a recreational asset within the county. They achieved a small measure of success by getting a 'motor-boat' ban lifted.

It was necessary, however, to view the retention of the canal in a wider context, an exercise that was probably beyond the expertise of the Associations' branch members. In 1954, the Inland Waterways Association commissioned the civil engineering firm of Cyril Boucher and Partners to report on the overall condition of the canal and the likely costs involved in phasing a restoration to full navigation. Surprisingly, they found the condition of the canal:

> … as a whole, comprising the waterway and the locks, remarkably good for a canal that has been without traffic for nearly fifty years. No extensive dredging or weed cutting is required, and no major repairs are necessary at any of the locks … the whole of the work could be carried out without difficulty, and completed within six months … at a cost of £12,500.

The 'fixed' swingbridge at North Newton in 1960. With their low headroom, or air-draught, most types of boats were restricted from using the canal for any great distance.

With such a rosy picture, it is understandable that the Association felt encouraged, particularly as the report raised the possibility that barges could still use the canal after some limited lengths had been dredged.

However, the British Transport Commission at the time had other ideas and did not see a future for the canal at all. They stubbornly resisted efforts to get the canal used again; traffic was barred from the canal and the locks were not allowed to be used and were padlocked. The canal, however, was kept reasonably clear of weed growth, fences were repaired and the banks and towpath maintained by a team of seven men kept permanently busy on the work.[4]

THE BOWES COMMITTEE OF INQUIRY

With a growing interest in the future of many inland waterways in this country, the Minister of Transport, Mr Watkinson, set up the Bowes Committee in 1955, assuring the House of Commons 'that we want to make the best use of our inland waterways'. Hugh Molson, his Parliamentary Secretary, suggested that 'the realisation of this aim might call for legislation to transfer the canals from the present authorities to local authorities or some other bodies'. The Ministry of Transport and Civil Aviation appointed the Committee of Inquiry into Inland Waterways with terms of reference requiring it to look at the economic use of canals, future administration, and the present law relating to their closure. The committee sought the views of interested parties and called for evidence on the state and condition of a number of inland waterways together with possible uses, before drawing up its recommendations.

No doubt heartened by the prospects offered by the Bridgwater and Taunton Canal at that time, a group of professional and businessmen at Taunton and Bridgwater drew up a proposal to buy back the canal into private ownership and operate it commercially for carrying goods. They believed that 'both the Dock and the Canal are not being used to the full advantage of the community and that the resources at present expended on the canal can be turned to profitable account'. They recognised that legislation would be needed to give effect to this example of de-nationalisation, which would have been the first of its kind in the country but claimed that by using the canal in this way, it would 'reduce substantially the price of coal and timber brought to Taunton and would develop the recreational use of the waterway'.[5]

In submitting their report to the Bowes Committee, the group stated that a prerequisite for the reopening of the canal would be to place both the dock and the canal under joint ownership and management. They added that the dock remained in use for the import of coal, sand and various minor shipments, but, whilst the canal has not been used for commercial traffic since 1907, it cannot be closed because of statutory requirements, as well as being important for land drainage, with its water being used for sluicing the dock as well as providing water for the railway troughs at Durston.

They mentioned that, apart from pleasure craft, traffic using the canal would be confined to timber and possibly coal. Taunton Gas Works would use approximately 250 tons of waterborne coal a week, at 5s 6d per ton from Bridgwater Dock, as opposed to

8s per ton by rail and 7s by road. For timber, canal transport would be 32s per standard (2½ tons), cheaper than rail transport and 6s per standard cheaper than by road. It was considered that a minimum of eleven barges would be required in the first instance, being 54ft x 13ft beam, and drawing not more than 3ft. Such craft could carry 60 tons of coal or fifteen standards of timber.

Although this proposal was a serious offer, it is very doubtful if it was either sufficiently researched or costed. Within a short time haulage of goods by rail or road would be infinitely cheaper than anything that could be undertaken on the canal, whilst the calculations over the capacity of the barges appear very suspect. With no mention of whether horses or motorised barges would be used, a cargo of 60 tons per barge appears optimistic when, in its hey-day, loads exceeding 25 tons were rarely recorded on the same sized barges drawing a similar depth of water.

It is, perhaps, not surprising that it had been submitted to the Bowes Committee, this proposal was taken no further. So soon after bringing the inland waterway network into public ownership, the committee would certainly not be attracted to the idea of selling off part to private interests. Furthermore, the future of Bridgwater Dock was far from certain and as the 1950s drew to a close, British Railways were giving serious thought as to whether they could continue to operate it commercially.

The Bowes Committee submitted its report in July 1958, and this was presented to Parliament, in the form of a White Paper, in February 1959. After carrying out a comprehensive survey of canals and inland waterways it proposed dividing them into three categories; those capable of carrying commercial traffic, cruising waterways and remainder waterways. The Bridgwater and Taunton Canal was relegated to the third category for it was considered that its usefulness for commercial traffic had disappeared, but it was still of value for drainage, water supply, recreation or amenity.

THE RIVER TONE FLOODS

The River Tone, and indeed the River Parrett, were notoriously prone to flooding but during the twentieth century the devastating effects of floods on the lowland to either side has been mitigated to a large degree, mainly through the building of heightened banks and a programme of dredging. However, within living memory there have been occasions of severe flooding along the Tone which have been equally disruptive and damaging as anything experienced in previous years.

In December 1929, for example, after days of continuous rain, the banks of the Tone burst near Curload and Athelney, causing great distress to the villagers whose houses were close to the river. The flooding lasted for many weeks and caused considerable damage on the Moors for the farmers as well. So isolated were the residents, with their village street under feet of water, that many were forced to stay in upper rooms for days on end. One resident can recall receiving her bread off the prongs of a pitchfork from a farmer below in a boat. A local newspaper, the *Evening World*, set up a distress fund, called the National Noah's Ark Fund, to help and raised over £30,000, an amazing figure in those days.

The River Tone floods at the Railway Inn, Athelney …

…and at Curload, December 1929.

Building the new sluice at New Bridge, River Tone, 1938. The 'old' bridge, built by the Conservators of the River Tone over 200 years before, seen to the left, was demolished in these works. (Courtesy of the National Rivers Authority)

The Somerset Rivers Authority carried out river-widening works and installed mechanically operated weirs and sluices at New Bridge during the 1930s. After 1945, there were many discussions on how best to create a River Tone flood alleviation scheme. The Tone's winding course to join the Parrett, its numerous obstructions in the form of weirs, locks and half-locks, and its shallowness, meant that after times of considerable rainfall it was often incapable of absorbing large volumes of water and dispersing them quickly. Before any measures were put in hand, a serious flood inundated the centre of Taunton during the last days of October 1960, causing damage and much disruption for many days. Station Road, the livestock market and the cricket ground were completely submerged, as was the A38 at Bathpool where a large area of low-lying land was also under feet of water.

The chief engineer to the Somerset Rivers Authority, E.L. Kelting, again investigated the possibility, already referred to, of using the redundant Bridgwater and Taunton Canal as a relief channel but, upon investigation, it was found that, apart from not being wide enough, the canal had too little 'gradient' along its length to get flood water away quickly. It was estimated that the work would cost around £1.7 million 'which was not considered commensurate with the probable benefits that would result'.[6] A scheme to scour out the River Tone, straighten it and remove obstructions was then considered, at an estimated cost of £660,000.[7]

Some idea of the obstructions to the flow of the river can be judged from an account of the Ham pound lock at the time:

When the lock gates at Ham fell into disrepair many years ago, one pair was replaced by a masonry wall across the lock with two openings in it. These openings were originally provided with timber sluice gates, but these, in turn, decayed, and in recent years, the openings have been closed in the summer by vertical timbers, to maintain the penning level. In March 1961, an 18 inch diameter penstock was fixed on one opening, and the other was blocked up.[8]

Repairing the river banks of the Tone after the 1929 floods. An intriguing solution that would most certainly be frowned upon today! (Courtesy Mrs N. Meade, Athelney)

Remains of the last barge on the River Tone submerged near Ham Mills. It was later blown up by Army engineers in November 1965. (Courtesy of the National Rivers Authority)

This comprehensive flood alleviation scheme for the River Tone was drawn up and provided for straightening out the course of the river below Taunton and giving considerable protection to the villages of Ruishton, Creech St Michael and Ham, as well as widening other stretches to Stanmoor Bridge. Work commenced in 1965, sweeping away many of the vestiges of the old line of the Tone navigation: its weirs, locks and half-locks that had caused generations of boatmen, and indeed the Conservators of the day, so much anguish and effort.

The Territorial Royal Engineers were called in to help the Somerset River Authority in carrying out the work:

> Over the past three weekends men of 205 (Wessex) Field Squadron RE (TA) from Weston-super-Mare and Bridgwater have demolished a half-lock at Ham. The work has included the blowing up of a quantity of masonry and concrete, so that the river can be widened and deepened. The Sappers have also blown up an old barge, waterlogged and filled with mud, which could not be moved by machinery. About 200 lbs of explosives have been used … these tasks provide valuable training experience as well as performing a useful purpose.[9]

It is certain that the present generation, with a more developed interest in conservation, would take a different view of this destruction. Apart from some old photographs, nothing remains today of the half-locks on the Tone and whilst these locks were probably difficult to retain, no doubt one could have been extracted and re-erected nearby as a permanent reminder of the way the river remained navigable over the centuries. As for the barge, a miraculous survivor of the years of barge traffic on the Tone, it is tempting to think that this could also have been carefully salvaged and, in time, repaired.

When all the works to widen and deepen the river had been completed, the Somerset Rivers Authority, together with the adjacent drainage boards, sought the abolition of the navigation functions on the River Tone, from a point at its junction with the Bridgwater and Taunton Canal to Stanmoor Bridge, at its confluence with the River Parrett.[10] The closure of navigation rights was confirmed in 1969,[11] thus bringing to an end an illustrious history of commercial traffic to Taunton of nearly 400 years.

The British Waterways Board is Established

Under provisions in the Transport Act, 1962, the British Transport Commission was abolished and canals and inland waterways became the responsibility of a new body, the British Waterways Board, charged with reviewing the whole canal investment in this country, together with the problems and liabilities of each waterway. The Board was to report in 1964 that the Bridgwater and Taunton Canal generated an income of about £6,500 each year, mostly from the sale of water to the Somerset Rivers Authority, whilst the annual cost of maintenance was around £11,000.

With a backlog of maintenance and repair work already pressing on some of the other 800 miles of canals, it would be some time before attention could be given to the Bridgwater and Taunton Canal although by 1963 the Board had established a depot at

The *Karlstad*, one of the many cargo boats using the dock in the 1950s. Wares Warehouse can be seen on the right-hand side. Loading and unloading was done using a travelling steam crane, but all the other features at the dock, such as the winches, the bascule bridge and the lock gates themselves, were worked entirely by manual labour. (Courtesy of D. House, Dykes Farm, Stoke St Gregory)

Durston, from where they directed the employment of a small team of men in continued maintenance which generally took the form of weed cutting and clearance in order to safeguard the water channel itself.

The Conservators of the River Tone who, since 1947, had still not carried out their annual inspection on the canal, decided in 1964 that in the coming year they would look at the canal again, although any question of achieving navigable condition would be premature in the circumstances; too much still had to be done. After a break of twenty-seven years, a visit was arranged for 1 September 1965, a feat made possible by the co-operation of the regional engineer for the southern division of the British Waterways Board, F.C.B. Clayton. The Board provided for the occasion an iron 'shoe', which was towed by a motorised weed cutter between Bathpool and Higher Maunsel lock. After that, the Conservators met annually, with the continued assistance of the Board, but these later inspections were usually carried out using small boats and a motor coach to get from one place to the next, as none of the locks were yet in working order.

BRIDGWATER DOCK – AN UNCERTAIN FUTURE

During the 1960s, the commercial viability of Bridgwater Dock declined considerably and its owners, British Railways, considered offering it for sale to any other public bodies that might be interested in running it on a commercial basis. They approached the Borough of Bridgwater who commissioned engineering consultants, Broughton and Partners, to look into the possibilities and to advise on what would need to be done to ensure a commercial future. Needless to say, if British Railways could not operate the dock successfully, it was unlikely that a local authority would be able to do so. It was a Victorian dock, with antique equipment, with few concessions to modern dock-handling techniques, and ill-suited to the needs of the larger vessels of the 1970s. Such were the estimated costs of both restoring the dock for continued commercial use and then running it, in view of the rapidly declining income from the few vessels that still docked there, that in their report of 1966 the consultants convinced the Borough that they should not proceed with any purchase.

Traffic at the dock in 1963 showed that there were 350 dockings by coasters, with a further fifty from vessels trading overseas, compared with over 660 dockings at the more modern facilities at Dunball, just down-river of Bridgwater, over the same period. As was to be expected, coal was the chief cargo to Bridgwater Dock, but even this only amounted to just 59,000 tons, with an additional 29,000 tons of sand and just over 20,000 tons of timber and woodpulp.[12]

A Remainder Waterway

The duties and powers of the British Waterways Board were revised by the Transport Act of 1968. In order to direct limited funds to the most deserving cases, Parliament used the three categories devised some years earlier, for maintenance purposes: commercial waterways, cruising waterways and remainder waterways.

The Bridgwater and Taunton Canal, as a 'remainder waterway', had become little more than a land drainage channel. The Board were required to carry out their works of maintenance and repair in the most economical manner possible, whilst constrained to keeping the canal only in a safe condition. Any works to achieve a recreational use would need to depend upon finance provided from other sources, such as local authorities and amenity societies.

Within months, and with cruel irony, as if the new custodians of the canal needed any reminder of the problems of inheriting an old canal, a major collapse of the retaining walls in the cutting between Albert Street and West Street in Bridgwater brought down hundreds of tons of earth, which blocked the canal and the towpath. It was not immediately clear what had brought about this collapse but the Board ultimately found it necessary to shore up the remaining walls in the cutting with both vertical and horizontal timbers, many of which are still in position today. The canal was later cleared of the debris, for the water channel had to be maintained to the dock, but the wall was not rebuilt and the earth from the slipped bank was left, blocking the towpath for more than nine years until cleared as part of the works to restore and reopen the canal.

The Conservators in an 'iron shoe', being towed by a weed cutter for their annual inspection.

A Year of Destiny

1969 was a critical year for both the dock and the canal. After years of poor trading, the owners of the dock, the British Railways Board, finally announced its closure. The necessary Parliamentary Act was secured to effect its closure, after the British Waterways Board had insisted that there be provisions included to safeguard their canal in the event of the dock being disposed of. These provisions required the installation of concrete walls across the lock at Newtown, separating the canal from the dock, and walls across the two dock entrances to the Parrett. Whilst the dock would now be effectively isolated from the canal and the river, sluices through the walls would allow a slight flow through to prevent the water becoming stagnant. Furthermore, a new weir was to be built by British Railways at Hamp, where the canal runs alongside the Parrett, which would act as an overflow between the two, now that the route through the dock was no longer available.

The dock, at the time of its closure, had been sadly neglected for many years and was in a poor and run-down condition, with lock gates inoperable and many of the dock-side features either broken or removed for scrap. The historic scraper boat (also known, misleadingly, as the dredger), now considered to be the oldest, working steam-operated vessel in the country, was removed to the Maritime Museum at Exeter.

To complete this distressing picture of the demise of the once distinguished and prosperous maritime industry in the town, the British Waterways Board applied successfully to be relieved of their responsibilities of ensuring navigation on the canal, a status it can hardly be said to have enjoyed since the swingbridges had been fixed in 1940.

RESTORATION OF THE CANAL

Towards the end of the 1960s, there developed a ground swell of public opinion that perceived a future for the abandoned waterway, if not for the dock itself. With the canal in public ownership and a growing awareness of the need to provide recreational facilities many saw that its restoration for leisure use, including boating, could well be possible.

The West Somerset Section of the Inland Waterways Association produced a report, 'The Bridgwater and Taunton Canal – Waterway with a Future'. Its principal authors were C.P. Clements and Mrs Rosemary Sixsmith, both redoubtable campaigners for the restoration of Somerset's waterways and founder members of the Somerset Inland Waterways Society, successor to the West Somerset Section of the IWA.

The report set out the case for the preservation and use of the canal as a 'linear' country park, affording potential for limited boating, angling and rambling, together with the protection and care of canal-side wildlife and habitat. The Countryside Act in 1968 conferred powers upon local authorities to provide rural recreational facilities for public enjoyment. The IWA Report was widely circulated throughout the county, particularly to those in local authorities. It confirmed the views then being formulated by the British Waterways Board and Somerset County Council, that a case could be made for arresting any further decay on the canal, and that its 'recreational' future should be planned for and, indeed, actively promoted.

THE FIRST STEPS: THE COUNTY COUNCIL TAKES THE INITIATIVE

As early as 1966 Somerset County Council asked the county planning officer to consider the possibilities of establishing a water-based recreation use of the canal. Subsequently, the Countryside Act, with its concept of country parks, and the imminent extension of the M5 motorway through Somerset, which, it was perceived, would bring more tourists into the county, provided the impetus to prepare positive plans for the canal.

By 1970, the county planning officer had reported to the county council that, 'it would be desirable that the county council should take an active interest in ensuring that … the present character and condition of the canal does not deteriorate'. Commenting upon the recent closure of Bridgwater Dock, he added that there was a need 'to retain the Dock as an attractive water feature', emphasising that the dock was an integral part of the recreational potential.[1]

Lower Maunsel, 1970. The use of concrete for the balance beams is interesting and was probably adopted shortly after the First World War. (Courtesy of Somerset County Council)

The cast-iron 'ball and chain' design for the counterbalance weights to the ground paddles at the lock chambers.

A drawing of Kings lock.

The report was adopted by Somerset County Council who, recognising the potential it offered for 'low-key' recreation, agreed to contribute funds to improve the general standard of maintenance, and more importantly perhaps, to offer grants to the British Waterways Board in order to ensure a programmed restoration of the four locks, at Higher and Lower Maunsel, Kings and Standards.

By this action, the county council signalled their belief that this abandoned canal did have a future and that it still represented a considerable capital asset within the county. Over time, it could be progressively restored to meet the ever-growing interest in water-based recreation, such as 'quiet' navigation in canoes and dinghies, angling, nature study or walking. The work to be done and the allocation of the necessary finance would all need careful planning and control, and to do this the county council set up a canal panel with a small number of members, which would meet quarterly to assess priorities and progress.

In April 1971, as a means of introducing these members to their new world of canals, the County Planning Officer, together with John Vincent, the Chairman of the County Planning Committee, and Ron Oakley, at the time secretary to the south-west branch of the IWA, organised a visit to the Monmouthshire and Brecon Canal in South Wales, where they were able to meet officers of the Brecon Beacons National Park and see for themselves the scope of canal restoration, and the work being done there. The visit obviously achieved the desired effect, for within the next three years, work was underway on the Bridgwater and Taunton Canal, with the restoration of the lock gates at both

Bathpool swingbridge, 1966. The deteriorating condition of this 'fixed' bridge caused increasing concern during the 1970s.

The 'tunnel' at Albert Street, Bridgwater, where the canal is in deep cut, with substantial retaining walls both sides.

Higher and Lower Maunsel, together with the renewal of their lock mechanisms, the work being carried out by the British Waterways Board and funded entirely by the county council at a cost of £2,500. By the end of the following year, over £15,000 had been allocated by the county council to meet the costs of additional maintenance to the towpaths, dredging and weed-cutting.

With the re-organisation of local government in 1974, the 'new' Somerset County Council sought to work closely with the new councils of Sedgemoor and Taunton Deane, through whose areas the canal flowed. At the same time, the work and duties of the Somerset Rivers Authority were transferred to a new body, the Wessex Water Authority. Early the following year, membership of the canal panel was extended to include representation from both district councils, for it was agreed that there would be a joint financial input into the work on the canal.

1974 also saw another change, for the West Country branch of the IWA was formed. Over the following two decades, this branch was to be keenly supportive of the work of the local authorities and the British Waterways Board, contributing precious funds and, perhaps of greater importance, organising boating festivals and canal functions as and when restoration permitted.

Somerset County Council Purchases Bridgwater Dock

The county council, after more than three years of negotiations with British Railways, purchased Bridgwater Dock in December 1974. Whilst of no commercial value, it possessed considerable historic and amenity quality as a relatively unaltered survivor of the industrial legacy of Victorian Bridgwater.

Throughout its 130 years it had accommodated the growth in river traffic, but by the early 1960s it came as no surprise that its owners had found it uneconomical to run and decided to close it down. Throughout the years it had made few concessions to modern dock-side handling; all its equipment, locks, flood gates, sluices and cranes were manually operated by gangs of men using chains and winches. Even the double bascule bridge, which carries a public highway over the dock, was operated in a similar manner, taking 15 minutes to raise and slightly less to lower!

With public ownership of the dock and the possibility of a barrage scheme across the River Parrett, a major recreational feature based on boating and water-based activities seemed possible. The dock would need a considerable amount of money spent on it and the existing industrial leases on the land alongside would need to be reviewed and, where necessary, terminated, before plans could be drawn up for an appropriate redevelopment of the area.

The area engineer to the British Waterways Board, Roger House, was able to advise on the extent of the restoration work his Board could undertake on the canal, as well as the works that it would be necessary for the county council to undertake at the dock in restoring the long-derelict lock gates to the River Parrett and to Newtown lock. As the boats that would use either the dock or the canal would probably have a beam of no more than 12ft, it was decided that restoration would be confined to the barge lock, leaving the ship lock closed. With the agreement of the Board, the concrete wall inserted across the barge lock at the time of its closure was removed, although the ship lock was retained, later forming a convenient footway across the dock at this point.

Throughout the late 1970s, work proceeded on restoring the locks on the canal and raising the bridges to give a headroom of 4ft, with Kings and Standards locks and the bottom gates at Newtown being finished by 1980. By this time over £50,000 had been contributed by the county council to the British Waterways Board to finance those works, including maintenance, that were over and above their responsibilities for a 'remainder waterway'.

In September 1978, the first major restoration work on the canal was carried out by contract labour funded by both the county council and Sedgemoor District Council. This involved the grading back of the steep west bank of the cutting between West Street and Albert Street, Bridgwater – the scene of the retaining wall collapse of nine years earlier. The work also involved the clearing and levelling of the towpath and lifting of some of the low-level horizontal timber shores that had been inserted to safeguard further collapses. An existing but abandoned ramp was reopened, providing a popular link at West Street for pedestrians to reach the canal towpath.

In 1981, Sedgemoor District Council sponsored an employment scheme, under the auspices of the Manpower Services Commission, which offered work to a small team of local people who were unemployed, in what was to be the first of many such schemes organised by both the district council and the county council to assist in the restoration of the canal. In this case they worked on a scheme devised by Ben Coles, of Sedgemoor

Fordgate Farm – the canal-side barns.

District Council, and with the site staff of the British Waterways Board in dredging the length of canal between the dock and Albert Street, widening the towpath and building an access ramp for wheeled maintenance vehicles to reach the canal bank from Victoria Road.

THE OLD BATHPOOL SWINGBRIDGE – A CHANGE OF ATTITUDE!

By 1975, the condition of the timber, fixed swingbridge which crossed the canal at Bathpool was very poor indeed and it was doubtful whether it could continue to carry even the lightest traffic loadings for much longer. Thought was given to removing the bridge, closing the road access, and substituting a fixed pedestrian footbridge. It would have the agreed headroom of 4ft, which was the standard practice of the British Waterways Board for remainder canals. A scheme was drawn up in 1977 and a planning application submitted to Taunton Deane Borough Council early in 1978, to which there were numerous objections. These were mainly from inland waterway enthusiasts and canal users who pointed out that the 4ft headroom was insufficient and would prevent the use of the canal by all but the smallest craft. Subsequently, the application was deferred to 'enable a review to take place over the appropriate navigational headroom'.[2]

The consequences of this decision were far-reaching, for there was now a growing interest in accommodating boating on the canal, for which the 'air-draught' under bridges would need to be far greater. Once limited headroom was installed there would be little chance of achieving navigation upon the restored canal. Here was an opportunity to rethink the whole approach to the canal restoration. The British Waterways Board, in consultation with the Council for Sport and Recreation and the Countryside Commission, agreed that they would carry out a 'canal-length' review and report on the problems of the present low bridges in the light of the Board's amended policy where, in future, they would require a minimum 7ft 6ins headroom for navigational and maintenance purposes.

An independent body, the Inland Waterways Amenity Advisory Council (IWAAC) set up under the Transport Act 1968 to advise the Secretary of State for the Environment and the British Waterways Board on certain aspects of the recreational development of the Board's waterways, inspected the canal in September 1978. They had a responsibility to advise on the desirability of increasing the mileage of the national network of inland 'cruising waterways'. Their report was to reinforce the work of the British Waterways Board in their review of the low bridges on the canal, for they stated that they were anxious to secure a future for the whole Bridgwater and Taunton Canal as a 'cruising waterway' and would support an application to the Secretary of State to that effect, when the time was right and the bridges raised.

These views were not only helpful but timely. The British Waterways Board themselves were undertaking their review and formed a Joint Working Group, with the assistance of officers from the three local authorities, to 'prepare both a Recreational and Restoration plan for the canal, taking into account the needs of recreation, the obstacles to navigation, the cost and the likely benefits'.[3]

The report, 'A Canal and its Future', set out three options:

1) Optimum Development. A long-term policy to restore the canal for navigation as opportunities arise and public finances allow and in the short term to carry out environmental improvements, provide low-cost recreation facilities and safeguard the canal's future with appropriate planning policies.

2) Interim Development. To provide facilities for quiet recreation only, to carry out environmental improvements, but to make no safeguards for long-term restoration.

3) No Further Development. No recreational facilities would be provided, no environmental improvements would be carried out, no safeguards would exist for long-term restoration and as local authorities would not assist the British Waterways Board financially, the standard of maintenance would fall.

The first two options were supported by a summary of the works that would need to be done and their estimated costs, the third option requiring no works and therefore no additional expenditure. Using 1979 costs, it was indicated that option 1 would cost around £533,000, with the British Waterways Board contributing £229,000 and the balance being found from the local authorities and other contributors. For option 2 the costs were far less, a total of £60,000 needing to be met by the local authorities and other contributors as there would be no input from the board.

The report invited public comment, and these, predictably, polarised between the angling and boating interests, although it was pointed out that experience on numerous canals had shown that both interests could happily live alongside each other if neither use was excessive. After considering all the representations that were made on what was, in effect, the first attempt to programme a future for the canal, the county council and the two district councils adopted the first option and requested that the Joint Working Group be reconvened to report further on formulating possible policies based on optimum development, with proposals for a phased programme of restoration with their estimated costs.

THE BRIDGWATER AND TAUNTON CANAL: RECREATION AND RESTORATION PLAN

This second report[4] contained a study of the cost implications involved and the mile-by-mile format adopted made it quite clear as to the amount of work that would be necessary, with a likely time-scale, and the breakdown of costs between the participating authorities. It was ready for presentation to the respective councils in the summer of 1983.

It set out a range of environmental and restoration works to be carried out over a period of six years. Whilst the Board was still constrained to meeting only their statutory responsibilities for a 'remainder waterway', they were prepared to organise their financial involvement so as to coincide, wherever possible, with other works financed by the local authorities. Accordingly it was possible to draw up a programme of works, phased over

Newtown lock, Bridgwater Dock. A volunteer group from the West Country Branch of the Inland
Waterways Association get down to a spot of practical cleaning, 1980. (Courtesy of IWA)

the six years, ranging from tree-planting schemes and towpath resurfacing to the more
expensive rebuilding of the swingbridges.

The budgetary allocations indicated that alongside a total capital investment of over
£25,500 and an annual maintenance contribution of £60,000 by the British Waterways
Board, there would be a capital expenditure over the six years by the county council of
just over £200,000, by Sedgemoor District Council £44,000, and by Taunton Deane
Borough Council a little over £25,000. Each authority after the first few years would
contribute a further £5,000 per year to provide an increased level of canal maintenance,
brought about by the installation of features such as the rebuilt swingbridges and restored
lock chambers. It was envisaged that the Countryside Commission would contribute an
estimated £40,000 for tree planting and assistance in the purchase of land for canal-side
picnic sites and car parks. The report also reviewed other aspects of the canal, apart from
navigation, such as angling, countryside recreation, wildlife and its habitat and water
supply and land drainage.

After more than forty years of closure and stagnation, at last the Bridgwater and Taunton
Canal had a fully costed plan for taking it into the 1990s. The Report was considered by
all three local authorities and the British Waterways Board during the following months

and, in June the following year, the Canal Panel was informed that all had resolved to support the recommendations along with the financial commitments involved.

The advantage to each of the three local authorities and the British Waterways Board of this procedure was that it enabled them to pre-plan their work schedules well in advance and to prepare forward budgets with the knowledge that the other contributors were doing likewise, a precaution that was to prove invaluable when the authorities were faced in later years with the difficulties of trimming their spending budgets.

The West Country branch of the IWA, now under the energetic leadership of their new chairman, Tony Rymell, also resolved to adopt the plan and offered both to finance and undertake some of the works required. Their Waterway Recovery Group – a team of mainly weekend volunteers – would concentrate on cleaning rubbish from parts of the canal, particularly the lock chambers, whilst others of the branch would assist in creating short usable lengths of waterway along parts of the canal, rather than concentrating all efforts from the Bridgwater end.

The recreational development of the canal needed to take place within the overall policies of the Somerset Structure Plan, where several policies were directly applicable to the canal and its environs, particularly those relating to improved access to the countryside, the provision of facilities that improve recreational opportunities and the need to safeguard important landscape areas from potentially damaging development.

RESTORATION WORK COMMENCES

It was clear that if the varied range of tasks were to be carried out effectively, it would be necessary to establish a workforce which would be separate from those employed by the British Waterways Board: a workforce that could be deployed on duties as and when necessary. The Manpower Services Commission saw possibilities in this canal restoration scheme for work training for men and women experiencing long-term unemployment, particularly as the phased and varied work pattern provided a range of manual, supervisory and clerical tasks.

As owners of the canal, the British Waterways Board drew up the necessary details of an employment scheme for the Manpower Services Commission, to which the three local authorities would make additional financial contributions. It was agreed that in order to achieve a common direction for the projects undertaken, the county council should prepare the various work programmes, liaise with the Commission and the Board on behalf of the three authorities, act as co-ordinator and 'pay-master' for the team, and appoint the necessary supervisory staff. Phil Stone, in the County Planning Department, would give day-to-day direction to the work.

By the beginning of 1984 a Community Programme Scheme had been set up in the Sedgemoor area with a team operating from an office above the Magistrates' Courts in Bridgwater. Within eighteen months this temporary space proved too small and it was necessary to move to larger premises which could accommodate, not only the increase in clerical and manual staff, but a training room and outside space for stores and materials, tools and the vehicles, including a caravan, necessary for providing a refuge for the workforce

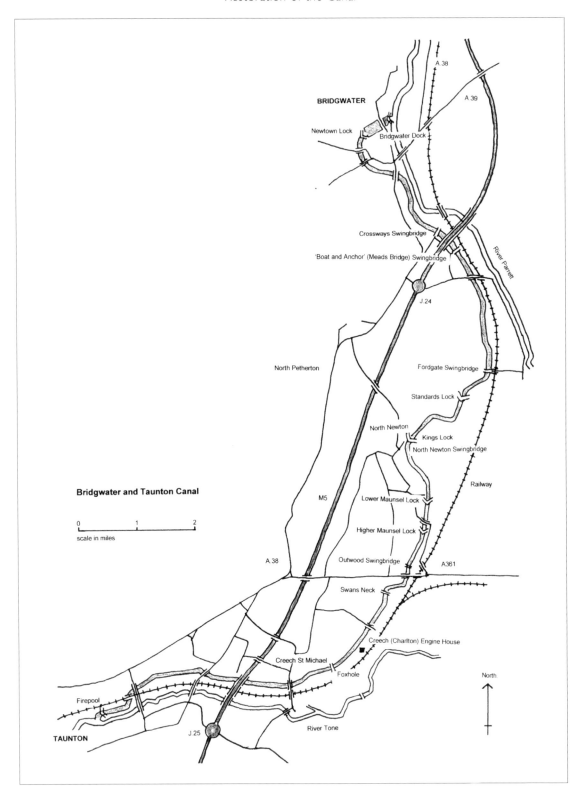

The Bridgwater and Taunton Canal.

Installed in 1981, the pedestrian swingbridge at Newtown lock replaced the earlier railway bridge.

during inclement weather. The county council possessed a property in Wembdon which was available at that time and which offered the appropriate temporary accommodation.

Over the next two years, a reliable workforce was established whilst the jobs they undertook consisted mainly of those over and above the responsibilities of the British Waterways Board, but which were necessary if the canal was to be restored to navigation. Before long the small tasks gave way to more demanding work as they all learnt new skills, and the team numbers rose, at one time reaching as many as thirty.

Considerable time and effort was put into resurfacing the canal towpath, for whilst the canal was unusable, its towpath was still a very popular walkway and in many places had become narrow, overgrown and muddy underfoot. Cutting back other undergrowth, bank stabilisation, and providing ramped approaches, as had earlier been done at the Victoria Road Bridge, was now carried out at Hamp Bridge so that mechanical plant could operate along the canal for maintenance. Clearing back vegetation and refashioning disused footpaths was also carried out at the neglected Browns Pond area just south of the canal, adjacent to the Taunton Road in Bridgwater, as well as at the Hamp clay pits area, where considerable numbers of trees were planted.

The work of the county councils' Dock and Canal Panel was now growing in complexity as it embarked upon a programme of restoration that would not be completed for another seven or eight years and there was the need to ensure continued employment for the workforce. In mid-1985 the decision was taken to establish the Panel as an

Advisory Committee, which, whilst having no executive powers would oversee the canal restoration and report directly to the County Planning and Transportation Committee.

User organisations, such as the Taunton and Bridgwater Angling clubs who had enjoyed fishing rights on the canal for over seventy years, ramblers, and those interested in the canal's unique historical importance would be able to meet British Waterways' Board's representatives annually to discuss problems and put forward their own ideas as to the future development of the canal. A few years later it was found more effective for representatives of the user organisations to be invited to attend the Advisory Committee meetings. The organisational framework was now in place allowing the major tasks in restoring the canal to be planned for and programmed into forward budgets with a certain degree of confidence.

THREE SWINGBRIDGES REBUILT – CROSSWAYS, BOAT AND ANCHOR AND FORDGATE

The major obstacle to reopening the canal to navigation was the presence of the twelve 'fixed' swingbridges, which had been closed since 1940. A further low railway bridge over the lock chamber at Newtown lock, owned by the Somerset County Council, had already been replaced by a pedestrian swingbridge in October 1981, but there still remained a concrete road bridge at Priorswood, on the eastern approaches to Taunton, also owned by the county council, that would need to be raised.

During 1986, a start was made on rebuilding the three swingbridges at Crossways, Boat and Anchor (also known as Meades Crossing) and, a little later, Fordgate. Each would require three phases of work: the provision of a temporary road crossing while the old bridge was removed and rebuilt; the renewal of the brick abutments, approaches and bases, the fabrication and positioning of the new bridge deck itself.

These would be major undertakings in themselves, and whilst the third stage of the work, the fabrication and positioning of the bridge deck, would be carried out by steelwork

The original design of the canal swingbridges at Bathpool, 1938.

The restored swingbridge at The Boat and Anchor, 1987.

The restored swingbridge at Fordgate, 1987.

specialists, it was considered that the workforce on the Community Programme Scheme was more than able to handle the other two stages. This would involve the installation of a temporary road bridge, which would first need to be assembled, using steel girders and timber decking, after which the old bridge could be removed, the brickwork to the abutments strengthened, and the bridge bases concreted in.

The design of the bridges was based closely upon the appearance of the originals which were shown in a number of old photographs. The county surveyor asked John Thomas and Dick Ambrose, engineers in his department's bridges section, to work with their counterparts in the British Waterways Board. They produced a design in steel with a timber deck, that was as near as possible identical in outline to the original, yet capable of carrying any vehicle licensed for British roads, although for frequent use a limit of 16 tons was considered suitable. The manufacture of the deck itself and the central trunnion mechanism upon which the bridge pivoted were of a specialist nature and involved complex engineering and were sub-contracted. After seeking competitive quotations, the contract was awarded to the engineering firm of White Horse Plant Ltd at Westbury, a firm that had, in 1981, provided the pedestrian swingbridge at Newtown, Bridgwater Dock. To meet present day highway requirements, each bridge had to possess a removable barrier so that the road could be closed on both banks while the swinging deck was in the 'swung off' position for navigational purposes.

At the time of the adoption of the Recreation and Restoration Plan, it was estimated that each swingbridge would cost £23,000; the cost being shared equally between the respective district council, the county council and the British Waterways Board. The reason that the Board were able to consider a financial contribution was that with an opening bridge, it was envisaged that this would allow weed cutting to be carried out from a boat using floating hoppers, thus greatly speeding up their own maintenance work.

The British Waterways Board agreed to lower the water level of the canal while the canal team inspected the brickwork to the bridges and where necessary, renewed and strengthened them, for they would now be receiving far heavier loads than hitherto and had not been maintained, perhaps, for more than 100 years. Whilst the decks were being fabricated, the team laid out and concreted the reinforced concrete bases for the central trunnion mechanism of the swingbridge. The three swingbridge decks were delivered in September 1987, the deck for Crossways being lowered onto its abutments on 24 September.

During the time when the rebuilding of the swingbridge at Crossways was underway, the Wessex Water Authority was itself carrying out works to the banks of the River Parrett, which required access over the Boat and Anchor swingbridge. As the old bridge was far too weak to carry this heavy equipment, the Water Authority provided their own temporary bridge, which they were able to leave in place at the end of the contract for a further few months. This enabled the canal team, after finishing at Crossways, to proceed immediately with the Boat and Anchor swingbridge contract without first having to provide their own temporary bridge. This speeded up the work considerably so that by December of that year, all the abutment work had been completed and the new deck installed, ahead of programme!

1987 also saw the installation of the third swingbridge, at Fordgate, fully a year earlier than originally planned. This stroke of fortune was brought about by a generous offer

The resurfaced access road and landing stage at Kings lock, with a small car park at the lock-side, built by the Canal Community Project team in 1988.

from the building firm Stansell & Son (Taunton) Ltd to carry out, at their cost, all the work necessary in building new abutments and reinforced concrete bridge bases. The attraction to all those involved in the canal restoration was that this firm could carry out these tasks in a couple of weeks, whereas the canal team would need possibly six weeks or more to do the same work.

Unlike the first two bridges, Fordgate carried no public road and was purely a farm accommodation bridge. With the agreement of the farmer, David Bere, who was prepared to forego vehicular access to his fields the far side of the canal during the month of December, it was possible to dispense with the need to erect a temporary road bridge. Within four weeks of starting work on site, the rebuilt abutments were finished and the new bridge deck was in position and working.

CAR PARKS AND PICNIC SITES

Since the days when it was agreed that the canal should be developed for recreational purposes, the search for suitable canal-side car park and picnic sites had continued, but with limited success. The undoubted appeal of this short canal is that it passes through quiet and attractive countryside, but this also means that access to it by vehicle is limited with few opportunities for parking.

Enhancement works at the lock chamber at Firepool, Taunton, carried out Taunton Deane Borough Council.

During the summer of 1986 an opportunity occurred at Lower Maunsel, where the owner of Brickyard Farm was prepared to sell a portion of the canal-side orchard for a car park and picnic site. It was an ideal location, for not only did the site itself contain a number of old and attractive trees, but it was within 50 yards of the lock at Lower Maunsel, perhaps one of the most popular spots on the canal. Site acquisition was completed by October of that year with grant aid from the Countryside Commission. The canal team carried out the levelling and surfacing work so as to have it open for the public by the following summer.

During 1987, two other important sites were laid out as car parks and picnic sites; one next to the British Waterways Board's canal depot at Bathpool and the other, a small car park adjacent to the Kings lock which, whilst not providing a picnic facility, at least allowed access to the canal-side and towpath. That year, with both sets of lock gates restored at Firepool lock by the British Waterways Board, Taunton Deane carried out an enhancement scheme there, laying paving around the locksides and providing sitting areas adjacent to Firepool Weir as part of an overall plan to improve the appearance of this once important, commercial part of the town. British Waterways Board constructed by-pass weirs at all the locks, so that they could control the flow of water through the canal once it was open to public use. Also, with an eye to public safety, ladders were fitted to each side of every lock chamber.

Maintenance Agreement

By this time the canal was navigable from Bridgwater Dock to Fordgate and discussions were held with Ian White of the British Waterways Board, who had taken over from Roger House as Aero Engineer, over the desirability of entering some form of agreement that, once the canal was navigable to Taunton, the canal could be upgraded from 'remainder waterway' to 'cruising waterway'. This improved status was important, for under the statutory limitations on expenditure placed upon the Board, a 'remainder waterway' was allowed only sufficient funds to ensure that the Board dealt with it 'in the most economical manner possible, consistent with the requirements of public health and the preservation of amenity and safety.'[5] If a successful application was to be made by the British Waterways Board for the canal to be reclassified they would need to show that these extra costs would be met by others and not fall upon their own budget: indeed, a programme of possible contributions by the public authorities was recognised in the 1983 Recreation and Restoration Plan, which outlined the annual costs each authority might be called upon to make.

The local authorities were therefore invited to enter into a Management Agreement with the board, which would set out the annual contributions expected of them, based upon the extra maintenance the board had carried out as each successive length of canal was opened to navigation. The board had used such agreements previously with the local authorities, and had, at that time, recently concluded a similar scheme with the county and district councils involved in the restoration of the Kennet and Avon Canal. With the completion of the swingbridge at Fordgate, at the end of 1987, the waterway was navigable as far as Standards lock, a distance of just under 4¼ miles from Bridgwater Dock. The maintenance agreement stipulated that the refundable costs to the Board would be based upon the mileage opened up to navigation. These were called 'step costs', and their amount would increase progressively as the canal restoration proceeded and it became available for boating. In April 1988 the three local authorities entered into a twenty-one-year agreement, a length of time not related to the completion of the works, but to the likely period required for a satisfactory reclassification to 'cruising waterway'. Once navigation to Taunton had been achieved, the British Waterways Board would be urged to initiate and support an application for such reclassification to the Secretary of State for the Environment.

At the beginning of 1989, a reorganisation by the British Waterways Board established a new regional structure, with Brian Rodgers at Gloucester being appointed Regional Manager. Richard Dommett, who had been associated with the canal since the mid-1970s, the Waterways Manager for the South West and South Wales, took responsibility for both the restoration programme and the canal's promotion, whilst Phil Cox was appointed his canal supervisor, based at Bathpool.

More Bridges

The rebuilding of the swingbridges had not been entirely successful in the early days, for their necessarily complicated design to accommodate heavy vehicles, while remaining

The farm accommodation bridge at Whites Dairy before being restored and raised to allow boats to pass under.

light enough to open easily, meant that some of the operating sequences were often not understood by the boating public. This resulted in the bridges being, at times, insecurely fixed for road traffic, and consequently damaged. The resultant delays while repairs were undertaken were not only frustrating but absorbed precious canal finance!

The problem was largely overcome when operating instructions were fixed to each bridge. It was decided, however, with some reluctance, that further farm accommodation bridges, where possible, would be raised to give the 8ft air draft which by this time had become standard policy elsewhere on canal restoration schemes, although it was appreciated that such a move would change the authentic 'historic' appearance of the canal. Those bridges where this solution could be adopted were at Whites Dairy near Standards lock, Cogload Bridge near Charlton (also known as Higher Buckland), North End and Foxhole, both near Creech St Michael, and Swans Neck and Black Hut, near Durston. The limiting factor in all cases was whether there was enough room on the canal bank to accommodate the increased length of the approach ramps. The building work involved was far simpler than for the conventional swingbridges and could easily be undertaken by the canal team with costs being reduced significantly. In January 1989, work started on heightening the abutments to the first 'raised' bridge at Whites Dairy, with the deck being positioned two months later. This was followed shortly afterwards by the raising of the bridge at Cogload, both being completed at a cost of around £5,000 each. During the late summer of that year, protracted negotiations to purchase a half-acre piece of land adjacent to the canal at North End, Creech St Michael, were finally resolved, and in October the canal team took a break from raising bridges for a short while and turned their attentions to laying out and landscaping what has since become a popular and well-used car park for those who like walking the towpath or taking part in canal-side angling. This work fitted in well with the restoration programme, for the next bridge to be raised was to be that alongside the new car park at North End. It had been agreed that it was desirable to try to open up a length of canal to navigation from Taunton in the same way as had been already established from Bridgwater. With Bathpool being a natural starting point on the outskirts of Taunton for boating on the canal, however, it offered less than 2 miles of navigable canal, unless North End Bridge could be raised.

By December, the team was ready to start work. The bridge was principally an agricultural crossing, but it also carried a public footpath for which a temporary bridge would need to be provided whilst work was in progress. When this work was underway, the British Waterways Board took the opportunity to make provision for 'stop logs' in the bridge abutments to the bridge. Stop logs are baulks of timber that can be slotted into grooves either side of the canal and built up one on top of another, so they form a dam to hold back water when repair works need to be done. They considered the 'pound' unacceptably long (between Firepool and the next lock at Higher Maunsel) and the bridge at Creech conveniently split this distance of 6½ miles in half.

The canal team experienced many frustrating delays over the work on this bridge, carried out over the winter months when a succession of hard frosts and generally bad weather slowed down progress on site considerably. It was finally completed in the early months of 1990.

Firepool Lock fully restored.

The Kings lock restoration complete, including the raising of the footbridge in 1989. The footbridge over the lock chamber was funded by the Inland Waterways Association.

The national Boat Rally at Crossways, April 1989, organised by the West Country Branch of the Inland Waterways Association. The swingbridge is seen 'swung off' amongst an armada of small craft.

The narrow boat *Croghall-Mor* easing slowly through Newtown lock to become the first vessel to re-enter the canal after its partial re-opening in April 1989.

The temporary bridge structure that had been originally used at Crossways the year before was, in June 1988, re-erected at North Newton, in readiness for the replacement of the bridge there the next year. Due to the lack of space on both approaches, it had to be positioned at an angle over the canal to allow sufficient manoeuvrability for milk tankers and other lengthy vehicles to approach the bridge.

Despite the growing preference for 'raised' bridges wherever possible, this lack of abutment space meant that at North Newton a replacement swingbridge would be necessary. With experience gained from the operation of the three earlier swingbridges, a revised design was produced. The modifications naturally affected the price which rose to nearly £40,000 proving, if proof was necessary, that the decision to raise bridges, instead of swinging them, was right in the circumstances! It took time to redesign the bridge and to prepare new contract documents and it was not until late in 1989 that work started on site, with the canal team alternating between this bridge and North End as weather conditions permitted.

A Partial Reopening of the Canal

The West Country branch of the Inland Waterways Association had consistently supported the progressive restoration of the canal and throughout the early years, involved themselves in various fundraising activities. These were to assist in financing the work as it progressed and were a much appreciated contribution.

In January, 1986, Branch members had raised just over £2,500, and with the Inland Waterways Associations' National Restoration and Development Fund matching pound for pound, a donation of £5000 was made towards the canal restoration, no mean achievement from a group of canal enthusiasts! It was originally earmarked for the reinstatement of the swingbridge at Bathpool, but as this bridge was not yet a priority in the programme of works, it was used to meet the costs of raising the footbridges over the chambers at both Standards and Kings locks, the work being completed by early 1988, in readiness for the opening of the length of canal to North Newton.

Another aspect of the Association's support manifested itself in 1989, when, with nearly 5 miles of the canal available to navigation, the branch organised a major Boat Rally at Crossways for the weekend of 22 and 23 April that year. The British Waterways Board also assisted by providing a temporary slipway and the occasion was supported by Sedgemoor District Council and the Somerset County Council.

The Rally provided, for the first time in nearly fifty years, the spectacle of craft using the canal. Boat owners, enthusiasts, and members of other organisations were joined by many members of the public who crowded along the towpaths as others took rides in the armada of small craft that spent two days cruising between Bridgwater Dock and Fordgate. It was an auspicious start and one which led subsequently to the decision to hold an annual canal festival at Bridgwater. The Somerset Waterways Festival, as it is now known, has been organised each year since by the Somerset Inland Waterways Society, under its chairman, Phil Heath, with assistance from British Waterways and the local authorities.

1989 also marked the centenary of the setting up of county councils in England and Wales, and the Association of County Councils that year promoted a national competition for recent county council schemes in the field of urban and rural conservation. The submission of the Bridgwater and Taunton canal restoration gained the Countryside Award, with a fine Wedgwood plate, specially designed to signify the achievement. These two events and later that year, an award from the Royal Town Planning Institute, meant that the efforts of so many were now gaining, not only local, but national recognition and support.

Unfortunately, 1989 was also the year that the Manpower Services Commission withdrew its funding and support nationwide for the various employment measures that had meant so much to both the people involved and to the chances of completing schemes such as the canal restoration. Without this help, it seemed that the impetus would be lost and the work never finished, an unthinkable idea after so much time and effort had been put into the restoration and expectations were so much closer to being realised.

THE ROYAL TOWN PLANNING INSTITUTE

AWARD FOR PLANNING ACHIEVEMENT 1989

Commended

Somerset County Council
Sedgemoor District Council
Taunton Deane Borough Council

in association with

British Waterways Board

for

Bridgwater and Taunton Canal

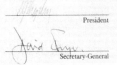

President

Secretary-General

Left and opposite: The significance of this canal restoration was recognised nationally by these awards.

SETTING UP A CANAL PROJECT TEAM

In February 1989, six months before the end of the MSC scheme, Somerset County Council had set up an Enterprise Training Scheme to promote training opportunities throughout the county. It was hoped that a team could be established for the canal that would not need to rely upon MSC funding but unfortunately, 'very few entrants came forward into the project, and the progress on the canal was very slow indeed – most work being carried out by the Employment Training supervisors themselves.'[6]

Clearly this state of affairs could not continue and the county council resolved 'that a small canal team be established on a two-year contract initially to complete the bridge restoration programme, jointly financed by "savings" on the swingbridge programme, and extended into the third year when the allocations for 1991–92 are agreed by contributors.'[7]

The team would consist of a supervisor and foreman with three manual workers and a clerical officer working part-time. The costs were estimated to be about £55,000 per year, a figure which included all office costs, rental, hire and travel costs. Over the three-year period of employment this was roughly equal to the estimated savings on the original swingbridge programme where raised bridges were substituted. It made sound sense, and by June the team, to be known as the Canal Project Team, was established, led by Ted Plumb as supervisor with Les Davis his foreman, both of whom had had considerable experience of working on the canal during the M.S.C. days. The county council could not act alone in funding this team and, as with the joint funding of the swingbridge programme, approaches were made to the other canal contributors and finance agreed.

The raised bridge at Foxhole.

Steps at Creech St Michael linking the towpath with the village street. The work was carried out entirely by the Canal Community Project Team.

The Canal Project Team Continues the Canal Restoration

The Canal Project Team's first priority, after completing the installation of a new swingbridge at North Newton, extending its approach ramps and building new side culverts, was to complete the work of raising the remaining bridges between there and Taunton. The bridge at Foxhole, near Charlton and a half a mile from North End, was chosen to be the next to be raised. The bridge proved to be a little more complicated than the other bridges attempted, in that it crossed the canal at a skew, which required not only some extra work in building up the approach ramps, but some particularly challenging brickwork to the abutments. However, the team, who daily became more skilled at this type of challenge, were up to the task and today, this raised bridge is perhaps the most attractive along the canal and every bit as fine as the work of the early canal builders!

By 1991, there remained to be raised the bridges at Black Hut, Swans Neck, Bathpool, Outwood and the low-level road bridge at Priorswood on the eastern outskirts of Taunton. Work on these was not going to be easy as each one possessed its own set of difficulties and site restraints.

Black Hut, near Durston, was the first raised that year. The old bridge carried a farm track across the canal which itself was high up on the Lyng embankment at this point. The approaches were already steep enough without increasing them for a raised bridge but the farmer who used the crossing was agreeable to additional land being made available so that the approach ramps could be lengthened without significantly increasing the gradient. It was necessary to re-site slightly an adjacent lengthsman's hut, a relic of the canal's operational days, but in so doing the chance was taken to repair it and now, with the rebuilt bridge, the group provides a pleasing example of sympathetic canal restoration.

Swans Neck, just south of Higher Buckland Farm at Durston, also posed problems for the Canal Project Team.

Not only was it necessary for the owner of the farm to continue to take heavy machinery over the canal but any question of extending the approach ramps for a higher bridge were hampered because of the sharp drop in ground levels immediately behind the towing path. With much ingenuity from the team, and not a little tolerance from the farm owner, it was agreed that a raised bridge and its ramps could be fitted in within the site limitations but the latter would require considerable earth works, including rock gabions for stability. Although access to the bridge site from the public highway was short, facilitating the transport of heavy materials, the bridge proved to be more expensive than the other bridges tackled up to that time. Nevertheless it was still cheaper than installing a swingbridge and the attractive design of the completed job is a worthy addition to the canal's structures.

1991 also saw the completion of a new housing estate at Tanpits, on the northern side of the canal at Bathpool, where the layout provided for a realigned road between Bathpool and West Monkton. With this new road it was now possible to close the existing vehicular crossing over the canal at Bathpool and for the Canal Project Team to remove the old swingbridge and replace it with a lighter, pedestrian-only swingbridge, similar to the one installed at Newtown lock at Bridgwater.

Higher Maunsel lock after restoration works.

Lower Maunsel lock.

The Bathpool bridge was opened on 28 March 1992, at a ceremony organised by the West Country branch of the Inland Waterways Association, by Christine and Pamela Jarvis of nearby St Quentin's Hotel who for more than twenty years had been keen and active supporters of the canal restoration. In the 1970s, when little activity had been possible on the canal, they operated a small boating centre alongside their holiday accommodation at St Quentin's in their own way introducing many visitors to the joys of canal boating, and keeping alive the hopes of an eventual reopening of the canal.

The limited amount of land available on either side of the swingbridge at Outwood, near Durston, again meant that a raised bridge was out of the question; there was simply not enough space to accommodate the increased length of ramps, particularly as the canal towing path ran close to the road at this point. It was reluctantly accepted that a swingbridge was the only practical solution and in July 1993 a design was produced for a cheaper version than that used at North Newton, where the hydraulics were replaced by a much more simplified 'landing' mechanism at the abutments. Another modification made was to build into the bridge deck itself an additional splay end which provided for an easier turning manoeuvre for farm vehicles. Whilst the bridge deck was fabricated by the Bridgwater firm of E.C. Harris, the other work of rebuilding the brick abutments, concreting-in the central trunnion and all the necessary safety barriers was carried out by the Canal Project Team.

Costing £28,000, the bridge was opened on 24 July 1993 as part of the many celebrations British Waterways were organising up and down the country that year in recognition of 200 years of canal building. Outwood, almost by coincidence, happened to be a propitious location for such an event, for it lies very close to the boundary between the two district authorities involved in the canal restoration. The opening was attended by the chairman of the Somerset County Council, the Chairman of Sedgemoor District Council, the Mayor-elect of the Taunton Deane Borough Council and representatives of British Waterways.

The raising of the bridge at Priorswood, now known as the Maidenbrook Canal Bridge and which carries heavy vehicular traffic to the Crown Industrial Estate, was always going to be one that would be most taxing for those working to open up the canal to Taunton. Built in the 1960s to headroom of barely 4ft, and at a time when navigation on the abandoned canal was scarcely considered, its removal and replacement would be an expensive undertaking, especially at a time when public money for such work was desperately limited. Without its raising, though, through navigation to Taunton could never be achieved, thwarting the whole restoration programme. In the Recreation and Restoration Plan of 1983, it had been anticipated that the costs for replacing this bridge would be in the order of £100,000, a figure which dwarfed all other costings on the canal although it was recognised at the time that, as it would be one of the last schemes to be undertaken, this figure would inevitably rise.

A design was prepared for a new, brick-faced in-situ concrete bridge, that echoed the appearance, even if not the form of structure, of many traditional canal bridges. It would have an elliptical arch, spanning both the canal and the towing path, with an air draught of 8ft 3ins above the water and a width of 34ft. Its cost was £178,000, a figure which included the removal of the old bridge, raising the level of the approach roads so as to achieve satisfactory forward visibility, and diverting gas, water, telephone and electricity

Priorswood Bridge before removal, October 1993.

The Maidenbrook Canal Bridge (previously known as Priorswood Bridge), Priorswood, Taunton, completed March 1994.

Above and left: Two views of Firepool Pumping Station at Taunton. Built upon the structure of earlier lime kilns (the flames from which are said to have given this place its name), this two-storey structure mounted a massive water tank to provide water for the the adjacent Taunton Station. In plans for the future, it is hoped that this building can be restored to provide canal-related facilities.

A trip on the canal at Lower Maunsel lock, June 1993. (Courtesy of Bill Sealey)

services. Both Taunton Deane Borough Council and Sedgemoor District Council each contributed £25,000 towards the work, which was carried out by the Exeter firm of P. Trant Ltd, and completed in March 1994.

From Priorswood, the canal threads its way to Taunton through unimaginative post-war industrial development, designed with little thought for canal-side amenity and which leaves limited scope for either towing path improvements or additional tree screening. At Obridge, however, as part of the Taunton Cycle Route, the towing path has been widened and resurfaced with ramps constructed to link the towing path to the adjacent road. Nearer to Firepool, the narrow tongue of land between the canal and the River Tone has been landscaped by Taunton Deane Borough Council as part of its enhancement work, providing a children's wood and a pleasant linear park as an attractive entry into the town.

During the mid-1980s plans were drawn up for restoring the fabric of the long derelict Firepool Pumping Station at Taunton and converting it into a canal-side restaurant and canal museum with a small boatyard alongside for the hire of canal craft. Rather like book-ends at each end of the canal, the Pumping Station was seen as complimenting the restored warehouse at Bridgwater Dock and provide an attractive venue alongside the canal and river at Taunton. Unfortunately these plans have not progressed; the structure continues to decay, and, if action is not taken shortly it may be beyond economic restoration.

NATIONAL TRAIL BOAT RALLY AT TAUNTON, 1992

With the three local authorities and British Waterways finalising the restoration of the canal, the Inland Waterways Association and their West Country Branch were keen to encourage, and be active in promoting, its widest possible use and enjoyment. The Association was persuaded to hold its Annual National Trail Boat Rally at Taunton during May 1992. As its name implies, this event attracts boaters and canal enthusiasts from all over the country and this was an opportunity to show off the restored canal. The site chosen for the rally was the Tone at French Weir, the Rally forming part of the West Country Waterways Festival. It attracted over 20,000 visitors during its three days and offered public boat trips upon the River Tone through Taunton for the first time for perhaps fifty years.

Such has been the interest generated by these annual waterway rallies since the first at Crossways in April 1989, that a Somerset Navigators' Boat Club has now been established by the West County branch of the IWA, with a present membership of over seventy persons. This all seems a far cry from those depressing days, barely twenty years ago, when the canal lay derelict and abandoned, with little interest from much of the public and when anyone who took a boat on the canal for pleasure was considered an eccentric!

CANAL TRIP BOATS BEGIN OPERATING

As the work progressed, private firms became interested and investigations were made into the possibility of 'off-line' moorings at Crossways and a marina and hotel complex at Huntworth.

Kings lock.

Swans and cygnets also find the canal attractive.

The West Country branch of the Inland Waterways Association decided that they would run limited summer boat trips on the short section of canal that was already open to navigation. Their *Ruby I* operated from Lower Maunsel during 1988 and two years later, in April 1990, the Grand Western Horseboat Co. of Tiverton was given permission by British Waterways to operate a regular summer boat trip service from North Newton to Fordgate, using their *Iona Gem*. This was an ex-naval cutter, built in 1945, and restored and adapted to carry public passengers. Operating for three years, the last two from Lower Maunsel while *Ruby I* operated from Bathpool, these two vessels gave many a taste of canal boating that will inevitably grow as the canal increases in popularity. In 1990 members of the local authorities who had been involved in the canal restoration were invited, along with the Commodore and Treasurer of the Conservators of the River Tone, to take a short trip along the canal from North Newton to Fordgate in the *Iona Gem*.

By 1991, these canal boat trips were carrying nearly 6,000 visitors and were becoming increasingly popular with local groups and organisations. At Easter 1992, members of the West Country branch started up regular Sunday afternoon trips on the canal from Bathpool, in their newly fitted out *Ruby II*, a larger vessel than its predecessor. *Ruby I* was transferred, interestingly enough, to operate upon the Bude Canal, the canal from whence the early navigators had come to cut the first sods of the Bridgwater and Taunton Canal way back in 1822.

LEISURE AND TOURISM STRATEGY FOR THE CANAL

With much of the restoration work now complete, it was necessary for the earlier Recreation and Restoration Plan to be updated, and in April 1993 British Waterways produced their Leisure and Tourism Strategy for the canal. This had been prepared in liaison with the three local authorities and set out a framework for future provision of leisure facilities and an improved tourism role. It envisaged that as the canal attracted increasing public interest from those enjoying the leisure and recreation opportunities afforded by the restored waterway, additional canal-side facilities would be required, although it was possible that some of these would be provided by the 'private sector' as part of their own commercial undertakings. It was always the intention since the first days of the restoration, that the public should gain as much pleasure as possible from taking part in those other leisure activities that the canal could provide, such as a leisurely walk along the towing path, enjoying the canal-side wildlife and participating in angling.

Much still remains to be done and this is set out in the Leisure and Tourism Strategy. Basic facilities for canal users have to be installed, such as additional slipways, increased car-parking and toilets, while landing stages need to be provided, as well as ensuring the towing path is upgraded so that it can be equally well used by the disabled. Whilst the occasional cyclist will still be able to ride between Bridgwater and Taunton along the canal towing-path, full cycle route status will be limited to the urban approaches to the two towns, thereby encouraging its use as a quiet, traffic-free route for those travelling to work from the towns' outskirts and nearby villages. Connections will be made to the neighbouring network of minor local roads to create circular routes. This valuable but limited promotion for cyclists using the towing-path, will go a long way to meeting the understandable concerns of anglers who fear a conflict of interest could develop along the other rural stretches of the canal-side.

ANGLING

Angling is a highly popular pastime on canals and rivers, and the Bridgwater and Taunton Canal is no exception, providing anglers in the region with excellent fishing. The Recreation and Restoration Plan made provision for maintaining and improving not only the quality of the fishing but the amenities for the anglers as well. It is an important activity that draws many to the canal and needs to be provided and planned for in a way similar to the provision for the boating enthusiasts. The anglers from both the Bridgwater and Taunton Associations have, for years, enjoyed these facilities and pay rents to fish, both for pleasure and in competition along its banks. The canal is regarded as nationally important and, being relatively shallow, it is considered to be safe for youngsters interested in the sport.

The canal holds a big head of carp, tench, bream and roach, whilst perch, the stickleback and the pike, the largest native fresh-water fish in the British Isles, are also plentiful. In the spring, it is possible to spot elvers, young eels, swimming up the canal, and even climbing the lock gates!

WILDLIFE AND PLANTLIFE

The canal banks and the adjoining fields are rich in flora and fauna and together form a wildlife site of considerable county importance for nature conservation. Work on maintaining the canal banks and the periodic weed and reed cutting need to take this into account, particularly at breeding times. The wetland habitat, with its clear and relatively unpolluted water, supports an interesting variety of plant and wildlife. The heron, with his statuesque pose and lightning reflexes is one of the most effective hunters to be seen at the waterside, his sharp eye scanning the scene for his varied diet of fish, frogs, beetles and various rodents. Many visitors on boat trips have already been fascinated by spotting a heron at such close quarters, either standing motionless or flying by with his slow, graceful, flight. The elegant swan and the colourful kingfisher are also to be seen throughout the length of the canal. Other birds include thrushes, blackbirds, chaffinches and wren, and, very occasionally, a tawny owl may be seen.

Frogs, together with toads and newts are all to be found along the canal, and amongst the long grass and reeds will be found sedge warblers; whilst on the water, the coot, with his distinctive white forehead, and the black-plumaged moorhen will be evident. The water will be shared with pond skaters, whirligig beetles and water voles. The voles, whose presence is often given away by a sudden 'plop' in the water are not always the best friend of the canal manager, for their tiny burrowings into the canal bank at water level can often be the cause of water loss, particularly on the embankments.

Both dragonflies and damselflies, with their vivid colours, can be seen flying close to the water; the dragonfly being the larger, and more easily distinguishable.

Willows, so characteristic of our river and canal banks, provide a home for a range of insect species as well as giving shade upon the waters from their drooping foliage, whilst alders help stabilize the banks, and provide valuable habitats for burrowing voles and nesting moorhens.

The clear water of the canal supports abundant plant life. Tall reeds overshadow rushes and clumps of yellow flag iris along the edge of the waterway, while the wide, leathery leaves of waterlilies float on the surface. At the waterside, bur reed and bulrushes will also be seen, as well as water flag, yellow iris and water forget-me-not, with its pale blue and yellow-eyed flowers.[8] Plant species alongside both the canal and the river are varied, and include many that are becoming less abundant than formerly. The observant visitor may also see species of bur-marigold, flowering rush, and the spiked water-milfoil.[9] The wildlife and plantlife of the canal and river bank are precious; they should not be wantonly harmed or destroyed, but left for our enjoyment and study.

Further information on this subject can be obtained from the Somerset Wildlife Trust, formerly the Somerset Trust for Nature Conservation, the Somerset Environmental Records Centre, the National Rivers Authority, which has published an illustrated pamphlet on the wildlife of the river, *Looking at the Tone*, and British Waterways which has produced a brochure on wildlife on this canal.

Approaching Standards Farm.

WALKING

The walk provided by the canal towpath is an attraction for those wanting an easy, level walk away from the noise and distractions of motor traffic and has become increasingly popular as the restoration of the canal has proceeded and the condition of the towing path improved. Over most lengths of the towpath it is possible to walk without much difficulty. With a number of small car parks now provided at intervals the walker is now able to enjoy short walks or circuits involving footpaths further afield in the adjacent countryside. The towing path provides an excellent route of some 12 miles for groups taking part in the ever popular 'sponsored walks' and for jogging for the more energetic. Disabled persons are not to be denied the canal facilities either, for the relatively flat towpaths are usually wide enough for wheelchairs with direct access from the car parks.

Apparently, the challenge of walking between Taunton and Bridgwater, for those who wish to test their strength and endurance, is nothing new, for, at the time the canal was being cut, the *Taunton Courier* carried the following account: 'A pedestrian, Townsend, a brushmaker from Taunton, commenced his arduous task of walking three times to and from Bridgwater in a day, for six successive days, being a total of upward of 70 miles'. He accomplished this feat, walking, it is recorded, a total of 432 miles in the six days and was presented with a sack of flour, weighing 280lb in reward for his trouble which he then carried with him to Bridgwater![10]

Bon Voyage

With the canal now restored and available for boating once again, it is all too easy to forget those days in the 1950s and 1960s when, with apparent official disinterest, it was in grave danger of sinking into total dereliction. That it survived up to this time at all was in large part due to the energies of the Conservators of the River Tone, who, with their statutory duty, still inspected the canal once a year to make certain it was in a navigable state, long after it had closed commercially. With this monument to the vision and daring of those early canal entrepreneurs now in public custodianship, it must never again be allowed to fall into disrepair or be abandoned. It has already been shown that the canal is a valuable asset to the county and one that can provide the fullest opportunities for outdoor recreation.

Slowly, over the years, public interest has been reawakened to the value of our canals in many parts of the country and there is no doubt that they have opened up increased tourism potential as well as providing for the individual a quiet refuge in which to enjoy boating, angling and all the other aspects of countryside recreation. For the Bridgwater and Taunton Canal, this slow and painstaking process of restoration is, at last, complete, and is there for us all to use and enjoy.

All that is needed to complete this story is for the Conservators of the River Tone to undertake, once again, their annual inspections. And why not? They are still in being as a body of guardians, and their canal inspections, reviving a 300-year-old tradition, would remind the town of the great debt it owes them.

UPDATE FOR THE NEW EDITION

The final chapter of the first edition of this book was written in late 1993, and published in 1994 to coincide with the official reopening of the Bridgwater and Taunton Canal, which took place some months later with a small ceremony in June of that year. It was held at Taunton with the ceremonial reopening of the lock at Firepool which links the canal to the River Tone, and thus enabled the small flotilla of craft that had gathered for the occasion to travel down to the small jetty on the waterside alongside the Brewhouse Theatre.

That day, just over twelve years ago, was memorably sunny, with many participants mingling with onlookers to see so many craft upon the River Tone once again, which up to that time rarely witnessed any craft upon its waters. It represented the culmination of many years of hard work, financial commitment and organisation by British Waterways and the local authorities, and many volunteer groups.

The work had taken just over ten years to complete, at a time when the restoration of canals, both locally and nationally, was slowly growing in the public's awareness as a vital part of our concern for the environment, and the role waterways could play in providing a valuable dimension to our recreational and leisure outlets in the twenty-first century.

The main part of the restoration work on the Bridgwater and Taunton Canal was carried out during the mid-1980s, at a time of severe economic belt-tightening throughout the country. For local authorities in particular, this timing was, to put it mildly, unfortunate, as demands on limited public finance were fierce. Yet, the four participating parties, British Waterways and the three local authorities, were steadfastly determined that financial allocations would need to be promised year on year so that the necessary programme of work could be completed on time. In this update it is important to emphasise this point, for when long-term commitments are undertaken, equally long-term budgeting commitments have to be made. Without this, projects such as this canal restoration could scarcely begin. The restoration of the Kennet and Avon Canal was largely carried out during this same period, and involved far more public bodies, but its eventual completion also underlines this point.

Over the past twelve years what has happened to meet those aspirations expressed at the ceremonial opening?

British Waterways and the local authorities have continued to invest in improvements to the canal to meet current needs. The towpath, already a very popular route for sponsored walks, as it is flat and traffic-free, is now part of National Cycle Route 3, and has been improved for recreational cycling, and, indeed, is well used for commuting both to work and neighbouring schools.

At the halfway point along the canal, at Lower Maunsel, a canal centre with refreshment and tea rooms and toilet facilities has been developed alongside an improved facility for

Recently installed landing pontoon at Taunton, adjacent to the Brewhouse Theatre.

boat moorings. The car park at Lower Maunsel is well used and shows the continued popularity of this part of the canal.

Substantial moorings have been built at Taunton town centre, adjacent to the Brewhouse Theatre and other landing stages and moorings have also been built or improved at Bathpool and at Bridgwater Docks. There are possibilities that have been long in the pipeline, to provide additional mooring facilities at the Taunton end of the canal, in the area close to Firepool lock. Again, at Firepool, a small, but quite adequate car park has been set aside for those wishing to visit the canal, a most important step in attracting people to come and see the canal and riverside.

Terry Kemp, until quite recently British Waterways' economic and social development manager, was keen to develop the aspect of 'people power', now that the canal is up and running. It needs managing and local involvement ensures that local needs are responded to. Mr Kemp gave the example that:

> ... for many years there has been a local canal wardens service along the Bridgwater and Taunton Canal. They do much for the safe navigation on the canal and the communities along the route. They give their time generously in giving talks locally, ensuring damage and litter are dealt with and generally informing the public of the benefits of this waterway to their locality.

The number of boaters using the canal has steadily increased over the years with over fifty boats moored on the canal and visiting boats launched at the slipways at Bathpool and Bridgwater. It has to be admitted that numbers will never be great, because the canal, being only 14½ miles long, and isolated from other navigable waterways, provides only a short length of water to enjoy.

To this end, studies have been made over the past few years to see whether links can be made with other stretches of waterway in the area to increase the length of navigable waterway. These could undoubtedly involve the use of the River Parrett in some form, together with the River Tone and some of the large drainage channels that penetrate the lowlands of Somerset to the east.

The Environment Agency is currently looking into the feasibility of some form of tidal control measure on the River Parrett, which would have the effect, if built, of providing permanent high water throughout the length of the river up as far as Langport. Together with the River Tone and the various branches, there are well over 50 miles of navigable waterway. If these could be economically joined together again, this would give waterway access to a number of historic towns and villages in Somerset, and could form an attractive 'canal circuit'.

The reopening of the Bridgwater and Taunton Canal has led to an increasing interest in examining the remains of two other canals that linked into Taunton, although both are now defunct. Perhaps the more important, historically, is the short, 14-mile, Grand Western Canal mentioned in chapter five. This was a tub-boat canal, built to limited width and using lifts and an incline.

Today, only very short lengths are in water, and many of the remaining structures are either listed structures or scheduled ancient monuments. The other canal is the Chard Canal, again referred to in chapter five. Both are being studied to record their features, structures, embankments and cuttings both from the point of view of recording their unique role in playing a part in Somerset's transport history, and to protect them from unnecessary damage.

In 2005, a new organisation was set up, in response to a growing need to look at the wider canvas of the county's waterways. The Somerset Waterways Development Trust is a Charitable Trust, and includes those who 'have their eyes and hearts set on conserving, protecting and improving the special assets within Somerset of canals, rivers and watercourses'. Indeed, 'Think waterways and you have the Somerset equivalent of the Eden Project', says Taunton Deane Councillor David Durdan, who is passionate about the future of waterways in the county and feels that, as a direct result of the reopening of the Bridgwater and Taunton Canal there is a deal of public expectation to build upon this work, with inland waterway tourism and recreational potential to follow.

The five objectives of the Trust are:

1. Promoting Somerset waterways.
2. Explaining to people about Somerset waterways.
3. Interpreting the history and landscape of Somerset waterways.
4. Protecting and conserving the environment, landscape, heritage and recreational resource of Somerset waterways.
5. Improving and enhancing in a sustainable manner the Somerset waterways.

Membership of the Trust will include those with interest in waterways and those with an ability to do positive works to fulfil the stated objectives. The Somerset Waterways

Development Trust was established during the summer of 2005 and, as a charitable Trust, has enabled it to seek funding from sources other than the local authorities. Furthermore, the Trust has the remit to purchase land for associated waterside purposes, including leisure and environmental reasons, if it is felt to be of public interest. Its setting up has already had one fortuitous outcome in that it has brought together a wider grouping of those already interested in the subject, with their own expertise and funding potential.

Although it is early days yet, and approach to national funding is not ruled out for approved schemes. With the Trust established, the future of the waterways in Somerset would appear to be on a far better footing.

As Val Whittcombe, who runs the canal centre and tea rooms at Lower Maunsel, says, 'The waterways of Somerset are not about boats and boating. They are about the environment, the landscape, our historic inheritance as well as a place to relax and slow down. We need an organisation to ensure this will be preserved'.

As part of the longer-term future development of Taunton, the borough council, together with the Somerset County Council, South West of England Regional Development Agency, and the Environment Agency commissioned town planning consultants, Terence O'Rorke, to prepare a 'Vision of Taunton – a twenty-first century town'. The river corridor was recognised as an important 'green' wedge within the town centre, and emphasised the importance of the waterway throughout the town in future planning.

As if to underline the growing interest in the waterway scene throughout the county, the Taunton and District Civic Society convened, in October 2005, a conference to bring together those with particular interests in canal and waterway restoration. This was a large undertaking for a relatively small society but, again, it marks the growing concern and, indeed, fascination for the subject that is now spreading further afield than just canal enthusiasts. Their chairman, Andrew Knutt, undertook the task and brought together over 100 delegates to hear speakers give an overview of the possibilities and opportunities that lie ahead, if the example and impetus set by the Bridgwater and Taunton Canal restoration is not to be lost.

It is indeed a coincidence, but perhaps a timely coincidence, that this update is being written exactly 100 years after the Bridgwater and Taunton Canal ceased operating commercially. Few at that time would have placed much money on its restoration in the coming century, indeed few would have harboured any thoughts that the canal, as they would have known it, could ever have an important role to play again.

The Bridgwater and Taunton Canal has now joined a growing number of canal restoration schemes up and down the country that have proved quite conclusively that there is a future for these waterways, one that provides for leisure, recreation and pleasure to countless people. 'You cannot wear out water', as one planning officer said, when bemoaning his county's continual battle against the erosion of landscapes and beauty spots by the incessant pressure of vehicles and feet!

If the restoration of this canal has brought about an awareness of our waterway heritage, then it has all been a wonderfully rewarding undertaking for all concerned. To our forefathers 100 years ago, it would be truly amazing!

Tony Haskell,
2006

REFERENCES

Abbreviations

BT – *Bridgwater Times*
LHL – Local History Library, Taunton
NRA – National Rivers Authority
SRO – Somerset Record Office, Taunton
TC – *Taunton Courier*
VCH – Victoria County History of Somerset

Chapter 1

1. LHL, Calendar of Manuscripts of the Dean and Chapter of Wells.
2. Ibid.
3. Ibid.
4. Ibid.
5. Malet, Hugh, *Octavius Warre and the Conservation of Taunton Castle* (Taunton 1987)
6. Farr, Grahame, *Somerset Harbours* (London 1954)
7. I am indebted to D.R. Culverwell for allowing me to publish this family research which adds considerably to our understanding of those early years of coal and barge traffic in the seventeenth and eighteenth centuries.
8. Malet, *Octavius Warre*.
9. SRO, Goodland, Roger, *A Short Account of the Conservators of the River Tone* (unpublished 1966)
10. Tone Navigation Act 10 & 11, William III (1699)
11. Ibid.
12. Ibid.
13. Morriss, Christopher (ed.), *The Ilustrated Journeys of Celia Fiennes 1685–1712* (London 1949)
14. SRO, DD/TC (2) 9.
15. SRO, DD/TC (2) 10.
16. River Tone Act 6 Anne (1708)
17. SRO, DD/TC (2) 10.
18. Prichard, Mari and Carpenter, Humphrey, *A Thames Companion* (Oxford, second edition 1981).
19. LHL, Redler, J. and Coombe, C. v GWR (1907)
20. SRO, DD/TC (2) 10.
21. Ibid.
22. SRO, DD/TC (2) (box 1)

23. SRO, DD/TC (2) 10.
24. SRO, DD/TC (1) 2.
25. SRO, DD/TC (2) 10.
26. Tone Navigation Act 10 & 11 William III (1699)
27. Hadfield, Charles, *The Canals of South West England* (Newton Abbot, second edition 1985)
28. Toulmin, Joshua, *History of Taunton* (Taunton 1791)
29. Ibid.
30. SRO, DD/TC 2 (box 1). 'Due to severe water shortage experienced during the summer months, the Conservators of the River Tone had to issue rules to all traders and boatmen from 24 June to 29 September, in each year, no boat shall traverse any part of the river between Curry Moor half-lock and the Town of Taunton having on board a cargo of heavier weight than 7 tons and a half.'
31. Hunt, T.J., lecture at Taunton Castle.
32. SRO, DD/MK 8/12.
33. TC, 2 January 1822.
34. TC, 13 February 1828.
35. SRO, D/RA 7/4/4.
36. Ibid.
37. Burrow Bridge Act (5 Geo. IV)

Chapter 2

1. *The Sun* newspaper (December 1824)
2. Buchanan, R.A. and Williams, M., *Brunel's Bristol* (Bristol 1982)
3. SRO, Q/RUp 4.
4. SRO, DD/TC 40.
5. SRO, Q/RUp 5 and 14.
6. TC, 8 February 1810.
7. SRO, DD/CM 36.
8. SRO, Q/RUp 30.
9. Ibid.
10. Hadfield, Charles, *The Canals of South West England*.
11. SRO, Q/RUp 32 and 35.
12. 51 Geo. III.
13. Priestley, *Historic Account of the Navigable Rivers, Canals and Railways throughout Great Britain* (London 1831)
14. Ibid.
15. Jessop, Henry, Report of Bridgwater Corporation (1829)
16. SRO, Q/RUp 71.
17. SRO, DD/TC 2 (box 1)
18. 5 Geo IV.
19. TC, 11 December 1822.
20. TC, 25 December 1822.
21. Ibid.
22. SRO, Q/RUp 68.
23. TC, 25 December 1822.
24. TC, 8 December 1824.

25. Ibid.
26. TC, 6 April 1825.
27. TC, 2 July 1828.
28. TC, 8 December 1824.
29. *Sherborne Mercury*, December 1824.
30. SRO, D/RA/9/11. DD/X/HUN 5, DD/WY/BX 175 and Q/RUp 78.
31. Rolt, L.T.C., *Victorian Engineering* (Harmondsworth 1970)
32. TC, 20 July 1822.
33. TC, 2 July 1828.

Chapter 3

1. Standing Order of House of Lords (50 136)
2. 7 Wm. IV and 1 Vict. c83.
3. SRO, DD/AH 23.
4. SRO, DDTC 19.
5. 5 Geo. IV (1824)
6. SRO, Q/RUp 71.
7. Ware, Michael E., *Canals and Waterways* (Aylesbury, 1987)
8. 5 Geo. IV (1824) C1 1X (2803)
9. A document, written by John Easton, describing a 'Chain for Measuring', is in the collection of the Institution of Civil Engineers, London.
10. TC, 8 January 1823.
11. Hadfield, Charles, *The Canals of South West England*.
12. TC, 15 January 1823.
13. 5 Geo. IV(1824)
14. TC, 20 September 1826.
15. TC, 16 August 1837.
16. SRO, DD/P, Creech St Michael.
17. TC, 28 June 1826.
18. TC, 2 August 1826.
19. TC, 24 May 1826.
20. TC, 3 January 1827.
21. Ibid.
22. Edward Goldsworthy, *Recollections of Old Taunton* (Taunton, 1975)

Chapter 4

1. SRO, Goodland, Roger, *A Short Account of the Conservators of the River Tone* (unpublished 1966)
2. TC, 23 December 1829.
3. SRO, DD/TC.
4. TC, 15 August 1832.
5. TC, 1 October 1828.
6. SRO, DD/TC box 2 (14 and 15)
7. SRO, DD/TC 25 and 26.
8. TC, 20 January 1830.
9. Robin Bush, *Jeboult's Taunton* (Buckingham 1983)

Chapter 5

1. Buchanan and Williams, *Brunel's Bristol*.
2. SRO, Q/RUp 19-21.
3. SRO, Q/RUp 38.
4. Gloucester was shortly to be linked by canal to the river Severn and Bristol Channel, in order to attract larger vessels to the harbour.
5. TC, 8 January 1825.
6. TC, 18 November 1829.
7. SRO, Q/RUp 108.
8. TC, 25 February 1835.
9. SRO, Parrett Navigation Bill (May 1836)
10. William IV, 7 (1837)
11. SRO, Q/RUp 133.
12. TC, 11 July, 8 and 15 August 1838.
13. William IV, 7 (1837) S 13.
14. A full account of the building of the dock can be found in Murless, Brian J., *Bridgwater Docks and the River Parrett* (second edition, Taunton 1989)
15. SRO, DD/TC.
16. Hadfield, Charles, *The Canals of South West England*.
17. BT, 2 February 1854.
18. Harris, Helen, *The Grand Western Canal* (Newton Abbot 1973)
19. Chard History Group, *The Chard Canal* (Chard 1967)
20. Harris, C.J., 'Bridgwater: its Docks, Canal, River Navigation and Railways,' *Journal of Railway and Canal History Society*, Vol.27 (July 1983)
21. Hadfield, Charles, *The Canal Age* (Newton Abbot 1968)
22. Hadfield, Charles, *The Canals of South West England*.
23. 51 Geo III (1811)
24. LHL, *Bragg's General Directory for the County of Somerset*, 1840.
25. LHL, *Slaters Directory* 1852–3.
26. TC, 13 June 1838.
27. I am indebted to Richard Goodland Hyde for information on the coal trade.
28. TC, 18 November 1835.
29. TC, 19 August 1829.
30. TC, 35 February 1835.
31. TC, 27 June 1838.
32. TC, 4 July 1838.
33. Fox, Charles H., *Chronicles of Tonedale: Two Centuries of Family History* (printed for private collection 1879)
34. Chard History Group, *The Chard Canal* (Chard 1967)
35. TC, 8 July 1835.
36. Chard History Group, *The Chard Canal*.
37. TC, 18 October 1837.
38. TC, 7 July 1839.
39. TC, 7 July 1841.
40. TC, 21 July 1841.
41. Curtis, W.E., letter in *The Somerset Countryman* (July 1934)

42. Hadfield, Charles, *The Canals of South West England*.

43. GWR Records, 25 June 1835.

44. 19 and 30 Vic. (1866).

45. SRO, DD/TC.

Chapter 6

1. Hadfield, Charles, The Canal Age.

2. SRO, Roger Goodland and Charles H. Goodland, *The Family of Goodland* (unpublished papers 1938)

3. TC, 6 June 1838.

4. TC, 1 July 1829.

5. TC, 4 December 1822.

6. BT, 25 June 1857.

7. TC, 6 October 1886.

8. TC, 6 July 1857.

9. Ibid.

10. BT, 19 March 1857.

11. BT, 23 July 1857.

12. *Taunton Courier*, 26 June 1839.

13. *Taunton Courier*, 18 July 1881.

14. Robert Ford, merchant and ship owner, in evidence given in the hearing into the Parrett Navigation Bill, May 1836.

15. Murless, *Bridgwater Docks and the River Parrett*.

16. SRO, Parrett Navigation Bill (May 1836)

17. Ibid.

18. VCH Vol. VI.

19. SRO, Parrett Navigation Bill (May 1836)

20. TC, 3 May 1826.

21. TC, 1 February 1826.

22. TC, 12 April 1826.

23. 5 Geo. IV.

24. SRO, D/RA 9/20.

25. TC, 8 November 1826.

26. TC, 31 January 1827

27. SRO, DD/TC.

28. LHL, Dugdale, James, *Somersetshire* (London 1819)

29. TC, 19 May 1841.

30. TC, 2 January 1828.

31. SRO, Parrett Navigation Bill (May 1836). The Parrett Navigation Co. had been authorised and set up in 1836 but it had limited success in maintaining commercial navigation on the river and was insolvent by 1860.

32. Bazelgette, J.W. and Whitehead, A., *Report on the Yeo, Parrett and the Drainage* (October 1869)

33. TC, 28 January 1829.

34. NRA.

35. NRA report 'The Old Pumping Stations on the River Parrett.'

36. Hanson, Harry, *The Canal Boatman 1760–1914* (Stroud 1984)

37. Legg, Philippa, *Cidermaking in Somerset* (Glastonbury 1984)

38. Paget-Tomlinson, Edward, *Britain's Canal and River Craft* (Ashbourne 1979)

39. I am indebted to Wallace Musgrave of Burrowbridge for this account, related to him by Henry Palmer when he was landlord of the New Bridge Inn during the 1930s.

40. LHL, Porter, Edmund, *Bridgwater Industries – Past and Present* (printed privately, 1970)

41. SRO, Parrett Navigation Bill.

42. Ibid.

43. TC, 30 August 1826.

44. VCH Vol. VI.

45. Ibid.

46. TC, 15 March 1826.

47. TC, 19 December 1832.

48. BT, 10 May 1855.

49. I am indebted to Roy Beck of Fivehead, whose grandfather, George Beck, was probably the last coal haulier to use barges on the Tone in the late 1920s, for these recollections.

50. TC, 13 April 1831.

51. TC, 18 July 1838, SRO Q/SCa 31–63 and Q/AGW 14/3.

52. TC, 10 June 1829.

53. FitzRandolf, Helen E. and Hay, M. Doriel, 'Osier Growing and Basketry' from *The Rural Industries of England and Wales* (Oxford 1926)

Chapter 7

1. TC, 8 February 1865.

2. TC, 23 October 1822.

3. Deane, Phyllis, *The First Industrial Revolution* (Cambridge 1969)

4. Ware, *Canals and Waterways*.

5. TC, 24 May 1826.

6. TC, 24 January 1827.

7. Hanson, *The Canal Boatmen 1760–1914*.

8. TC, 6 January 1830.

9. LHL, Porter, *Bridgwater Industries – Past and Present*.

10. TC, 11 January 1837.

11. TC, 17 January 1838.

12. TC, 10 January 1850.

13. TC, 23 January 1828.

14. TC, 27 January 1830.

15. TC, 18 October 1837.

16. SRO, *Bridgwater and Taunton Canal Navigation: Rules, Bye-laws and Regulations*.

17. VCH Vol. VI.

18. TC, 20 February 1828.

19. TC, 10 May 1837.

20. TC, 3 February 1836.

21. TC, 18 July 1838.

22. TC, 22 August 1838.

23. BT, 13 March 1856.

24. TC, 20 March 1837.

25. Bush, Robin, *Jeboult's Taunton*.
26. TC, 8 June 1859.
27. TC, 8 February 1865.

Chapter 8

1. 29 and 30 Vic. (1866) 5 24.
2. SRO, DD/TC.
3. Ibid.
4. Ibid.
5. Ibid.
6. LHL, information researched by Somerset Industrial Archaeological Society (1988)
7. SRO, DD/TC.
8. 29 and 30 Vic. (1866)
9. SRO, DD/TC.
10. TC, 10 August 1881.

Chapter 9

1. LHL, Redler, J. and Coombe, G. v GWR (1907)
2. Ibid.
3. Ibid.
4. TC, 29 July 1874.
5. LHL, Redler, J. and Coombe, G., v GWR (1907)
6. Ibid.
7. Ibid.
8. Ibid.
9. Ibid.
10. SRO, DD/IC 25 and 26.
11. TC, 26 March 1812.
12. *The Courier*, 22 September 1915.
13. LHL, Redler, J. and Coombe, G., v GWR (1907)
14. TC, August 1829.
15. TC, 26 July 1828.
16. LHL, Redler, J. and Coombe, G., v GWR (1907)
17. *The Courier*, 22 September 1915.
18. *The Courier*, 22 September 1915.
19. TC, 27 January 1830.
20. 'The Bridgwater and Taunton Canal', *GWR Magazine* (September 1920)
21. SRO, DD/IC minutes.
22. Ibid.
23. I am indebted to T.H. Stagg for allowing me to quote from his father's account of a Conservators' inspection.
24. Helles, John, 'The Taunton Stop Line', *Fortress* No.14 (August 1992)
25. Hawkins, Mac, *Somerset at War 1939–1945* (Wimborne 1988)
26. British Railways, Comprehensive Engineering Survey (1965)

Chapter 10

1.   SRO, DD/TC (letters)
2.   Ibid.
3.   Ibid.
4.   *Western Morning News* (1 April 1955)
5.   *Somerset County Herald* (24 November 1956)
6.   Williams, Michael, *The Draining of the Somerset Levels* (Cambridge 1970)
7.   NRA.
8.   NRA, Minute Book 1959–63.
9.   *Somerset County Gazette* (13 November 1965)
10. Land Drainage Act (1930) s41. Communication from Ministry of Agriculture, Fisheries and Food, 13 December 1966.
11. The Variation of Navigation Rights (River Tone) Order 1969 (S.I. 1969, No.1604)
12. Prepared from figures supplied by Bridgwater Harbourmaster and used in report by Broughton and Partners, civil engineers (1966)

Chapter 11

1.   Dale, R.W., county planning officer, *The Bridgwater and Taunton Canal – a Recreational Study* (September 1970)
2.   Somerset County Council, Dock and Panel Minutes (April 1978)
3.   British Waterways Board, *Bridgwater and Taunton Canal – A Canal and its Future* (June 1980)
4.   British Waterways Board, Somerset County Council, Sedgemoor District Council and Taunton Deane Borough Council, *The Bridgwater and Taunton Canal: Recreation and Restoration Plan* (August 1983)
5.   Transport Act 1968, s. 107.
6.   Somerset County Council, Joint Report Planning, Highways and Transport Committee (19 April 1989)
7.   Ibid.
8.   Somerset County Council and Inland Waterways Association, *West Country Waterway Guide (No.7): The Bridgwater and Taunton Canal* (1988)
9.   Lindi Wilkinson for Somerset Wildlife Trust (formerly the Somerset Trust for Nature Conservation), *An Ecological Survey of the Bridgwater and Taunton Canal.*
10. TC, 24 November 1824.

INDEX

If you are interested in purchasing other books published by Tempus,
or in case you have difficulty finding any Tempus books in your local bookshop,
you can also place orders directly through our website

www.tempus-publishing.com